BLACK CHRONOLOGY
from 4000 B.C. to the
Abolition of the Slave Trade

*A
Reference
Publication
in
Afro-American
Studies*

Charles T. Davis, *Editor*
Henry-Louis Gates, Jr., *Associate Editor*

BLACK CHRONOLOGY

from 4000 B.C. to the
Abolition of the Slave Trade

ELLEN IRENE DIGGS

G.K.HALL &CO.

70 LINCOLN STREET, BOSTON, MASS.

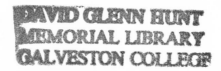

Library of Congress Cataloging in Publication Data

Diggs, Ellen Irene, 1906-
   Black chronology from 4000 B.C. to the abolition of the slave trade.

   Rev. ed. of: Chronology of notable events and dates in the history
of the African and his descendants during the period of slavery and
the slave trade. 1970.
   Bibliography
   Includes index.
   1.   Africa—History—Chronology.   2.   Blacks—History—
Chronology.   3.   Slavery—History—Chronology.
4.   Slave-trade—History—Chronology.   I.   Title.
DT17.D5   1983   960′.02′02   82-21353
ISBN 0-8161-8543-3

To the Memory of
My Mother and Father and
to the Hopes of
My Nieces and Nephews

Contents

The Author

Ellen Irene Diggs is a noted writer whose credits include several dozen scholarly articles on various cultures and black history. She is also a widely published author of travel literature; accounts of her travels and field studies in Cuba, Haiti, Israel, Egypt, Africa, South America, and the U.S.S.R. have appeared in major U.S. dailies.

Educated as an undergraduate at Monmouth College and the University of Minnesota, she pursued graduate studies at Atlanta University, where she was a student of and research assistant to W.E. Burghardt Du Bois. She received her masters degree from Atlanta University, and her doctorate from the University of Havana. At Atlanta University, she was cofounder of Phylon, the Atlanta University Review of Race and Culture.

Dr. Diggs has been active in several civic areas, most notably in the fine arts as a member of the Women's Committee of the Baltimore Museum of Art and the Women's Board of the Peabody Institute of The Johns Hopkins University, as the author of the Minority Report on the Maryland Department of Correction and the Department of Parole and Probation for the Governor's Task Force.

She was a Roosevelt Fellow, Institute of International Education, to the University of Havana, and, sponsored by the U.S. Department of State, she was an exchange scholar resident in Montevideo, Uruguay. Dr. Diggs has been a fellow of the American Anthropological Association, the American Association of Physical Anthropologists, and the American Association of Applied Anthropology, has been an Associate in Current Anthropology, and is a fellow of the American Association for the Advancement of Science.

Preface

Motivated by the favorable reception of my seventy-one-page paperbound monograph entitled A Chronology of Notable Events and Dates in the History of the African and His Descendants during the Period of Slavery and the Slave Trade, published in 1970 by the Association for the Study of Negro Life and History, and with the idea of a revised edition, I collected and added additional items to my personal copy.

In consultation with the late Charles T. Davis, professor of English and Master of Calhoun College, and later with Henry-Louis Gates, Jr., assistant professor of Afro-American Studies and English, Yale University, the monograph was revised to include "every major book written by blacks from the sixteenth century"; "a host of specific abolitionist titles crucial to the formation of the image of the black in the Western mind"; and "all the slave narratives, as well as collections of poetry, novels, histories." I also added other pertinent events, legislation and court decisions, inventions by blacks, conspiracies, rebellions, uprisings, papal bulls, statistics, ideologies, and personalities. The arrangement of this book is chronological from 4777 B.C., when the first of three successive Egyptian empires began, to 1888, when all the slaves in Brazil were emancipated. This chronology demonstrates that the documented history of Africans and Afro-Americans began more than six thousand years ago.

It is clarifying to have a reference book that arranges events in chronological order. A calendar orients and guides one's thinking. Dates are landmarks; they give generalized ideas of beginnings and endings of eras and movements. Dates divide up the past, and when the fragments of the past are put back together one gets a more comprehensive view of the unity of human history. In the introduction to the original edition, Charles H. Wesley wrote that "dates are important pegs on which to hang events, and when the long sweep of history is taken into consideration, they bring meaning and a rationale into the study of people and the events which concern them. . . . They are the guidelines pointing out the past. . . . Students interested in black folk should remember the important dates

and devise the means of using them through the principles of association and parallelism. Note these in connection with these dates
which follow and the association and parallels in other phases of
history previously learned. . . . It is most significant because it
embraces not only the United States but also the Americas, Africa
and all the world where black people lived and achieved. It spans
the Ancient and Medieval world from 3500 B.C."

This chronology puts what we know in focus; it enriches and in-
creases our knowledge and understanding of the Afro-American past.
A rather inclusive history of Africans and their descendants might
be written using this chronology as a guide. It shows that the
suppression of the slave trade and the abolition of slavery were due
directly to agitation by blacks as well as whites; that agitation
for full social, civil, economic, and political equality in the United
States did not begin in the 1950s and 1960s; that the fifties and the
sixties represent an acceleration of the struggle that began shortly
after the arrival of the first twenty blacks to this continent. This
chronology attempts to destroy myths, presents documented facts, indicates who was contemporary with whom, what happened where and when;
how diverse the events involving Afro-Americans have been; how, and
sometimes why, events affecting Afro-Americans have emerged out of
each other.

The Chronology is concerned with slavery and the slave trade as
inhuman institutions, their impact on whites as well as blacks, how
emancipation came about, and the part played by blacks in their
abolition. Riots, insurrections, uprisings, revolts--all the things
that indicate dissatisfaction, desire for, and attempts to gain,
freedom are included. Whether successful or unsuccessful, planned
or spontaneous, these attempts were motivated by a desire to be free.

This Chronology provides a comprehensive view based on facts
selected from a mass of material in numerous sources. These facts
enable the reader to perceive the interrelation of events in the
history of blacks in various parts of the world and to observe the
way in which the slavery of blacks in the United States was integral
to worldwide financial, cultural, religious, technological, and
scientific conditions.

Every effort has been made to give credit to all sources, by
enclosing direct quotes in quotation marks and, when quoting or
paraphrasing, by citing author, date, and page number.

Introduction

The importance of organizing and making readily available the record of events and personalities in the history of Africans and their descendants can scarcely by overemphasized. Social policy and social reform to a large extent depend on accurate and complete information. The revolution in research and scholarship and the reconsideration and reexamination of old research regarding blacks, demand a chronology that includes relevant events in the history of blacks from a new perspective; the mere questioning of the labeling of people, such as Ethiopians and Egyptians previously considered white, is itself significant.

A chronology of Afro-American history is important because there is so widespread a belief that Africa and Africans have no history, have not achieved, have made little or no contribution to culture; that Africa is a dark, mysterious continent, isolated and insulated from the rest of the world; that what happened in Africa does not matter.

The history of Africa has been suppressed and distorted. North Africa is often viewed as separate from the rest of Africa and its population as not including Africans, or, when Africans are included, they are not identified as blacks. What most people believe about Afro-Americans is that all of their ancestors were slaves, when as a matter of fact the twenty blacks who arrived in Virginia in 1619 were free men, free in Africa and free under the laws of Virginia.

Although slavery has existed throughout history, although slavery was practiced throughout Europe, and although dungeons were common all over Italy, where sixty thousand slaves worked in chains, writing about slavery is often confined to blacks in the United States and Africans in Africa, which tends to lead the reader to the conclusion that only blacks have been slaves.

Blake writes in his preface to The History of Slavery and the Slave Trade Ancient and Modern that "it is strange that a system which pervaded and weakened, if it did not ruin, the republics of Greece and the empire of the Caesars, should not be more frequently

noticed by historical writers. They refer, only incidentally, to
the existence of slavery. An insurrection or other remarkable event
with which the slaves are connected, occasionally reminds the reader
of history of the existence of a servile class." Slaves "numbered,
in the age of the Antonines [Roman Empire], sixty millions! . . .
How few of the historians of England refer to the existence in that
country of a system of unmitigated, hopeless, hereditary slavery.
Yet it prevailed throughout England in Saxon and Norman times. In
the time of the Heptarchy, slaves were an article of export. 'Great
numbers were exported, like cattle, from the British coasts.' The
Roman market was partially supplied with slaves from the shores of
Britain. Pope Gregory the Great, struck with the blooming complex-
ions and fair hair of some Saxon children in the slave market, sent
over St. Augustine from Rome to convert the islanders to Christianity."

Two hundred years after the suppression of slavery in Europe,
Europeans began enslaving Africans, bringing them to Europe, to
North and South America, and the isles of the Atlantic. They estab-
lished forts and factories on the coasts of Africa.

Only a relatively small number of persons in the United States
owned large numbers of slaves or any slaves at all. In some cases,
especially in cases of ownership of a few, the owners were little
better off than their slaves. The fears of many whites of the
period covered here, however, are apparent from the legislation
enacted: against slaves using African languages; against attempts
by blacks and whites to teach blacks to read and/or write; against
amalgamation of the races by interbreeding and intermarriage except
when producing more slaves.

There was severe, brutal punishment of slaves: death, castration, whipping, cutting off an ear, slitting the nose, putting out
an eye, branding with a hot iron. Blake records that to destroy
their dignity and sense of personal worth, slaves, except livery
servants, were prohibited from possessing or wearing any apparel
"finer than negro cloth, duffils, kerseys, osnaburgs, blue linen,
check lines, or coarse garlix or calicoes, checked cotton or Scotch
plaid; and any constable seeing any negro better clad, might seize
the clothes and appropriate them to his own use."

The memory of slavery as an institution still disturbs the descendant of an owner of a human being and the descendant of the one
who was owned.

Black Chronology

from 4000 B.C. to the Abolition of the Slave Trade

c.4777 B.C.

"About 4777 B.C. Aha-Mena began the first of three successive Egyptian empires. This lasted two thousand years, with many Pharoahs, like Khafra of the Fourth Dynasty, of a strongly negroid cast of countenance. At the end of the period the empire fell apart into Egyptian and Ethiopian halves and a silence of three centuries ensued . . ." (Du Bois 1915, p. 33). "The great Sphinx at Gizeh, so familiar to all the world, the Sphinxes of Tanis, the statue from the Fayum, the statue of the Esquiline at Rome, and the Colossi of Bubastis all represent . . ." blacks, "and are described by [William Flinders] Petrie [an expert in the field of Egyptology] as 'having high cheek bones, flat cheeks, both in one plane, a massive nose, firm projecting lips, and thick hair, with an austere and almost savage expression of power'" (Du Bois 1915, p. 34; Du Bois 1939, p. 25).

3500 B.C.-1723 B.C.

A protohistoric period in history of Ethiopia; includes two periods corresponding with the Old and Middle Kingdoms of Egypt and a third period corresponding with the New Egyptian Empire. An historic period, from 1723 B.C. to 335 A.D., includes:
A. The Napatan Period--1723 B.C. to 308 B.C.
B. The Middle Meroitic Period--308 B.C. to 10 A.D.
C. The Late Meroitic Period--10 A.D. to 355 A.D.
(Du Bois 1939, p. 27).

3064 B.C.

The middle empire arose and lasted nearly twenty-four centuries. Under pharaohs whose African descent is plainly

(c.3000 B.C.)

> evident, such as Amenemhat I and II and Usertesen I, the
> ancient glories of Egypt were restored and surpassed.

c.3000 B.C.

> Imhotep, a learned black physician, the earliest known physi-
> cian and history's earliest known scientific genius, lived in
> Egypt. In the course of time, he was deified and became for
> later generations the special god of medicine.

c.2660 B.C.-22 B.C.

> In c. 2660 B.C. Usertesen III drove back the black tribes of
> the Upper Nile Valley and attempted to confine them to the
> edge of the Nubian Desert above the Second Cataract. Hemmed
> in here, they set up the state of Napata. Less than one
> hundred years later an African from the south, Ra Nehesi, was
> seated on the throne of the pharaohs and was called "the King's
> eldest son" (Du Bois 1947, p. 114; Du Bois 1915, p. 35). This
> may mean that an incursion from the far south had placed a
> black conqueror on the throne. The whole empire was in some
> way shaken, and two hundred years later the invasion of the
> Hyksos began. The domination of Hyksos kings, who may have
> been Negroids from Asia, lasted for 500 years (Petrie 1902,
> 1:52, 53; 237; cited in Du Bois 1947, p. 35).

c.2300 B.C.

> The plains of the Tigris and Anzan-Susinka were ruled by a
> dynasty of black kings.

2160 B.C.-1100 B.C.

> The monarchy centering at Thebes lasted 1,000 years. By the
> time of the Eighteenth Dynasty, the courts had become centers
> of social law and a state socialism had been established.

c.2000 B.C.

> "Around 2000 B.C.--because of a diminishing flow of airborne
> moisture from southern Europe or some other climatic change--
> the Sahara started drying up. Animals and humans began to
> disperse, but the paintings--protected by dry air and nests
> of pit vipers--remained" (Davidson 1966, p. 43).

"It was under Usertesen III circa 2,000 B.C. that there arose
one of the earliest flares of the race and color question,
for after he had defeated the Nubian-Ethiopian forces, he set
up a huge granite stele--an advertising medium similar, in a
way, to modern highway advertising signs--on which the hiero-
glyphics stated the following: 'No Black man whatsoever
shall be permitted to pass this place going down stream (the
Nile) no matter whether he is travelling by desert or journeying in a boat--except such Blacks as come to do business in
the country or travelling on an embassy. Such, however, shall
be well treated in every way whatsoever. But no boats belonging to Blacks shall, in the future, be permitted to pass
down this river.' Usertesen III charges his successors to
keep up the fight against Nubia and Ethiopia so the boundary
would be made permanent. The stele was set up at Semnah, the
modern Sennar in the Anglo-Egyptian Sudan" (Huggins and
Jackson 1969, p. 55).

c.1546-1525 B.C.

Amenhotep I, son of Aahmes I (Ahmose I) and Nefertari was,
along with his mother, worshipped by the Egyptians as a saint
or demigod for generations following his death. Amenhotep I's
successors were Thutmose I (c.1525 B.C.-1508 B.C.), Thutmose
II (1508 B.C.-1504 B.C.) and Queen Hathshepsut (1504 B.C.-
1482 B.C.). Hathshepsut's successor, Thutmose III (1482 B.C.-
1450 B.C.), one of the greatest militarists of antiquity,
appears to have been the son of a Sudanese woman.

1500 B.C.

Hathshepsut reigned conjointly with her half-brother Thuthmosis
II for two or three years. After the death of Thuthmosis II,
Hathshepsut assumed full power as ruler of Egypt. She completed the temple of Deir el Bahari (Sublime of the Sublime)
one of the most dramatically situated in the world. It was
designated some say by Thuthmosis II and others her favorite
architect, Senenmut. A tree-lined avenue of sphinxes led up
to the temple and ramps led from terrace to terrace. Reliefs
on the south side of the middle terrace show the queen's expedition by way of the Red Sea to Punt. Throughout the
temple there are statues of the queen. The king and queen of
Punt are represented as of the modern Hottentot type, and the
queen as having the characteristic steatopygia (Du Bois 1947,
p. 128).

3

(c.1420-1412 B.C.)

c.1420-1412 B.C.

> King Tut's fraternal grandfather, Thutmose IV (1425 B.C.-
> 1412 B.C.), the successor of Amenhotep II, it is believed
> married a black woman, Mutemua. Amenhotep III, whom King Tut
> stated was his father, was apparently black.

1411-1375 B.C.

> Amenophis III (Amenhotep III), son of a black woman, Mutemua,
> reigned (some say 1402 B.C.-1365 B.C.).

1580 B.C.-1350 B.C.

> Aahmes defeated the Hyksos and founded a new empire, the
> Eighteenth Dynasty, which lasted about 1500 years. Black
> Nefertari, "the most venerated figure of Egyptian history"
> (Du Bois 1947, pp. 114, 128) and cofounder of the Eighteenth
> Dynasty, was his queen; styled the wife of the god Ammon, many
> monuments were erected in her honor. Nefertari was known for
> her beauty, strong personality, and unusual administrative
> skills. For many years Nefertari was joint ruler with her son,
> Amenhotep I, who succeeded his father (Du Bois 1939, pp. 26,
> 27). Nearly 300 years later (c.1420 B.C.) one of Nefertari's
> descendants, Thothmes IV, married black Queen Mutemua, whose
> son was the celebrated Amenhotep III (reigned c.1400 B.C.),
> the builder of the great temple of Ammon at Luxor and the
> Colossi at Memnon (Du Bois 1939, p. 27). According to some
> authorities, Nefertari was the grandmother of Thothmes I
> (Thutmose I, c.1525 B.C.-1508 B.C.) and the great-grandmother
> of Hathshepsut and Thothmes III (Thutmose III)--two of the
> greatest sovereigns that ever sat on an Egyptian throne.
> Thutmose III fought seventeen campaigns in twenty years. If
> there ever was an Egyptian Empire he was the Emperor (Du Bois
> 1939, p. 27).

c.1365-1359 B.C.

> Nefertiti, wife of Akhenaton and daughter of Segenenra, should
> not be confused with Nefertari. Akhenaton, often called the
> "Heretic Pharaoh," was originally Amenophis IV but changed his
> name in honor of the Aten, the disk of the sun, the basis of
> his form of monotheism. He was particularly detested because
> he tried to establish monotheism in a new capital at Tell
> el-Amarna. Akhenaton was apparently black; his facial features

duplicate most of the characteristics of the stereotype for a
black male. Nefertiti was one of the most famous beauties of
the ancient world and is most widely known for the celebrated
portrait head of her now in the Berlin Museum and the un-
finished head now in the Cairo Museum which was excavated
from a Tell el-Amarna studio (Maroon and Newby n.d., p. 52).

1122 B.C.-249 B.C.

In the earliest Chinese history several texts in classic
books spoke of diminutive blacks; thus the Tcheu-Li, composed
under the dynasty of Tcheu, gives a description of the inhabitants with black and oily skin. . . . The Prince Liu-Nan,
who died in 122 B.C., speaks of a kingdom of diminutive blacks
in the southwest of China. "H. Imbert, a French anthropologist, who lived in the Far East, has said in Les Negritos de
la Chine (Imbert 1923): 'The Negroid races peopled at some
time all the south of India, Indo-China, and China. The
south of Indo-China actually has now pure Negritos as the
Semangs, and mixed as the Malays and the Sakais. . . . In the
first epochs of Chinese history, the Negrito type peopled all
the south of this country and even in the island of Hai-Nan,
as we have attempted to prove in our study on the Negritos,
or Black Men, of this island. Skulls of these Negroes have
been found in the island of Formosa and traces of this Negroid
element in the islands of Liu-kiu to the south of Japan"
(Du Bois 1947, pp. 179, 180).

1050 B.C.

Early legendary history declared that a queen, Maqueda, or
Nikaula of Sheba, a state of Central Abyssinia, visited
Solomon in 1050 B.C. and had her son, Menelik, educated in
Jerusalem. This was the supposed beginning of the Auxmite
kingdom, the capital of which, Axume, was a flourishing center
of trade.

900 B.C.-c.200 A.D.

Nok culture existed in the Central Nigerian plateau.

750 B.C.-355 A.D.

Seventy-six rulers reigned in Ethiopia.

5

(750 B.C.-308 B.C.)

750 B.C.-308 B.C.

When Shesheng I, the Libyan, usurped the throne of the
pharaohs in the tenth century B.C., the Egyptian legitimate
dynasty went to Napata as king priests and established a
theocratic monarchy. Gathering strength, the Ethiopian kingdom under this dynasty expanded north about 750 B.C. and for
a century ruled all Egypt. During the early Napata period
there were twenty-six kings. The first king was Piankhy
(Piankhi) and some of his successors were Kashta the Kushite,
Shabaka, Tarharqa (Taharka), and Tanutamen. Napata was an
administrative center and became the first capital of Kush
(Du Bois 1915, p. 39; Du Bois 1939, p. 29).

744 B.C.-710 B.C.

Piankhy reigned. He inherited from his father, Kashta,
dominion over Egypt as far northward as Thebes, perhaps 200
or 300 miles farther, and he served as governor or viceroy
over Egypt under the Ethiopian crown before the conquest
(Du Bois 1939, p. 30).

732 B.C.

Piankhy was informed by courier that a Libyan prince from the
Delta was marching south. Piankhy waited for the Libyan to
get as far as possible from his base. When he reached
Hermophlis, 400 miles south of the Mediterranean, Piankhy
started the attack, assembling an army at Napata, and ordered
them to march northward to Thebes. Finally, he joined his
armies, swept through Egypt, and received the submission of
sixteen princes (Du Bois 1939, p. 30).

c.710 B.C.

Piankhy died having completed the conquest of Egypt, and
ruled over a land that stretched from the shores of the
Mediterranean to the borders of modern Ethiopia--almost a
quarter of the African continent.

700 B.C.

Pharaoh Necho of Egypt sent out the Phoenician expedition that
circumnavigated Africa.

688 B.C.-663 B.C.

Reign of "the greatest of the Ethiopian kings," Taharka. His reign, with all its wars, was an era of prosperity and cultural advancement. It has been said that he, with four other kings, led expeditions as far as the Straits of Gibraltar. Arthur E. P. B. Weigall calls his reign "that astonishing epoch of nigger domination," and Randall-MacIver says "It seems amazing that an African Negro should have been able with any sort of justification to style himself Emperor of the World." Taharka died in 663 B.C. and was succeeded by his nephew Tanwetamani, during whose reign the Assyrians drove the Kushites out of Egypt (Du Bois 1939, p. 31; Du Bois 1947, p. 137).

620 B.C.-560 B.C.

Two of the most illustrious writers of Greece were called blacks by the Greek Orthodox humanities scholar, Maximus Planudes: Aesop and Sappho. Ovid makes it clear that the ancients did not consider Sappho white. She is compared with Andromeda, daughter of Cepheus, black King of Ethiopia. Ovid says: "Andromede patriae fusca colore suae." In Epistle XV of the Heroides of Ovid (translated by Ridley), Sappho says to Phaon, "I am small of stature but I have a name that fills all lands. I myself have produced this extended renown for my name. If I am not fair, Andromeda, the daughter of Cepheus, was swarthy though the complexion of her country was pleasing to Perseus. White pigeons, too, are often mated with spotted ones and the black turtledove is often beloved by a bird that is green." Paul Lacroix says of Sappho: "Although Plato graces her with the epithet of beautiful and although Athenaeus is persuaded of her beauty on the authority of Plato, it is more probable that Maximus of Tyre who paints her for us as little and black is in conformity with more authentic tradition."

c.600 B.C.

It is probable that Hindus were trading with East Africa about this time and settling on the coast.

c.593 B.C.-567 B.C.

Aspeluta, whose mother and sister are represented as African, ruled.

(550 B.C.)

550 B.C.

King Amasis of Lower Egypt substituted wax figures for the
human victims sacrificed daily at the temple of Ammon.

500 B.C.

Rise of Kushite kingdom of Meroe, a busy iron-working center
on the Middle Nile in the northern part of the modern Republic
of Sudan.

Sabaeans from southern Arabia settled in northern Ethiopia and
with the local peoples began to build a new culture that was
to be the parent culture of Axum.

The gradual replacement of stone by iron for essential weapons
and tools began. By c.200 B.C. the metal founders of Meroe
had built a major industry in iron. But the actual setting up
of iron-extractive and forging industries south of the Sahara
seems not to have occurred until soon after 300 B.C. The
existence of an iron-using industry over a fairly wide area of
the Niger and Benue rivers (in north central Nigeria) has been
validated by archaeological evidence (Davidson 1968, p. 16).

431 B.C.

As early as 431 B.C. the trade of Egypt was well known in
Athens. Sails and papyrus rolls came from Egypt and ivory
from Libya. The slaves were usually not from Africa but from
Asia (Du Bois 1947, p. 140).

430 B.C.

Herodotus "had no difficulty in concluding that Egypt's cultural origins lay in continental Africa" (Davidson 1968,
p. 12).

c.430 B.C.

Herodotus wrote that the Kushites bound their prisoners with
gold chains and used weapons tipped with stone, while for
them bronze was the rarest metal. The oldest Iron Age dates
come from central Nigeria where over 2000 years ago some of
the people began to make iron (Davidson 1968, p. 9).

Black Chronology

c.372 B.C.-361 B.C.

Horsiatef made nine expeditions against the peoples south of Meroe.

332 B.C.

Alexander the Great conquered Egypt. He had blacks in his armies; one of the most illustrious was Clitus, whom he made King of Bactria and commander of his cavalry. Clitus's mother, Dropsica, was Alexander's nurse, and Clitus is mentioned by Plutarch and others as Clitus Niger, that is, Clitus the Negro (Du Bois 1947, p. 140).

328 B.C.-308 B.C.

Nastasen, successor of Horsiatef, moved the capital from Napata to Meroe although Napata continued to be the religious capital and the Ethiopian kings were still crowned on its gold throne.

308 B.C.-225 B.C.

During this period there were ten rulers, five reigning at Napata and five at Meroe. While the Ethiopian kings were still crowned at Napata, Meroe gradually became the real capital and supported at one time 4000 artisans and 200,000 soldiers. It was here that the famous Candaces reigned as queens. Pliny tells us that one Candace of the time of Nero had had forty-four predecessors on the throne, while another Candace figures in the New Testament (Acts 8, 27). Pseudo-Callisthenes tells the story of the visit of Alexander the Great to Candace, Queen of Meore. Candace told him not to scorn her people because they were black; she would not let him enter Ethiopia (Du Bois 1939, pp. 32-33).

250 B.C.-100 A.D.

The greatest period of the Kushite kingdom. It was during this time that the pyramids were filled with the finest objects and many great monuments were built. Trade with other countries was at its height.

(225 B.C.-200 B.C.)

225 B.C.-200 B.C.

Ergamenes united the kingdoms of Ethiopia. He was strongly
influenced by Greek culture which from the fifth to the
second century B.C. penetrated Africa from the east. At the
same time he began to employ the Ethiopian speech in writing
and used a new Ethiopian alphabet.

c.1 A.D.

The skills of metal-working began to be understood and practiced, perhaps beginning with copper in the regions of modern
Katanga and northern Zambia. They soon began working in iron.
Population was small. There is evidence of early farming and
cultivation of millet.

Sailors from Egypt and Arabia visited the East Coast of Africa
for trade, buying African ivory, tortoise shell, and other
products. There is increasing evidence that African slaves
were being transported to India before and at the beginning
of the Christian era. There were African sultans in Bengal
before the Portuguese arrived, at which time Africans were
already living near Madras. Janjira, a state south of Bombay,
is of African origin.

Kush was still rich and powerful.

Axum, in northern Ethiopia, became the center of a trading
kingdom that developed rapidly. Its main port, Adulis, was
visited by ships from Egypt and India.

64-68

The Roman Emperor Nero planned to invade Ethiopia and sent
some scouts to report. They penetrated as far as the region
of the Sadd.

100

Gradual spread of early techniques of metal-working across
the wooded uplands of Central Africa, and probably into East
Africa. In both regions the Late Stone Age continued for
several more centuries.

c.189-199

Pope Victor I, an African, unified the church by fixing the present date for Easter and making Latin the official language. Victor was the first of three African popes in the early Catholic Church.

120

A Greek merchant of Egypt wrote a guide to the Indian Ocean trade, the <u>Periplus of the Erythraean Sea</u>, which included the earliest description of life along the East Africa Coast between the Horn and southern Tanzania.

210

"Black people have been living in Britain since at least Roman times. We know of one individual African legionary, 'famous among buffoons and always a great joker,' who went down in history for making fun of the Emperor Septimius Severus outside Carlisle around the year 210 A.D. Significantly, the Emperor was 'troubled by the man's colour' and ordered purifying sacrifices to be offered, which turned out also to be black. Africans continue to appear unexpectedly in British history" (Edwards 1981, p. 33).

300

Kingdom of Awkar emerged under a chief named Gana.

311

Melchiades, an African, was elected Pope.

320

Earliest Iron Age settlements at Zimbabwe. Gradual spread of Early Iron Age Leopard's Kopje culture across central plateau south of Zambezi, and Ziwa culture across eastern plateau.

Axum completed destruction of Kingdom of Kush (Meroe). King Ezana of Axum accepted Christianity. Axumite port of Adulis continued as important center for the western trade of the Indian Ocean.

(400)

400

Seafaring Indonesians from Java and Sumatra arrived in Madagascar and settled there. They introduced a new kind of banana from Asia, which was widely accepted in Africa.

Rise of new X-Group culture in land of Kush. This became the parent of a brilliant Christian culture in Nubia between 600 and 1200.

c.450

The earliest version of the Mauritius story, upon which all later versions depend, is found in the Writings of Eucherius, Bishop of Lyons. According to this account Mauritius was a duke in Egypt (in the Thebaid), an early domain of Christianity. He was the commander of a Roman legion stationed there. By order of the Emperor Maximianus his troop of 6,600 men was dispatched to Gaul and ordered to participate in the persecution of Christians there. Being Christians themselves the "Legio Thebaica" refused obedience, and was finally, after gradual decimation, executed with its leaders. This event is said to have taken place in Switzerland, near what later became Saint Maurice in Valeis, on 22 September in either 280 or 300.

492-496

Gelasius, born in Rome of African parents, died four years after his election to the papacy. A writer of letters, books, and hymns, he taught the presence of Christ in the sacrament, and the supremacy of the pope over all the churches.

c.498

Artists flocked to Egypt from Asia Minor. Poets and writers lived at court. The Thousand and One Nights stories were collected. Indian stories and European romances were combined with Egyptian materials. A companion collection of poems was written by Antar-bin-Shaddad. Antar was born c.498, the son of a black slave girl, Zebbeda, and of Shaddad, a nobleman of the tribe of Abs. One of his works is the sixth poem of the Mo'allagat--the "golden verses"--which are considered in Arabia the greatest poems ever written. The story is that they were hung on the ka'bah at the Holy Temple at Mecca so

12

that all the pilgrims who came there might know them and do
obeisance to them. The Mo'allagat belongs to the first school
of Arabian poetry--to the Gahilieh--"time of ignorance." The
Antar poem belongs to the time of the War of Dahis, and like
the five poems that preceded it in the epic, it lauds the
victors of the battlefield, describes the beauties of nature,
and praises the camel of the desert. The main theme, however,
is love. The Romance of Antar was published in Cairo in
thirty-two volumes. There are two editions of the work: one
known as the Syrian Antar, the other as the Arabian Antar.
The deeds of prowess described in the poems of Antar compelled
his father to acknowledge him as his heir (Du Bois 1947,
pp. 189ff).

618-907

Evidence of blacks in China is given by Professor Chang Hsing-
lang in "The Importation of Negro slaves to China under the
T'ang Dynasty, A.D. 618-907." "The Lin-Yi Kuo Chuan [Topog-
raphy of the Land of Lin-Yi] contained in Book 197 of the
Chiu T'ang Shu [Old dynastic history of T'ang] says: 'The
people living to the south of Lin-Yi have woolly hair and
black skin.'" Chinese folklore speaks often of these blacks,
and mentions an empress of China, named Li (373-397), consort
of the Emperor Hsiao Wu Wen, who is spoken of as being black.
He adds that according to the writings of a later period--the
seventh to the ninth century--black slaves were imported into
China from Africa (Du Bois 1947, p. 180).

622

Prophet Muhammad journeyed with three companions from Mecca
to Medina. From this journey, or hegira, the world religion
of Islam was introduced by its soldiers, teachers, and merchants all the way across North Africa and southwestern
Europe and in the east as far as Malaysia and China (Davidson
1969, p. 81).

639

"The Arabs invaded African Egypt, taking it from the Eastern
Roman Emperors and securing as allies the native Negroid
Egyptians, now called Copts, and using Sudanese blacks,
Persians, and Turks in their armies. They came in 639 under
Amr-ibn-el-Asr, partly as friends of Egyptians against the

(690–1335)

> tyranny of the Eastern Roman Empire, partly even as defenders
> of the heretical Coptic Church. It must be remembered that
> they were related by blood and history to the Negroid peoples.
> One of Mohammed's concubines was a curly-haired Coptic woman,
> May. Nubians from the Sudan took frequent part in these wars.
> Alexandria surrendered in 642. . . ." (Lane-Poole 1901, pp. 22,
> 28, 29).

690–1335

> The African kingdom of the Songhay, with its capital at Gao,
> had a dynasty called the Dia, or Za, which remained in power
> on the western Niger from 690 to 1335. The known history of
> Songhay covers 1000 years and three dynasties, and centered
> in the great bend of the Niger. There were thirty kings of
> the First Dynasty. During the reign of one of these, the
> Songhay kingdom became the vassal kingdom of Melle, then at
> the height of its glory. The Mossi plundered Timbuktu in
> 1339 and separated Jenne, the original seat of the Songhay,
> from the rest of the kingdom.

700

> Early Iron Age peoples of the Bantu language family settled
> in small villages in many parts of East as well as Central
> Africa.

> Expansion of Indian Ocean trade as Muslim Arabs established
> trading stations in Northwest India, Ceylon, Southeast Asia,
> Southern China, and East Africa.

> Groups south of Zambezi began to move southwards across the
> Limpopo River. They carried the Iron Age into South Africa
> and initiated an agricultural revolution using their own iron
> implements for the systematic cultivation of crops. With
> this dispersal came the development of many different Bantu
> languages.

> Growth of a new Christian culture in Nubia (Northern Sudan);
> three kingdoms appear.

> Early origins along the East Coast of Swahili culture, and of
> the Swahili language, a Bantu language influenced by Arabic
> and other African languages. Development of trade and more

permanent settlements along the coast, including that of
Unguja Ukuu in Zanzibar.

Development of Iron Age "Kisale" culture in Katanga; increase
in importance of copper mining and trading.

Rise of trading state of Ghana in western part of Western
Sudan. More trade across the Sahara. Beginning of European
Middle Ages.

Foundation of the Empire of the Franks.

711-712

Moorish conquest of Visigothic kingdom in Spain under the
leadership of Tarik at the battle of Guadalete. Arabs split
their forces into two columns. One of them crossed the
Strait of Gibraltar to invade Spain. The other traveled
southward, following the caravan routes across the Sahara to
seek the source of Sudanese gold.

713

Portugal conquered by Moors.

746

One of the first events in the history of the Africans in
Spain was the attempt of Ibn Horaith, son of the chief of the
Jadhamite tribe of Arabs, by an African woman, to gain the
emirate in Spain. Thoaba, the emir, died in the year 746 and
his son, Amr, claimed his father's place. Ibn Horaith disputed the succession. Ibn Horaith had such a dislike for the
Syrian Arabs that he said: "If one bowl contained the blood
of all the Syrians I would drain it to the dregs" (Gould 1914,
p. 298). For this reason Sumayl, the leader of the Syrians
in Spain, used his influence to have Yusuf, of the tribe of
Fihrites, appointed emir, and to console him, Ibn Horaith was
made prefect of Regio. Sumayl, by treachery, had Ibn Horaith
deprived of his prefecture in January 747, after he had en-
joyed that honor only a short time. Ibn Horaith allied himself with Abu'l Khattir, another pretender to the emirate, who
reluctantly gave up his claim because the tribe to which Ibn
Horaith belonged was most numerous in Spain. This open
quarrel revived a feud of very remote antiquity between the

(757)

> Northern and Southern Arabs, and the nobles enrolled them-
> selves under the banners of the opposing clans. The battle
> took place at Secunda, a suburb of Cordova, and the remains
> of an old Roman walled town. There were only two or three
> hundred on each side, and they fought in the manner of the old
> chivalry. Initially, they tourneyed until all the spears were
> shattered, then they drew their swords, and when these broke
> they fought with clubs and bare fists. Toward evening Sumayl,
> the Syrian, departed and sent to Cordova for reinforcements of
> tradespeople. By force of numbers the party of Ibn Horaith
> was conquered and in the dusk he sought to escape by hiding
> under a mill. His former ally, Abul'l Khattir, pointed him
> out to Sumayl and, with a taunt for Ibn Horaith's hatred of
> the Syrians, said, "Son of a black woman, is there one drop
> left in your bowl?" (Gould 1914, pp. 298ff). Sumayl beheaded
> Ibn Horaith and slew seventy of his followers.

757

> Sidjilmessa, the last town in Lower Morocco toward the desert,
> was founded by an African who ruled over the Berbers (Du Bois
> 1947, p. 203).

758

> Abdurrahman, a Prince of Omayyads, arrived in Spain and after
> thirty years of fighting, founded an independent government.
> In the tenth century it became the Caliphate of Cordova. His
> power passed to black Sarakolles with whom Semites had amal-
> gamated.

800

> East African coastlands came under influence of Islam and
> Arabs.

800–1076

> Kingdom of Ghana. At Ghana there were forty-four white rulers,
> half coming before the hegira and half after it. Then the
> power passed to black Sarakolles with whom Semites had amal-
> gamated.

846

> Sefawa dynasty founded; Kingdom of Kanem emerged near Lake
> Chad.

16

(c.900–1054)

850

People of Ingombe-Ilede, in southern Zambia, were wealthy enough to bury their chiefs with many gold ornaments.

Four hundred black East Africans were enrolled in the army of Abu'l Abbas, ruler of Bagdad. They rose in revolt with a black called "Lord of the Blacks" as their leader.

862

"In 862 A.D. the Annals of Ireland record the landing of black slaves ('blue men' they are called in both Irish and Norse) by Vikings returning from raids on Spain and North Africa" (Edwards 1981, p. 33).

869

The Persian adventurer, Al Kabith, summoned the black slaves to revolt, and they flocked to his side in tens of thousands. In 871 they captured Basra and for fourteen years dominated the Euphrates delta. When Masudi visited this country fourteen years later, he was told that this conquest by famine and sword had killed at least a million people (Du Bois 1947, p. 187).

883

The Zeng blacks of East Africa revolted and some settled in Mesopotamia.

891

Levantines and Persians bought African slaves. At the close of the seventh century there were enough slaves in Mesopotamia to stage a revolt. They revolted again in 868.

c.900

"A skull confidently identified as that of a young black girl has been found in a tenth-century Anglo-Saxon burial at North Elmham in Norfolk" (Edwards 1981, p. 33).

c.900–1054

The influence of Ghana extended from modern Mauretanian

(916)

> frontier in the west, eastward to the bend of Niger, and north to the fringe of the Sahara.

916

> Al-Mas'udi, tenth century Arab historian, visited the east coast of Africa; in 943 he wrote in his book, The Meadows of Gold and Miners of Gems, about an important African kingdom that was perhaps near the mouth of the Zambezi. According to Al-Mas'udi, if a king departed from the rules of justice, he was killed and his heirs barred from succession.
>
> Continued spread of the Iron Age. Kalomo culture in this period in southern Zambia (middle and later stages: 900-1200).
>
> Early Iron Age in Malawi.

935-936

> Ikshid ruled Egypt as governor. He was succeeded by a black Abyssinian eunuch, Abu-1-Misk Kafur, (Musky Camphor) for whom Ikshid named a celebrated garden in Cairo. "Kafur was a clever man of deep black color with smooth shiny skin, who had been guardian of the sons of Ikshid. . . . He attracted men of learning and letters and began an era of art and literature which placed Egypt as a cultural center next to Bagdad, Damascus, and Cordova. . . ." (Lane-Poole 1914, 6:89). Kafur ruled Egypt for twenty-two years from 946 to 968. He conquered Damascus and Aleppo and incorporated Syria under Egyptian rule. He died in 968 (Du Bois 1947, p. 188).

961

> Abdurahman III's power passed into the hand of Almansur, of African descent, who kept order with his army of Berbers and other Africans, making fifty invasions into Christian territory.

975

> From the founding of Kilwa until its capture by the Portuguese in the fifteenth century, forty sovereigns ruled there. Kilwa eventually became the most important commercial port on the East African coast.

980

A sultanate, with its seat of government at Kilwa between
Cape Delgado and the Island of Mafia, was founded by Ali,
son of Hassan, Prince of Shiraz. It had as vassals the sultans of Sofala, Angoshe, Mozambique, Zanzibar, Pemba, Mombaz
or Mombasa, Melinde or Malindi, Kismayu, and Magadoo (Benadir).
These diverse Arab and Persian sultans were not, properly
speaking, governors of states. Their authority was exercised
only over Mussulman colonies of Asiatic origin established
around their respective residences and over the Africans
living in the proximity of these residences. Their principal
occupation was to recruit slaves from African chiefs, with
whom they conspired. Slaves were procured by means of raids
and sold to them. They in turn sent the slaves to the ports
of the Gulf of Oman and the Persian Gulf or resold them to
Portuguese slave traders. Slave trading constituted almost
the only commerce and the only excuse for the Mussulman
settlements of East Africa and was the source of their prosperity.

c.990

An attempt at independence on the part of the chief of the
Lamtuna led to an expedition of the King of Ghana, who captured Howdaghost and reaffirmed his authority over the
sedentary Berbers and the veiled Zenaga of the desert.

998

Muzaffar, the son of the Caliph Almanzor, fought a battle
near Ceuta, in North Africa, against Ziri, the Berber. The
combat was waged from dawn to sunset and Muzaffar was on the
verge of defeat. An African whose brother had been put to
death by Ziri's command avenged himself by wounding Ziri
three times and then retreated to the Spanish lines. At first
the African's story was not believed because the banner of the
Berbers still floated aloft. Finally, Muzaffar was convinced
and ordered an attack that put the Berbers to flight. Three
years later Ziri died when his wounds were reopened (Gould
1914, p. 298).

1000

Many trading settlements on East Coast. Most important were
Zanzibar, Pemba, Kilwa, and those of the Banadir (later

(1000)

Somali) Coast. The ruling prince from Shiraz arrived from
Persia and made numerous treaties with African rulers along
the coast. Central African ivory and gold trade with East
Coast was already in existence; imports of Indian cottons,
beads, and other goods.

Period of great age of Islam, which continued for three more
centuries.

Ghana at height of its power as a trading empire. Other important states, including Kanem, appeared.

Almoravid invasion of Ghana.

East Africa was known to the Chinese as Po Pa Li; there was
extensive trade between Mo Lin (Malindi) and Canton.

Along the southern bank of the Limpopo, in what is now northern
Transvaal, Shona peoples established themselves and built a
series of Iron Age settlements which were further developed by
new groups from north of the Limpopo in later centuries. They
worked finely in cast and beaten gold, produced good hand-
turned pottery, and traded their products for Indian cottons
and other Indian Ocean imports. They buried their kings with
a wealth of gold ornament. About 1600 they were displaced by
another set of rulers from across the Limpopo, relatives of
the Karanga called the Venda, who remained until they were
ruined by the devastations of the early nineteenth century
(Davidson 1969, p. 69).

c.1000–c.1100

Ancestors of the Yoruba crossed the Niger river from the
northeast and established the village of Ile Ife.

1000–1200

Ghana was on the edge of the desert in the north; Mandingo-
land was between the Niger and the Senegal in the southern
and western Sahara; the Wolof were in the west on the Senegal;
the Songhay were on the Niger, in the center.

1009

The sixteenth king of the Songhay was converted to Mohammedanism; since then all Songhay princes have been Mohammedans.

1020-1158

Nedjeh, a black slave, and his descendants ruled Arabia.

1021-1026

Zahir ruled Egypt; his wife was a black Sudanese woman. After the death of her husband, she largely influenced the rule of her son who came to the throne in 1036 and ruled until 1094, the longest reign in the dynasty. This son, M'add, took the name of Mustansir and is regarded as the best and ablest of the rulers of his time. He loved and encouraged learning and had a library of 120,000 volumes. The "Black Dowager," who had great influence over him, sailed the Nile in her silver barge and imported additional black troops from the south, until Mustansir had in his escort 50,000 black soldiers and swordsmen, 20,000 Berbers, 10,000 Turks, and 30,000 white slaves. For years all Upper Egypt was held by black regiments (Du Bois 1947, p. 188).

1023

Kasim Ibn Hammud was joined by his faithful Africans, and on 12 February took advantage of Yahya's absence in Malaga to enter the city. On 16 September the Cordovans again expelled his forces, but with his African troops he beseiged them and cut off their supply of food. On 31 October the Cordovans, in a concentrated force, sallied out and put the attenuated line of beseigers to flight, but the Africans made a desperate resistance and only surrendered when Kasim had fled. Kasim was later captured by Xeres. Yahya Ibn Hammud was impressed by the loyalty of the Africans to his uncle, so he employed them to garrison Carmona, a city he had captured from the cadi of Seville [a cadi is a minor Moslem magistrate or judge] (Gould 1914, p. 299).

1035

Muslim Almoravid movement developed on an island in the Senegal river.

Ismail, the son of the cadi, lured Yahya from his secure position within the city walls and slew him in battle. Nevertheless, the Africans who held the city gates and walls would

21

(1038)

not surrender to Ismail or Ibn Abdallah, the former ruler of
Carmona, and they were nearly annihilated by their foes. At
Algeciras African soldiers played the role of king-makers and
proclaimed Mohammed, a cousin of Yahya, caliph, but this venture was unsuccessful (Gould 1914, p. 299).

1038

Zuhair, of Almeria, was unpopular among his subjects because
he was a so-called Slav prince--that is, a descendant of
Northern mercenaries, such as the mamelukes of more recent
times. Ibn Abbas, his vizier, induced him to make an expedition into Granadan territory. On 3 August he found himself
surrounded. His Slav cavalry fled when their leader, Hudhail,
was dismounted, and his Andalusian troops were dispirited and
useless. His 500 African infantry thereupon seized the armory
and went over to the enemy. It is possible that their de-
sertion was prearranged, for Badis, king of Granada, was
devoid of religious and racial prejudice and had a Jew, Samuel
Ibn Nagdela, for vizier, and an African, Kodam, as provost-
marshall (Gould 1914, p. 299).

1040

A movement of Mussulman propaganda arose among portions of
the Lemtuna people, who inhabited principally the Tagant and
the district of Howdaghost, and that of Goddala or Jeddala,
who led a nomadic life between the Mauritanian Adrar and the
Atlantic; a federation was formed. From a monastery situated
on an island of the lower Senegal, the famous sect of the
Almoravides set out to preach Islam and to wage war from the
Sudan to Spain.

1047

Idris II of Malaga was deposed when the African troops who
garrisoned his citadel declared for his cousin, Mohammed.
The inhabitants of Malaga were eager to attempt to storm the
heights, but Idris declared them impregnable and said he
would submit to the decree of fate without further bloodshed.
Days later Malaga was annexed by Badis of Granada who continued the employment of an African garrison. The blacks
were very loyal to him, whereas the Arabs, who were numerous
in Malaga, disliked the rule of a Berber and conspired with
Mutadid of Seville. Mutadid sent his son, Al Mutamid, to aid

the Arabs of Malaga. Al Mutamid was dilatory in pressing the
seige and the Africans in the citadel managed to get word
through the hostile lines to Badis, who sent strong reinforce-
ments and defeated Al Mutamid (Gould 1914, p. 299ff).

1050

The <u>mansa</u>, or king of Manding, was converted to Islam by an
Almoravid. He made a pilgrimage to Mecca and began to enter
into relations with the neighboring states which were favorable
to the growth of his power and to the development of his
country. He also ceased considering himself a vassal of the
Empire of Ghana. Until then it was principally the Bambuk
who furnished the gold dust for the commerce which enriched
Ghana. They undertook an active and continual exchange of
the products between the Sudan and North Africa. After the
Almoravides learned the road to Manding and taught it to the
Moroccan caravans, the Boure became the principal source of
production for gold. This contributed substantially to filling
the treasury of the King of Manding and opened up new horizons
for its people.

Mossi State founded by an adventurer named Ubri.

1054

Howdaghost (Ghana's most important market), though the capital
of a Berber kingdom, was attacked, taken, and pillaged by
Abdallah ben Yassine, under the pretext that the town paid
tribute to the King of Ghana.

1057

Death of Ibn Yacin, founder of the Almoravid sect. After his
death Abubekr assumed leadership of the Almoravid forces in
the southern Sahara. He began the conquest of southern
Morocco with the aid of Abdallah ben Yassine.

1058

After restoring peace among the Berber and reasserting his
authority, Abubekr gave all his efforts to the destruction of
the empire of Ghana. Ghana did not succumb until fifteen
years later, after desperate resistance in the course of
which the Berber troops experienced more than one defeat.

(1067)

1067

Al-Bakri, an Arab scholar, wrote that the King of Ghana "can put 200,000 warriors in the field," more than 40,000 of them being armed with bow and arrow (Davidson 1966, p. 101; Hull 1972, p. 27).

1076

The Almoravides captured the old Sudanese city of Kumbi and put to the sword all the inhabitants who would not embrace Islam.

1086

Yusuf Ibn Tashfin, the leader of the Almoravides, fought and won a battle with Alfonso VI of Castille, at Zallaka. Alfonso was hemmed in on both sides, but resisted stubbornly. At a crucial moment Yusuf ordered his black guards, whom he had held in reserve, to charge. They did terrible damage; one of them cut his way through to Alfonso and wounded him in the thigh with a dagger. This fight won the victory and Alfonso could only save a small remnant of his forces. In Moslem Spain cooperation between Arabs and Berbers or Arabs of different tribes was impossible except in the face of a common danger. Jews and blacks were given opportunities to serve the state because they were neutral regarding the feuds between Arab and Berber, and because they had no connection with tribes, they had more personal loyalties. It was an age of each for himself and there are instances of blacks looking out for their own advantage regardless of the side for which they fought. On the whole, though, in that age of treachery and low standards the black soldier was unusually grateful and faithful to those who used him well. His physical courage was never called in question.

King of Kanem-Bornu converted to Islam.

1087

Shortly after the taking of Seville by Yusuf Ibn Tashfin, which gave Spain to the Almoravides (already masters of Morocco), Abubekr was killed in the Adrar during the course of a new revolt by his most direct subjects. The power of his sect and his dynasty, which had just asserted itself in

such a brilliant manner in the North of Africa and the South
of Europe, disappeared from the very country that had constituted its point of departure.

From the Thirteenth to the Seventeenth Dynasties, Egypt was
conquered by the Hyksos kings, who were probably from the
Arabian desert. At the end of the kings of the Thirteenth
Dynasty came Ra Nehesi, the king's eldest son, who was clearly
black. Ra Nehesi, Pharaoh of Egypt, although black and a
member of an Ethiopian clan, had little cultural connection
with blacks (Du Bois 1939, p. 26; Du Bois 1947, pp. 114-224).

1091

The Saracens called in the aid of the Moors from Africa, who
seized the dominions they came to protect, and subdued the
Saracens.

1100

There is an increasing amount of evidence that African slaves
were being transported to India before and at the beginning
of the Christian era, and before 1100 regularly exported from
the Lake Chad region to Mecca, Egypt, and other areas.

First stone mosques on East Coast of Africa. End of the
Daybuli period; Shirazi movement southward from Banadir coast.

New Iron Age period on plateau south of Zambezi associated
with Shona peoples. First stone buildings at Great Zimbabwe.

Ayyubids attacked and undermined the Nubian Christian kingdoms, which began to disappear.

Continued growth of Iron Age populations in many parts of the
East African inland. These were now moving out of the Early
Iron Age, and were beginning to form larger units of self
rule.

1170

Mossi State organized by Ya in memory of whom it was called
Yatenga (land of Ya). The two Mossi states, one founded in
1050 and the other in 1170, were always distinct and independent of each other.

25

(1171-1250)

1171-1250

    Egypt ruled by Ayyubid kings.

1180

    The southern branch of the Soninkes established a rival king-
dom around the city of Soso.

1193-1805

    Mameluke slaves ruled in Egypt for six centuries. The Mame-
lukes were white slaves bought by the thousands in the
Balkans, Greece, Turkey, and the Near East. "All through the
European Middle Ages, from the ninth century until the fourteenth, European kings and merchants were in the business of
selling European slaves to the kings and merchants of North
Africa and Western Asia" (Davidson 1969, p. 145). They were
used primarily as soldiers and shared in the conquests of
Islam and especially in the capture and holding of the Nile
Valley. At first they were auxiliary troops under strong and
ambitious sultans, several of whom were of African descent
(Du Bois 1947, pp. 192; 193). They defended Egypt, holding
off invaders from Asia and expelling the Crusaders from the
footholds they had gained. The foremost of these Mameluke
rulers were Sultan Baybards (1260-77) and Sultan Kala'un
(1279-90). During this period Egypt prospered with steady
growth of trade with many lands including the coastal areas
of East Africa (Davidson 1969, p. 77).

1200

    Rise of Kilwa to commercial wealth and political power along
the southern coast. King Ali bin al-Hasan of Kilwa began to
mint coins. Trading city of Kisimani on Mafia Island was as
important as Kilwa, and may have been the seat of King Ali
bin al-Hasan.

    Continued expansion of gold and ivory trade with the East
Coast--mainly with the Mozambique trading city of Sofala.

    Ghana collapsed under Almoravid and other attacks. Rise of
Mali after about 1230. Mali became an even larger trading
empire than Ghana had been, and flourished for about 150 years.

(1235)

Ancestors of Chewa are established in village groups in Malawi.

Groups of villages began forming into small states in southern Uganda and regions to the south.

1203

Sumanguru overwhelmed Ghana, reduced the descendants of the former suzerains of Soso to the state of vassal, and held it for a few years. In the same year, he brought his army to Koumbi and conquered it.

1213

A mansa of Manding, named, according to some, Mussa, and according to others, Allakoy, made a pilgrimage to Mecca. During his reign he returned there three times; his travels increased his prestige and his fortunes.

1215

Magna Carta in England.

c.1224

Sumanguru conquered Manding and annexed it to his state.

c.1230

Most of Spain was overrun: Valencia in 1243, Seville in 1248, Cadiz in 1262. Only the little southern kingdom of Granada held out until 1492.

1230

Sundiata, grandson of Mussa, proclaimed King of Mali after defeating Sumanguru.

1235

Melle, the Mandingan kingdom, was founded.

(1238)

1238

The kingdom of Granada established by the Moors.

1240

Sundiata destroyed Ghana. He developed agriculture and encouraged the raising and wearing of cotton. He, or one of his generals, completed the destruction of the Soso Empire by plundering the city of Koubmi, once the great capital of Ghana.

1255

Sundiata died.

1285-1300

Sakura, Malian emperor.

1285-1468

Mellestine was the leading power in the territory of Melle. The territory of Melle was southeast of Ghana and about 500 miles north of the Gulf of Guinea (Du Bois 1965, pp. 206, 207).

1300

"There are known to have been African sultans in Bengal before the Portuguese arrived, at which time Africans were already living near Madras, and at about 1300 A.D. a ruler near Bombay was an African. Janjira, a native state south of Bombay, is of African origin" (Singer 1953, pp. 637, 638).

1307-1332

Power of the Mandingo empire, Melle, brought to its apogee by Gongo-Mussa or Kankan-Mussa, the greatest of all the Mali emperors.

1324

Gongo-Mussa made a pilgrimage to Mecca with a caravan of
60,000 persons, including 12,000 young slaves gowned in
figured cotton and Persian silk; 500 slaves with golden
staffs. Mussa brought to Egypt no less than eight camel loads
of tibar (gold dust), each weighing 300 pounds, to defray his
expenses. He brought back with him an Arab, al-Kati, who
initiated a new style of architecture. While Gongo-Mussa was
away, Timbuktu was sacked by Mossi; he rebuilt the city and
filled the new mosque with learned blacks from the University
of Fez. On his way to Mecca, Gongo-Mussa passed by Tuat and
Cairo; his caravan aroused interest and curiosity everywhere
along the route.

1325

The troops of the Mandingo Emperor Gongo-Mussa captured Gao
and the Songhay became vassals of the Mandingo.

1326

Gongo-Mussa, after his capture of Timbuktu, took two young
Songhay princes to the court of Melle to be educated. These
boys, when grown, ran away and founded a new dynasty in
Songhay, that of the Sonnis, in 1355.

1327

Two hundred Moors arrived to assist the king of Granada as
soldiers.

1331

Moroccan traveller, Ibn Battuta, visited Mogadishu, Mombasa,
and Kilwa. Later ruled by King Hasan bin-Suleiman II, Kilwa
had several fine stone buildings, including the great palace
of Husuni Kubwa, "an enormous structure of well over 100
rooms, with galleries, patios, elaborate washing arrangements
and a fresh-water bathing pool" (Davidson 1966, p. 88).

(1331)

Development of early chieftainships in Malawi, ancestral to
Undi and others.

The Tonga spread across southern Zambia.

Christian Ethiopians survived many wars against Muslims and
other Africans. They began to build foundations of later
Ethiopian Empire.

Mali at height of its power.

1332

Gongo-Mussa died. The Mandingo empire occupied nearly the
same area as the whole of the territories of French West
Africa and the foreign colonies enclosed by them. The ex-
ceptions to this were the southern countries covered by dense
forest and the regions situated at the center of the Bend of
the Niger.

1333

The Mohro-naba of the Yatenga attacked Timbuktu and sacked the
city.

1335

The first Sonni prince of the Songhay, Ali-Kolen, shook off,
in part, the tutelage of Manding.

The dynasty of the Dia was replaced by that of the Sonni,
Soun, San, or Chi, whose first act was to break the lines of
vassalage that attached the Songhay to the Mandingo. Timbuktu and Walata remained in the power of the Mandingo as did
also the region of the lakes, the Massina, and Jenne.

1336

Shortly before his death, Gongo-Mussa sent an embassy to Fez
to congratulate Abul-Hassane on the victory he had just had
over Tlemcen. The sultan of Fez, in return, dispatched one
to Manding, where it arrived in 1336.

1339

The Mossi crossed the valley, plundered Timbuktu, and separated Jenne, the original seat of the Songhay, from the main
empire.

1346

By 1346 echoes of the African empires' wealth and trading had
begun to filter to the medieval merchant cities of southern
Europe. Several of them, notably Marseilles, Genoa, Florence,
and Venice, had long made efforts to link their commerce with
the Western Sudan. They tried to reach the empires by sea.
In 1346 a Catalan captain named Jaime Ferrer set out in a
galley from Majorca to find "the river of gold," which was
thought to lie somewhere far down the Atlantic coast. But
Ferrer never returned. Europeans as yet possessed neither
the necessary skill nor instruments for ocean voyaging
(Davidson 1966, p. 34).

c.1350

Kongo dynasty established.

1350-1500

The Chwezi established a kingdom called Bunyoro-Kitara
(Davidson 1969, p. 42). Much of Southern Uganda was ruled by
Chwezi Dynasty, with new methods of central government.
Kimera, a Bito, ascended the throne. The Bito line of kings
ruled for eighteen generations (Davidson 1969, p. 48).

1352-1353

Ibn Battuta, a Moroccan and a celebrated traveller of the
fourteenth century, was acquainted with East Africa. On his
way to India and China he visited the coasts of Somalia,
Kenya, and Tanzania. In 1331 he went as far south as Kilwa
and in 1351 he crossed the Sahara to the empire of Mali and
other lands of West Africa (Davidson 1969, p. 86). Ibn
Battuta wrote that among the admirable qualities of the
people, he noted a high sense of justice. "'Of all peoples,
the Negroes [sic] are those who most abhor injustice. The
Sultan pardons no one who is guilty of it. There is complete
and general safety throughout the land. The traveller here

31

(1353)

> has no more reason than the man who stays at home to fear
> brigands, thieves or ravishers.' Furthermore . . . the
> blacks do not confiscate the goods of any North Africans who
> may die in their country, not even when these consist of
> large treasures. On the contrary, they deposit these goods
> with a man of confidence . . . until those who have a right
> to the goods present themselves and take possession'"
> (Davidson 1966, pp. 82, 83).

1353

> Ibn Kaldoun, historian, when at Biskra, learned from well-
> informed persons that the power of the mansa of the Mali ex-
> tended over the entire Sahara. The King of Wargla showed
> deference to him and all the Tuareg paid him tribute.

1355-1591

> Kingdom of Songhay.

c.1359

> Mali reached its zenith under Mansa Sulayman.

1375

> The Majorcan cartographer Abraham Cresques produced a map of
> Africa from information probably given to him by his fellow
> Jews, who, unlike Christian merchants, were often permitted
> by the Moslems in North Africa to journey through their terri-
> tory. Cresque's map showed the mighty Lord of the Blacks
> seated on his throne in the midst of Mali, bearing aloft a
> ceremonial orb of gold. A white-veiled merchant rode on a
> camel toward him (Davidson 1966, p. 85).

c.1380

> Royal families in the Hausa states were converted to Islam.

1380

> The Bulala group forced Sefawa into exile and he established
> a new political base at Bornu on the west shore of Lake Chad.

32

c.1400

The community of Iron Age ideas and structures reached from the fringes of the Sahara to the Antarctic-facing shore of southern Africa. It had almost touched its greatest possible geographical extension.

Development of strong chieftainship among the Karanga of southwestern country south of Zambezi. Soon the Karanga would build an empire.

Rise of Songhay and new city-states in Hausaland (northern Nigeria) and in Yorubaland and Benin.

Ntemi kingships spread through western Tanzania.

Coastal states flourish. Older cities become richer. Newer cities, such as Gedi, acquired fine stone buildings.

1415

Expedition of Prince Henry of Portugal sailed for Morocco and captured Ceuta, the first of a series of conquests and voyages of exploration in Africa. Ceuta fell after one day of heavy assault and Portugal, as Bailey Diffie has written in Prelude to Empire, "was now launched on the imperial road from which there was no point of voluntary return. . . . The hope for profit, the conquest of souls, the cutting off of Castile, were identified with Portugal's national spirit" (Diffie 1960, p. 89). The fifteenth century is the period of African coastal exploration. After the fall of Ceuta, Henry, the third son of João, directed the maritime thrust of Portugal which was to culminate at the end of the century in Vasco da Gama's first voyage to India (Diffie 1960, p. 2).

1417

Benedetto Dei, a Florentine agent of Portinari, relating his travel to Nigeria, stated that he had been to Timbuktu, a place south of the Kingdom of Barbary, and one of the most arid in the world. He mentioned that trade is carried on there in the sale of cloths, serges, and material alongside those made in Lombardy.

(1417-1421)

1417-1421

Two Chinese fleets visited Banadir and Kenya coasts.

1420

Portuguese exploration of Africa promoted by Henry the Navigator.

1423

"Africans also turn up during the period as the familiars of witches, for instance in the trial of Alice Kyteler of Kilkenny in 1423, in which she was accused of having intercourse with an 'Ethiop' who could also turn into a black cat or black shaggy dog. Thus there are hints even as early as this of a dual social role for Africans--people to be laughed at and people to be feared" (Edwards 1981, p. 33).

c.1425

Mutota, King of the Karanga, organized a vast and victorious campaign of conquest designed to extend his rule over the whole inland plateau between the Zambezi and the Limpopo--the main gold-bearing area--and afterwards through Mozambique to the harbors of the East Coast trade. All this was substantially achieved by Mutota and his son Matope, so that Matope became the most powerful sovereign in the central-southern continent during the 1470s and was honored as such by the rulers and chiefs of the East Coast ports. They called his empire Wilayatu 'l Mu 'anamutapah after his indigenous title of Mwanamutapa, or lord of the plundered lands. The Portuguese corrupted it to Monomotapa (Davidson 1968, pp. 132ff).

Troubled periods began in government of Kilwa; conflicts between rulers and senior governors (emirs).

Portuguese began sailing down the Atlantic coast of Africa. In 1483 they made contact with the Angolan kingdom of the Kongo people.

Greatest expansion of early empire of Mwanamutapa. Matopa died, c.1480. Some years later (c.1490) the Karanga (Rozwi) chief Changa of Guniuswa (Butua) broke away from overlordship of Mwanamutapa, and began forming the new state of Urozwi.

34

Askia Muhammad became powerful emperor of Songhay.

1433

The Tuareg chief Akil succeeded in driving the Mandingo garrison from Timbuktu and in making himself master of the city.

1434

Antonio Gonzales, a Portuguese captain, sold African boys in the south of Spain.

The Tuareg chief Akil captured Arawan and Walata.

1437

African slaves were introduced in large numbers into western India.

1440-1473

Benin City became famous as a cultural center.

1441

The Portuguese reached the River of Gold. It was believed that their leader seized certain free Moors and the next year exchanged them for ten black slaves, a target of hide, ostrich eggs, and some gold dust. The trade was easily "justified" on the ground that the Moors were Mohammedans and refused to be converted to Christianity, while the "heathen" Africans would be better subjects for conversion and strong laborers.

1441-1442

Portuguese navigators Antonio Gonzales and Nuno Tristan journeyed to Rio de Oro. They brought back some gold dust and ten Africans whom Prince Henry the Navigator handed as slave gifts to Pope Martin V. The pope conferred to Portugal the right of possession and sovereignty on all lands to be discovered between Cape Blanco and India.

1443

Two hundred Africans introduced into Portugal.

(1443-1444)

1443-1444

The coast of Rio de Oro explored by Portuguese navigators Affonso Goncalves Baldaya and Gil Eanes; settlement made on Arguin Island just south of Cape Blanco near the site of modern Port Etienne.

1446

The Portuguese ships of Henry the Navigator arrived in Senegal.

Sierre Leone rediscovered by Alvaro Fernandes.

1447

Up until this year approximately 900 African slaves had been introduced into Portugal.

1448

Prince Henry established fort (slave market) on Arguin Bay, south of Cape Blanco.

1450

The Portuguese introduced 200 Africans from Arguin into Portugal.

Renewed excavations of Great Zimbabwe show that the early stone building culture gave way in about 1450 to another related culture, which promoted much larger structures.

1450-1850

Europe carried on a systematic trade in human beings of such tremendous proportions that the physical, economic, and moral effects are still plainly observable throughout the world. To this must be added the large slave trade of Mohammedan lands, which began with the seventh century and continued almost unchecked until the end of the nineteenth century (Du Bois 1939, p. 135).

(c.1473)

1455-1460

Between 700 and 800 Africans were brought annually from
Arguin into Portugal.

1455-1492

Little mention is made of slaves in the trade with Africa.
Columbus is said to have suggested blacks for America, but
Ferdinand and Isabella refused.

1459-1474

King Rukn-ud-din-Barbak, who ruled at Gaur, possessed 8000
African slaves and was the first king of India to promote
them in large numbers to high rank in his service.

1462

Factories were founded at Cacheu and the district became a
center of slave trade in the seventeenth and eighteenth centuries.

1464

Sonni Ali, called the Great, ascended the throne--the last and
greatest of seventeen Songhay kings.

1468-1469

Sonni Ali captured Timbuktu from the Tuareg.

1471-1480

Portuguese explorers discovered the Gold Coast, the delta of
the Niger, Fernando Po, and Gabon.

c.1473

By the intermediary of the Portuguese officers Rio de Cantor
(Gambia) and Elmina (Ghana), there took place an exchange of
presents, messages, and embassies between the Emperor of
Manding, who was then called Mamoud for Mamudu, according to
João de Barros, and the King of Portugal, John II, who came
to the throne in 1481 and reigned until 1495.

(1473)

1473

Sonni Ali entered Jenne as conqueror and took away from the authority of the mansa a good part of the Massina. He made himself master of Jenne and of the Massina, after having annexed to his kingdom the region of the lakes and Walata.

1474

African slaves were common in Seville. There is a letter from Ferdinand and Isabella to a celebrated black, Juan de Valladolid, commonly called El Conde Negro, nominating him to the office of Mayor of the blacks in Seville. Soon the population of Algarve was almost completely African. By the middle of the sixteenth century, blacks outnumbered whites in Lisbon.

c.1475

Songhay superseded Mali as the most powerful and important state in the Western Sudan.

1477

The King of the Mossi of Yatenga came to ravage the Massina and advanced as far as Walata, which he pillaged in 1480.

1480

Matope died.

Spain and Portugal partitioned the ocean horizontally.

1481

The Mali established the first direct Sudanese contact with Europeans through Portuguese sailors who had arrived on Mali's Atlantic coast. Mali sought an alliance with the Europeans to hold back the Songhay advance from the east.

1482

Pope Pio II condemned the slave trade.

The Portuguese built the first slave-trading fort at Elmina, Gold Coast (São Jorge da Mina), by initial consent and paid rent. They extended their trade down the West Coast and up the East Coast. The traffic grew larger and larger until it became the most important of all the commerce of the Zambezi basin. There could be no extension of agriculture, no mining, no progress of any kind where it was so extensively carried on.

1482-1485

The mouth of the Congo River, "the Mighty," and the coast of of Angola were discovered by Diogo Ção.

1483

The Portuguese captain Diogo Ção anchored in the waters of the Congo. The Kongo people had built a large and closely articulated state in the northern region of modern Angola. Their king willingly entered into trade with the Portuguese, exchanged ambassadors with Lisbon, and received Christian missionaries.

1486

The King of Benin sent an emissary to John II of Portugal to request the dispatch of missionaries to his kingdom.

Scholars and explorers such as Diogo Ção reached the Congo for the second time. Ção brought specimens of ivory sculpture from the King of the Congo to the Court of Portugal. D'Elbee ("Memoirs of D'Elbee" in Labat's Voyage du Chevalier des Marchais), Marchais, Pigafetta, and others not only wrote erudite memoirs on the splendors of the palaces, the habitations of the people, the internal moats of the castles of the nobility, their high degree of culture, and their exquisite knowledge of Portuguese and Castilian, but also brought tangible evidence and confirmation of their stories and travels in the form of art treasures and gifts from the West Coast of Africa. These art treasures are still to be seen in the old Royal Art Chamber at Dresden, the Weydmann Collections in the City of Ulm, and the National Museum at Copenhagen. Duke Ferdinand Albert I of Brunswick-Luneburg obtained numerous treasures from West Africa through the intermediary of Dutch traders in West Africa and his collections may be studied in

(1486)

the Municipal Museum of Brunswick. Before the collections of
The Dauphin of France and the princes of Europe, whether they
be of calabashes, garments, gold and silver, of copper or
bronze, bejewelled bows and arrow, treasure box or wigs, of
carved wooden figures, terra cotta or bronze heads, or of
reliefs from mural decorations of African homes, some modern
scholars stand in outraged awe at the greatness of a people
now so much reviled.

Black slaves in India rebelled, killed Fath Shah, and set
their leader on the throne with the title Barbah Shah. Another African, Indil Khan, remained loyal to Fath and, returning from a distant expedition, killed Barbah and accepted
the crown under the title of Saif-ud-din-Firuz. Firuz quelled
the disorders of the kingdom and restored the discipline of
the army. He was succeeded in 1489 by Fath Shah's young son
under a regency exercised by another African; but before a
year was out still another black, Sidi Badr, murdered both
child-king and regent and usurped the throne. He reigned
three years. In 1493 he was killed at the head of a sortie
against rebel forces that were besieging Guar, and with his
death this remarkable black regime in Bengal came to an end.
An Asiatic from the Oxus country was elected to the throne,
and one of his first acts was to expel all the Africans from
the kingdom. The exiles, many thousands in number, were
turned back from Delhi and Janupur and finally drifted to
Gujarat and the Deccan, where the slave trade had also
created a considerable black population (Coupland 1938, pp.
32, 33; Du Bois 1947, p. 197).

1488

A gift of one hundred Moro slaves to Pope Inocenio VIII by
the Catholic kings.

1491

Christianity was introduced into the Kingdom of Congo by the
Portuguese.

1491-1540

Leo Africanus, born a Moor, was captured by pirates when
journeying on the Mediterranean. The pirates, finding he
knew a great deal about Africa, which seemed very remote,

gave him to Pope Leo XI in Rome as a present. The Pope set
him free and as a special favor gave him his own name, Leo.

1492

According to legend, Pedro Alonzo Nino, one of Columbus's
crew on his first voyage, was a black.

Sonni Ali drowned.

Granada taken after a two years' siege; the power of the
Moors is extirpated by Ferdinand.

Immediately after the fall of Granada, about 100,000 Spanish
Moors passed over into Africa. Some ruined and deserted
cities on the sea coast, the remains of Carthaginian and
Roman power and enterprise, were allotted to the exiles.
Although they were of the same religion, and almost of the
same race and language as the people they sought refuge among,
they were strangers in a strange land; the African Moors
termed them Tigarins (Andalucians). They dwelt and inter-
married together, and were long known to Europeans by the
name of Moriscos (Blake 1859, p. 70).

1493

The Sonni dynasty was overturned at Gao by a Sarakolle
general, Mamadu or Mohammed Toure, of the Silla group, who
became invested with the sovereignty under the title of Askia.
He was the first prince of a new dynasty which was to last a
century. The Askia Mohammed reigned from 1493 to 1529.

Various problems concerning ownership of land discovered by
Spain and Portugal's explorers arose. The Spanish pope,
Alexander VI, was asked to solve the problem of ownership of
the New World. The Papal Bull of Demarcation (Papal Dona-
tion) donated the New World and the East to Spain and Portugal. The Pope's Bull debarred Spain from African possessions
and compelled her to contract with other nations for slaves.
This contract was in the hands of the Portuguese in 1600; in
1640 the Dutch received it, and in 1701 the French. The War
of the Spanish Succession was motivated not so much by royal
rivalries as to bring the slave trade monopoly to England
(Du Bois 1939, p. 137).

(1493)

Sugar cane was planted on the island of Hispaniola (Santo
Domingo); by 1520 there were more than twenty-eight sugar
mills. Brazil was the first to recognize and develop the
possibilities of sugar cane as a commercial plantation crop
produced by black slaves. Before the sixteenth century sugar
had long been known in Europe as an expensive luxury, sometimes prescribed in small quantities as medicine. But when
the Portuguese planters of Pernambuco began to put sugar on
the market at lower prices the taste for sugar began to spread
rapidly. Sugar cane became the main agricultural product of
the islands of Puerto Rico, Jamaica, and Cuba. The sugar
economy of the seventeenth and eighteenth centuries was based
on the institution of slavery. Capital was required for the
establishment of a plantation, construction of sugar mills,
and the purchase of slaves. The profit for the plantation
owners was enormous.

1493-1591

The dynasty of the Askias ruled in Songhay.

c.1495

Mohammed Abou Bekr, who was Sonni Ali's prime minister and
best known as Mohammed Askia, made a pilgrimage to Mecca
accompanied by a brilliant group of scholars and politicians.
They studied matters of taxation, weights and measures, trade,
religious tolerance, and manners. He was made Caliph of the
Sudan by the authorities of Mecca. During his reign, Askia
conquered and consolidated an empire 2,000 miles long by
1,000 miles wide at its greatest extent--a territory as large
as all Europe.

Five shiploads of Indians sent to Seville by Columbus to be
sold as slaves.

1497-1498

Vasco da Gama doubled the Cape of Good Hope and discovered
Natal. He also arrived at Sofala da Gama, Mozambique harbor
(island), and Malindi. On this voyage he discovered a passage
to India.

1498

From southern Sudan, Luo migrations in progress. New rulers
in southern Uganda. Rise of Bunyoro-Kitara. Kintu period
in Buganda.

Kikuyu and neighbors firmly established in central Kenya.

Great Zimbabwe becomes capital of the Karanga kingdom of
Urozwi, ruled by kings (mambos) who take the dynastic title
of Changamire.

Expansion of Songhay under Askia Muhammed. Growth of trading
cities of Timbuktu and Jenne. Expansion of new gold trade
between these cities and central region of modern Ghana
(Asante).

c.1500

A kanta reigned who was considered master of Katsena, Kano,
Zaria, the Gober, and the Zanfara; he also extended his power
over Air, a strategic market town.

Discovery of Brazil by Portuguese admiral, Pedro Alvares
Cabral; Cabral was the first European to visit East Africa
(Kilwa).

The first city to suffer a Portuguese attack was Mozambique.
In the years closely following 1500, Kilwa was forced to pay
tribute to the King of Portugal.

"Something like a black community appears in the account
books of the Scottish court at Holyrood shortly after 1500.
Reference is made to two women, Ellen or Helenor More and
Margery Lindsay, and to a number of men—Peter, Nageir and
Taubronar, the last being a married man with a child at Court.
Some of them probably came from Portugal, where trading in
Africans had been going on throughout the previous century.
In 1505 a payment is recorded in the accounts to William
Wood, one of the Scottish king's principal ship's captains,
'for the fraucht of the Portugall quhit hors, the must cat
and the jennet and the Moris,' and there are numerous items
such as payment for the transport of 'the More lassis' from
Dunfermline to Edinburgh in 1504, for a dance-entertainment
organised by Taubronar 'be the Kingis command', and expensive

(c.1500)

gowns, slippers and gloves, not only for the black ladies but
for their personal maidservants too: and the King's New Year
gift is recorded in 1513, 'to the twa blak ladeis, X Franche
crounis'" (Edwards 1981, p. 33).

Part of Kilwa's wealth was used to reinforce its power over
its neighbors but it was also used to embellish the daily life
of its people. "When the Portuguese first sailed into Kilwa's
harbor in 1500 under the command of Pedro Alvares Cabral they
marveled at its fine houses of coral stone, many of them
three and four stories high. The anonymous scribe who accompanied Cabral wrote 'In this land there are rich merchants
and there is much gold and silver and amber and musk and
pearls. Those of the land wear clothes of fine cotton and of
silk and many fine things, and they are black men'" (Davidson
1966, p. 88).

1501–1503

Ovando, Governor of Spanish America, objected to black slaves
and prohibited them from being sent to Hispaniola. He asserted that they fled among the Indians, taught them bad
customs, and never could be captured. He imported 40,000
Indians from the Bahamas to replace the local Indians, who
were rapidly disappearing. Despite Ovando's objections,
Africans began to be imported as early as 1501; by 1522 the
new blacks had staged a rebellion. A royal edict authorized
transportation of African slaves from Spain to Hispaniola via
Europe, where they were Christianized.

1502

Berbers and Moors in Spain driven back into Africa.

1504

License of Medina del Camo to Ojeda provided for white slaves--
no black slaves.

1505

Ovando sailed from Seville with seventeen African slaves and
some mining equipment to be used in the copper mines of
Española.

(c.1507)

Acquilon introduced sugar cane in America.

Sofala was occupied and the Portuguese East African Empire began.

A letter to Ovando, from the king in Segovia, dated September, read "I will send more black slaves as you request; I think there may be a hundred. At each time a trustworthy person will go with them who may have some share in the gold they may collect and may promise them ease if they work well." There is no record of one hundred slaves being sent that year (Du Bois 1939, p. 153).

Portuguese sacked Kilwa and Mombasa. They extended their domination along the coast, but concentrated their trade at Kilwa, Mombasa, and Malindi.

Malawi peoples formed a strong confederation under separate chieftainships of Undi, Karonga, Mwase, and others. These were strong enough to keep the Portuguese at arm's length.

c.1506

"One of the poems of William Dunbar, 'Of ane blak moir', is about the part played by Helenor in a parody tournament of around 1506-7 called 'the turnament of the black knicht and the black lady'" (Edwards 1981, p. 33).

1506

Madagascar discovered by the Portuguese.

By royal decree the following were not permitted to enter Española: Berber slaves, free persons and new converts, un-ruly black slaves, servants with Moors.

c.1507

Leo Africanus visited the Songhay. He wrote of the state of Mohammed Askia who made intellectual centers at Gao, Timbuktu, and Jenne, where writers and students from North Africa came to study. A literature developed in Timbuktu in the sixteenth and seventeenth centuries. The University of Sankore became a center of learning in correspondence with Egypt and North Africa; there were a large number of black Sudanese students.

(c.1507)

Law, literature, grammar, geography, and surgery were studied.
Askia the Great reigned thirty-six years and his dynasty continued until after the Moorish invasion of 1591 (Du Bois 1939,
p. 48).

Portuguese fort established in Mozambique.

1508

Importation of Africans to the Spanish possessions in the
West Indies, where they were used in the mines.

1510

Blacks brought from Spain to Puerto Rico by Micer Geron.

Ndongo, now Angola, flourished on the European-stimulated
slave trade.

Nuflo de Olano, a black, was with Balboa when he discovered
the Pacific Ocean. Thirty blacks helped Balboa direct the
work of over 500 Indians in transporting the material for his
ships across the mountains to the South Sea. Cortez carried
blacks and Indians with him from Cuba to Mexico and one of
these blacks was the first to sow and reap grain there. There
were two blacks with Velas in 1520, and 200 with Alvarado on
his expedition to Quito. In 1525 Almagro and Valdivia were
saved from death by blacks.

Frequent notices show that blacks were common in the New
World. When Pizarro was slain in Peru, his body was dragged
to the cathedral by blacks. After the Battle of Anaquito,
the head of the viceroy was cut off by a black; during the
great earthquake in Guatemala a most remarkable figure was a
large black seen in various parts of the city. Núnez had
thirty blacks with him on the top of the Sierras and there
was rumor of an aboriginal tribe of blacks in South America.
The first considerable response which Ferdinand made to the
appeal for laborers seems to have been in 1510, when he
ordered the Casa de Contratacion to send out 250 blacks.
This is the date which some take as the beginning of a traffic
in blacks between the Old and the New World. These were
Christian blacks to be purchased in Lisbon (Saco 1938, p. 67).
One of the last acts of King Ferdinand was to urge that no
more blacks be sent to the West Indies, but, under Charles V,

Bishop Las Casas drew up a plan of assisted migration to America; in 1517 he asked for the right of each immigrant to import twelve black slaves, in return for which the Indians were to be freed.

An order of black monks was inaugurated by the Catholic Church in Spanish America early in the sixteenth century. By the middle of the seventeenth, a black freedman and charcoal burner saw his son, Francisco Xavier de Luna Victoria, become Bishop of Panama, the first indigenous Catholic bishop in America.

A black landed with the first Spaniards in Peru and blacks were among those who later welcomed Drake and offered him aid. They repeatedly led rebellions and furnished one saint for the Catholic Church, Brother Martin de Porres.

Spain was accustomed to the enslavement of "Moors, Jews, and other white peoples. Voluntary manumission of slaves was common," and black freedmen early began to appear in the lists of persons licensed by the Casa de Contratación to go to the colonies. Francisco, a black, sailed for Santo Domingo in 1510 (Schurz 1954, pp. 162ff). "In 1512, female mulatto, Juana, who declared herself to be the daughter of Francisco Martín de Cazell, and a freedwoman, named Christina, with her three-year-old daughter, received permits for passage to the islands. The register of passengers for the next year includes the names of six freed persons of color. In 1527, a former slave of the Archbishop of Tarragona crossed the Atlantic with his wife, Francisca. In 1536, 'Maestre Jorge,' and his wife, María López, and his son Jerónimo, received permission to return to Santo Domingo, where he had been a slave of the bishop" (Schurz 1954, p. 163).

1511

Fifty <u>piezas</u> <u>de</u> <u>ebano</u> (black slaves) brought to work in mines of Santo Domingo.

1512

First blacks brought to Cuba from Spain.

(1512–1515)

1512–1515

 The Portuguese trader, Tome Pires, found in Malacca East
Africans as well as Indians and West Asians, and mentioned,
among others people from Kilwa, Malindi, Mogadishu, and
Mombasa. Maritime links between East Africa and Southeast
Asia were many and of great antiquity.

1513

 First blacks found in the New World at Qugrequa by Vasco
Nuñez were supposed to have been shipwrecked.

 The Hausa states made alliance with Askia Mohammed of Songhay,
but afterwards regained their independence. The Hausa were
converted to Mohammedanism about the beginning of the nineteenth century.

c.1516–c.1597

 Juan Latino, black Latinist of Granada, slave humanist,
author of <u>Ad Catholicum</u>.

1517

 Bartholome de Las Casas appealed to King Ferdinand of Spain
that Africans be sent to America to substitute for Indians
in the mines.

 African conspiracy in New Segovia (Venezuela).

 The Emperor Charles V granted a charter to a Flemish merchant
for the exclusive importation of African slaves into Spanish
America, thus, definitely founding the slave trade. Gareboot,
Mayordom of Charles V, obtained a monopoly for the slave trade
for eight years and sold it for 25,000 ducados to Genoese
merchants.

 As soon as the plan to import twelve black slaves per immigrant to the West Indies was proposed, a Savoyard, Lorens
de Gomenot, Governor of Bresa, obtained a monopoly of this
proposed trade and shrewdly sold it to the Genoese for 25,000
ducats. Other monopolies were granted in 1523, 1527, and
1528 (Du Bois 1939, p. 134).

Emperor Carlos I conceded first <u>asiento</u> to Lorenzo de Garrevod to transport 4,000 African slaves to Española, San Juan, Cuba, Jamaica.

The Order of San Jeronimo solicited from the Cortes the privilege of buying African slaves.

Las Casas was but one of several petitioners for the importation of Africans as slaves. The Jeronimite Fathers also petitioned, the difference being that Las Casas sought Spanish or Christian blacks, while the Jeronimites wished <u>bozal</u> blacks directly from Africa (Donnan 1969, p. 15).

1518

Ship in Spanish service carried the first cargo of Africans directly from the Guinea coast to Americas.

Gold discovered in Jamaica.

Africans from Cuba used in the conquest of Mexico.

Fray Luis de la Mejorada and Fray Alfonso de Ortega pleaded for the introduction of slaves into Santo Domingo and Española.

1519

There were several reasons why tales about Africa continued to circulate during the slave trade: "One was the secrecy practiced by royal chanceries and business houses, which were reluctant to publish, for the benefit of rivals, what they now began to know about the lands beyond the seas. A second was the dishonesty of literary hacks who concocted all sorts of nonsense for a gullible public. A third reason was the debasing effect of the slave trade. The records of the slaving centuries are full of references to Africans as 'children who never grew up,' and of paternalistic assurances about the good that was being done for them by non-Africans. Out of this carefully nurtured misconception came the great theme of the colonial epoch, the idea of 'the white man's burden.' . . . But there was also a fourth reason why Europe continued to misjudge Africa. Africans were different. They were a different color, they dressed differently and, probably most important of all, their values were different. To Europeans beginning to be caught up in an age of machinery

(1519)

and science, it was easy to assume that Africa's technological simplicity was indicative of backwardness in everything else. . . . Nineteenth Century Europeans thought that social order was a step ladder of racial virtue, with white peoples on the topmost rung and black peoples down at the bottom" (Davidson 1966, pp. 21, 22, 60).

The oldest text written by a West African was begun: the Tarikh al-Fettach of Mahmout Kati (Timbuktu). We find in it a codification of first-hand accounts of the Sudanese oral traditions and histories of the royal houses and dynasties of the sixteenth century. In it the myth of the origin of the Songhay, Manding, and Sarakole peoples is told. They descended from three brothers, the sons of the king of Yemen, chased away by the harshness of their father. They emigrated towards the Atlantic, taking their wives with them. This origin of the Sudanese peoples was mysteriously revealed in the presence of spirits during an interview obtained with Askia by Sherif Es-Seqli. The same myths exist for other peoples who were descendants of the giant Oudj, a contemporary of Noe. A little further, in the same Tarikh al-Fettach, we find a legend concerning the origin of the kings of Songhay. But we learn more from the codification of the tradition concerning the kings of Ghana, the Kaymagas, and the empire of Mali. We must note that the author reported facts happening five centuries before his time, in the first case, and two centuries earlier in the second. It is from him that we learn that twenty kings of Ghana had been ruling before hegira. There were twenty-two before the hegira and twenty-two afterwards; their capital was called Koumbi. There are also details about their wealth and magnificence.

c.1520

Chronicle of Kilwa written in Arabic.

Voyage undertaken for slaves at the suggestion of Lucas Vasquez de Ayllon; exploration of the east coast of North America; sale of Africans in the Americas legalized by Spanish crown.

Rise of Luba states in region of Katanga; extension of Luba forms of government to Lunda peoples of central Congo grasslands.

Spanish conquests in Caribbean and Central America. Beginning
of trans-Atlantic slave trade.

The Sultanate of Bagirmi, southwest of Lake Chad, was founded;
it reached its greatest power in the seventeenth century.
This dynasty was overthrown by the Negroid Mabas, who established Wadai about 1640.

1520

Two blacks were with Velas in 1520, two hundred black slaves
with Alvarado on his expedition to Quito. Almagro and
Valdivia were saved from death by blacks in 1525 (Du Bois
1939, p. 126).

1521

Henrique, son of Alfonso, first and last African bishop of
the Congo, returned to Mbanza after thirteen years in Europe.

1522

Slave revolt in Santo Domingo started by slaves belonging to
Diego Columbus, the discoverer's son, then governor of Santo
Domingo. It was put down with great severity (Schurz 1954,
p. 175). After 1522 "punitive laws of savage rigor were
issued by the Council of the Indies to discourage future revolts by the slaves. A graduated scale of penalties was
fixed for fugitive slaves, ranging from fifty lashes and the
pillory for an absence of four days to hanging for those who
remained away for six months in the company of 'seditious
Negroes.' After Spaniards had resorted to the cruel punishment of mutilation, one law ordered that 'in no case is there
to be carried out against fugitive Negroes the penalty of
cutting off their parts, which out of decency cannot be
named'" (Schurz 1954, pp. 175, 176).

1523

Blacks accompanied Don Pedro de Alvarado in the conquest of
Guatemala.

1525

Silver deposits discovered at Tasco.

(1526)

1526

Slave revolt in South Carolina.

Black accompanied Francisco Pizarro to Peru.

Real Cedula prohibited introduction into American of <u>Negros</u> <u>ladinos</u> (blacks who had lived two years in Spain or Portugal).

Kongo King Affonso complained in a letter to his royal brother in Lisbon that "we cannot reckon how great the damage is . . . and so great, Sire, is the corruption and licentiousness that our country is being completely depopulated." In the beginning the Portuguese found it necessary to respect the sovereignty of the strong kingdom of Kongo and presented themselves as friends and allies just as they had done along the coast of Senegal, at the mouth of the Gambia, at Elmina and at Benin while extracting the greatest number of captives for enslavement. Yet almost from the beginning the slave trade was accompanied by violence and despair. Instead of fighting the Africans, as they had done in the beginning, they sought to make them trading partners. "The Portuguese were impressed by the trading opportunities they found along the African coast, but they were no less impressed by their African allies' military power" (Davidson 1966, p. 101).

Lucas Vasquez Ayllon had blacks in his expedition to the coast of what is now Carolina and used them in the construction of the first ship made in America.

1526–1589

Saint Benedict the Black, born San Fratello, near Messina, Italy. His African parents were slaves of a rich landowner whose name (Manasseri) they were given according to the prevalent custom. He never learned to read and write. He was chosen as patron by the blacks of North America and as protector by the town of Palermo. He was beatified by Pope Benedict XIV in 1743 and canonized by Pope Pius VII in 1807. He was buried in the friary church in Palermo. In 1611 King Philip III of Spain provided in the same church a new shrine where his remains were transferred. His veneration became especially popular in Italy, Spain, and Latin America.

1527

Slave rebellion in Puerto Rico.

1528

Blacks were part of the expedition of Panfilo Narvaez in the conquest of Florida.

Enrique Eynger and Jeronomi Sayller received permits to introduce 4,000 blacks in four years in the Indies.

By this date there were about 10,000 Africans in the New World.

An expedition started out from Mexico to discover the land which is now New Mexico. It was led by Steven Dorantes or Estevanico, a black man who came to America with the Narvaez expedition in 1527. He and three Spaniards survived a succession of disasters and reached Mexico from Florida by the overland route. Because of his knowledge of Indian languages, Estevanico guided the expedition to the "Seven Cities of Cibola" as the land of the Zunis was supposed to be. He reached the pueblos but was killed by the Indians and the expedition following him turned back. It was forty years before other attempts were made to penetrate New Mexico.

1529

Askia Mohammed was dethroned by his son, Mussa.

Slaves set fire to Santa Marta, capital of Magdalena department, northern Colombia, on a small bay of the Caribbean.

1530

Slave revolt in Mexico; later, the followers of the black insurgent, Ba ya No, were captured and sent back to Spain.

Portuguese began the colonization of Brazil.

By royal decree only black slaves were to be sent to America (no se introdujesen en America esclavos mulatos, mestizos,

(1531)

turcos <u>ni</u> <u>moriscos</u> <u>sino</u> <u>solamente</u> <u>negros</u> <u>atezados</u>) (transla-
tion: solamente negros atezados=only black blacks) (Saco
c.1938, pp. 92, 146).

1531

Royal cedula, making slavery of the Indians illegal, proclaimed at Santiago.

Slave revolt in Panama.

1532

First Africans arrived in Brazil.

1533

First blacks arrived in Mexico, brought by the Germans
Ehinger and Cuon.

Uprising of blacks in mines of Jobabo, Cuba.

1534

Spanish expedition including 200 blacks left Nicaragua for
Quito.

Rodrigo Contreras, governor of Nicaragua, authorized by a
special decree to import two white slaves.

Real Cedula granted twenty licenses to import white slaves in
Indies; one of these licenses was granted to Domingo de Irala.
The license also permitted him to carry with him to the Rio
de la Plata 200 blacks.

1535

Crown of Spain permitted Pizarro to bring with him four white
slaves.

1536

First blacks arrived in Chile from Peru with Diego de Almagro.

1536-1545

Slave insurrection in Cartagena.

1537

Vadello accompanied by blacks on his expedition to Cartagena.

1537-1670

Slave insurrections in Mexico in 1537, 1546, 1548, 1570, 1608, 1670.

1538

First Africans arrived in Bahia, where they aroused the protest of Father Nobrega (Schurz 1954, p. 163).

Slave uprising in Santiago de Cuba.

1539

Blacks accompanied De Soto to New World. One of them stayed among the Indians in Alabama and became the first settler from the Old World.

1540

Importation of "mulato" and other "colored" slaves again prohibited by Real Cedula.

Mutilation of sex organs of cimarrones prohibited in West Indies.

Regulation of meat eating for slaves and Indians. Not abolished until 1928 in Maryland: "Legal restrictions against feeding one's Negro slaves terrapin meat more than once a week, cursing before a justice of the peace, dueling, and other practices which are not practiced so much any more will be removed at the next session of the Legislature if present plans of an 'obsolete law' committee are adopted" (Baltimore Sun, 5 November 1978).

A black slave of Hernandez de Alarcon carried a message across the country to Zunis of New Mexico.

(1542)

1542

Estimated number of fugitive slaves in Española 2000-3000 out of an estimated 30,000. Estimated 100,000 slaves in the Indies.

Blacks in Peru used in army against Diego Almagro.

An agreement between Hernan Cortes and the Genoese slave trader Leonardo Lomelin signed in Valladolid for 500 slave licenses.

1543

Royal decree prohibited importation in the Indies of Moors converted to Christianity and their children.

1545

Morocco claimed the principal salt mines at Tegazza but the reigning Askia refused to recognize the claim.

1546

Gonzalo Pizarro used 600 blacks in the battle of Anaquito, Peru.

1548

Arrival in Congo of the first Jesuit mission--three priests and a lay teacher.

Slave revolt in the mining district of the interior of Colombia; twenty whites were killed and hostages taken.

Portuguese settlement in Madagascar.

Slave insurrection in Honduras.

1549-1583

Daoud, successor of Askia Mohammed of the Songhay, reigned. The Songhay empire extended from the Atlas mountains to the Cameroon forests. Daoud renewed agriculture and science and

was closely associated with the Sultan of Morocco but already
the empire was on the decline.

c.1550

Kanem-Bornu captured Air from Songhay.

1550

Slave revolt in Peru. Slaves burned the town of Santa Marta
on north coast of South America.

Two hundred fifty black slaves in Nicaragua used in rebellion
against Spain.

Not until 1550, when Leo Africanus's (Hassan Ibn Muhammed)
report to Pope Leo X was published by Giovanni Battista
Ramusio, secretary in the Venetian government, did the
European bankers, traders, and merchants have detailed information of Africa because the Portuguese considered their information a state secret and hid it in the royal archives
(Davidson 1966, pp. 85ff).

1550-1551

Blacks in Peru prohibited from carrying arms or being in the
streets from 10:00 a.m.-4:00 a.m.

1550-1590

The Hausa tributary states staged a successful revolt. The
Bornu empire captured from Songhay the strategic market town
of Air on the fringe of the Sahara.

1551

Carlos I prohibited blacks from being served by Indians:
penalty for first offense, 100 lashes publicly administered;
second offense, cutting off ears. If free, first offense 100
lashes; second offense, banishment. Neither blacks nor
"mulatoes," slave or free, permitted to wear gold, silk, or
pearls.

Blacks prohibited from selling certain articles in the
streets of Havana.

(1552)

1552

First Jesuit mission departed from Congo.

Slave insurrection in Panama.

Slave uprising in Venezuela.

1553

The first British ships arrived in Africa.

Blacks used in Spanish Civil War.

In the woods near Nombre de Dios, Panama, were several pueblos of perhaps 800 black cimarrones.

Black uprising in Peru lasted over a year; battle of Pucara.

British came in contact with Benin and dealt in ivory, palm oil, and other goods. The Dutch established factories near Benin and engaged in the slave trade.

1554

Blacks participated in the rebellions in Honduras and Guatemala.

1555

An English expedition to West Africa returned with a cargo of 400 pounds of gold and 250 ivory tusks, comfortably multiplying its capital investment many times over. Other Englishmen quickly followed and returned with equally satisfactory results. In 1561 Queen Elizabeth herself invested in African trade and made a 1000 pound profit on one voyage (Davidson 1966, p. 86).

Three expeditions were carried out against the black cimarrones of Panama.

Slave revolt in Peru led by black Bayano.

In Santiago de Chile, a free black owned land in the town.

1556

Whites forced to travel in groups of twenty men in Panama.
The ratio of blacks to whites was about fifteen to one.

Viceroy of Mexico complained that 20,000 blacks in Mexico,
together with mestizos, outnumbered the Spanish.

1560

In the middle of the sixteenth century, maroons attacked the
treasure trains across the Isthmus of Panama and under a black
leader, Bayano, organized a regular government. The colony
started a campaign against them in 1560 and eventually captured Bayano and sent him to Spain. His followers founded
the city of San Diego de Principe.

1562

The first recognition of the slave trade by the English
government; an act was passed legalizing the purchase of
blacks, yet, as the earlier attempts made by the English to
plant colonies in North America were unsuccessful, there did
not, for some time after the passing of this act, exist any
demand for blacks sufficient to induce the owners of English
trading vessels visiting the coast of Africa to make blacks a
part of their cargo (Blake 1859, p. 98).

Sir John Hawkins, the first Englishman who transported slaves
from Africa to America, sailed from England for Sierra Leone,
and in a short time obtained possession of 300 blacks, partly
by the sword and partly by other means. He proceeded directly
to Hispañiola, and exchanged his cargo for hides, ginger, and
sugar and arrived back in England after an absence of eleven
months. The voyage was very prosperous and brought him great
profit (Blake 1859, p. 106).

"The Mossi had two kingdoms founded in the eleventh and
twelfth centuries among the Negroes inland from the Gulf of
Guinea. They are of interest because of the type of state
which they invented, and which was widely copied over Negro

(1562)

Africa and still persists. The main Mossi empire had four
vassal kingdoms besides the kingdom of the ruler. In the
ruler's kingdom there were five provinces whose governors
made up the imperial council and were the chief officers of
state. Associated with the council were eleven ministers
ruling the army, religion, musicians and collecting taxes.
The Mossi empires were peculiar in having little or no Berber
or white influence. They did not make extensive conquests,
but at one time attacked Timbuktu and later resisted Sonni
Ali" (Du Bois 1939, pp. 48, 49).

Desultory trade was kept up by the British until the middle of
the seventeenth century, when British chartered slave trading
companies began to appear.

1565

East Africa declared a Portuguese territory.

Felipe II permitted Pedro Menendez de Aviles to introduce 500
blacks into Florida. Menendez had a company of trained black
artisans and agriculturists when he founded St. Augustine.

1569

Audencia Real of Lima ordered curfews for slaves; they were
not permitted to carry arms or be served by either male or
female Indians. There were severe penalties (lash and pillory)
for breaking these rules.

1570

Blacks founded the town of Santiago del Principe.

Real Cedula prohibited black slaves married in Spain from
being carried to America without wives and children.

The most famous of the kings of Bornu, Idris Aloma, came to
the throne.

One can not be positive that Juan Ortiz de Zárate took with
him to the Rio de la Plata 100 African slaves as he was authorized to do in 1570. But the first indisputable evidence of
the arrival of an African in the Rio de la Plata dates from
this trip by Zárate. Accompanying him was "un portuguese

mulato marinero." But it is not known whether this Portuguese sailor of mixed ancestry settled in the region (Diggs
1951).

1571

"No negra, whether free, or slave, or mulata, may wear gold,
pearls or silk; however, if a free negra is married to a
Spaniard, she may wear gold earrings with pearls, and a small
necklace, and on her skirt a fringe of velvet. None may wear
mantos of burato or of any other material, except short cloaks,
which may reach to a little below the waist, under the penalty
of having them, as well as any gold jewelry or silk clothing,
taken away from them" (Leyes, L.i.t.5, law no. 28).

1573

Juan Latino, professor of poetry at the University of Granada
during the reign of Philip V, published his verse on the return of the Spanish prince from the battle with the Turks at
Lepanto twenty years before the first of Shakespeare's writings.

1573–1603

Under Idris III, the empire of Bornu was at its height. It
ruled over Kano, the Air, Kanem, and land south of Lake Chad.

1574

Paulo Diaz, grandson of Bartolomeso the explorer, visited
Angola and was deeply impressed with the high culture of the
inhabitants.

Portugal established the colony of Angola; Luanda followed in
1576.

1575–1605

Series of Angolan-Portuguese wars. Abundu and Imbangala resisted Portuguese attempts to seize fertile lands and mythical
silver mines.

(1577)

1577

Slave code decreed in Chile.

1578

Dom Sebastiao, King of Portugal, defeated and slain at the Battle of Kasr-al-Kabir (Alcazar); the Portuguese Empire over Morocco soon crumbled.

Slaves revolted in Lima when Sir Francis Drake arrived there in 1578.

1580

The Dutch visited the Coast of Guiana.

1584

Turkey attempted to wrest from Portugal the Zanzibar Coast, but was defeated by the Portuguese Admiral Thome de Sousa Coutinho.

c.1585

The Portuguese discovered Benin, one of the most carefully organized African states on the West Coast, and traded with it in slaves and other produce.

Turkey and Bornu exchanged diplomats and military personnel.

1585

The Sultan of Morocco seized the salt mines at Taghaza from the Songhay empire.

Swahili towns revolted against Portuguese in alliance with Turkish adventurer, Ali Bey.

Portuguese moved inland up the Zambezi and penetrated the empire of Mwanamutapa in northern part of the country. They founded settlements on the Middle Zambezi at Sena and Tete, and used these increasingly as bases from which to interefere in affairs of Mwanamutapa.

Dutch, English, and French competed with Portuguese and
Spanish for overseas loot, trade, and conquest. Brazil had
14,000 black slaves and non-Indian population of 57,000
(Schurz 1954, p. 163).

Kanem-Bornu at height of its power under Mai Idris Alooma.

Bitter wars by Portuguese against Angolan kingdom of Ndongo;
gradual ruin of this kingdom.

1586

Drake attacked San Domingo City and secured a ransom of
$30,000; by the beginning of the seventeenth century, the
commerce between San Domingo and Spain had been practically
destroyed.

1586-1655

More than 13,000 Africans . . . were imported into Buenos
Aires. Nevertheless there were not enough Africans to satisfy
the demand. Throughout the seventeenth century appeals from
the Cabildo, the audiencia and governors of Buenos Aires fell
upon the seemingly deaf ears of the kings.

1587

Zimba wrecked Kilwa.

"An English ship encountered two Portuguese sail off the
mouth of the River Plate in 1587. Between them they carried
eighty slaves. . . . The ships and cargo had been bought in
Brazil by an agent of the Bishop of Tucumán, who was then
building a new monastery. The Jesuit Gervasoni reported that
in 1729 the college of his order in Buenos Aires had over 300
slaves. At that time, he estimated that a third of the city's
population of 24,000 consisted of Negro slaves. In the latter
part of the same century, the itinerant 'Inca' Concolorcovo
wrote that in Córdoba he witnessed an auction of 2,000 blacks
from the properties of the religious colleges who were sold
in family lots. Among them were musicians and others with
special skills. The nuns of Santa Teresa had a farm in the
neighborhood with 300 slaves, and some families possessed
thirty or forty domestic slaves. The learned Indian added
the comment that the female slaves were famed as laundresses.

(1588)

Writing long afterwards of the same locality, the anticlerical Sarmiento said: 'Each· convent and monastery owned an adjoining property, on which there were bred eight hundred slaves of the Order, Negros, Zambos, and mulattoes.' The young female mulattoes, the testy Argentine president described as 'blue-eyed, fair-haired, slow-moving, with legs polished like marble; real Circassians, endowed with all the graces, who served as a whip to the human passions, all for the greater honor and profit of the convent to which these houris belonged'" (Schurz 1954, p. 165).

1588

Spanish Armada defeated.

In outfitting and maintaining the Invincible Armada, Philip II exhausted his credit with the Genoese bankers. The asiento (license) system promised larger and steadier revenues. Everyone coveted the Spanish asiento because it was much more than a license for supplying slaves. It was a screen to hide contraband goods.

1590

Simon Bolivar obtained authorization for importing 3,000 slaves.

A company of 3,000 Spanish renegades with muskets, led by Judar, attacked the Songhay. They overthrew the Askias at the Battle of Tondibi in 1591 and thereafter ruled at Timbuktu.

1591

Moroccans invaded and overran the empire of Songhay. The Songhay, with their bows and arrows, were helpless against powder and shot, and were defeated at Tenkadibou. Askia Ishak, the king, offered terms, and Djouder Pasha referred them to Morocco. Firearms were in use in Bornu a few years before Judar and his desert army used them with devastating effect on the Songhay.

Timbuktu, founded in the eleventh century, became Mohammedan.

Duarte Lopes, whom Philip II of Spain and Portugal sent to the Congo, related his experiences to Filippo Pigafetta, a Papal official who published his accounts in Rome.

1593

Fort Jesús at Mombasa, greatest of the old Portuguese citadels along the east coast, was begun but not completed until 1639.

1595

With the union of Spain and Portugal in 1580, the privilege of importing slaves fell to the Portuguese. In 1595 a detailed grant was given to Gomez Reynal. During nine years he was to deliver 38,250 slaves, at the rate of 4,250 annually. Of these 3,500 had to be landed alive. For his concession he was paid 900,000 ducats; for every black short of the quota he forfeited 10 ducats. The blacks were to be fresh from Africa and were to include no mestizos, Turks, or Moors. In 1600 Reynal died and the contract was transferred to Juan Rodrigues Cutiño, and extended to 1609 (Saco 1938, pp. 240-45, 247).

Dutch expedition to the Coast of Guinea.

"In 1596 Queen Elizabeth wrote to the mayors of various cities that 'these kind of people should be sent forth from the land.' The Queen issued licenses to deport Africans mainly on two grounds: because of economic pressures 'in these hard times of dearth,' and because 'most of them are infidels, having no understanding of Christ or his Gospel'" (Edwards 1981, p. 33).

1597

Monastery of Augustinian friars established in Mombasa.

1598

Several thousand blacks who worked in the rich gold mines near Zaragoza in Nueva Granada (now Colombia) wrecked the mines and killed the Spanish administrators and miners; they then defied the Spanish authorities from behind palisades that they had thrown up. The rebellion was suppressed with systematic ruthlessness by the colonial government (Schurz 1954, p. 176).

(1598–1610)

1598–1610

"The Moors lingered in Spain for a little more than a century. By 1610 through expulsion and migration, a million--among them many Jews--had returned to North and West Africa" (Huggins and Jackson 1969, p. 114).

c.1600

The first known King of Ashanti, a part of the Akans, reigned. He had been preceded perhaps by at least two kings. Gold was then unknown and iron was currency.

1600

Revolt of Maroons.

1602

The Dutch East India Company received a charter; it established a settlement at the Cape of Good Hope in 1652.

1607

Dutch attacked Portuguese on Mozambique.

Continued fighting between Moroccan invaders and soldiers of Songhay.

1609

Slave uprising in Mexico led by Yanga.

1610

Royal officials of Buenos Aires denounced by king for smuggling slaves.

c.1612

By the middle of the sixteenth century there were 20,000 African slaves in Cuernavaca and Veracruz. They caused the Spaniards more uneasiness than the more numerous Indians. The Viceroy Mendoza hanged a number of them as an example, but the Spaniards were still unable to take blacks for granted. Early in the seventeenth century the rumor spread through Mexico City that the blacks were going to rise and slaughter all the Spaniards on a certain day. One night the nervous Spaniards mistook the noise of a herd of runaway hogs in the streets for the sound of barefoot blacks bent on their destruction. The next day they executed more than thirty blacks in sheer panic (Schurz 1954b, p. 175).

1612

The British established themselves in Bermuda to conduct trade, including slave trade.

1614

Spanish law prohibited any person from buying anything from slaves.

1616

The Dutch supplanted the Portuguese as slave traders on the African coast and brought the first slaves to the North American continent. In South America they settled Guiana in 1616 and began the cultivation of sugar cane. Later, to curb the rebellious blacks, they brought in East Indians. The so-called "Bush Negroes" in the interior of Guiana were descendants of runaway slaves who had established villages and an organized government. By the end of the seventeenth century, they had large settlements on the Surinam River and before the middle of the eighteenth century they were making repeated raids on the plantations.

1617-1621

Formation of Dutch West India Company.

1618

James I of England granted exclusive charter to Sir Robert Rich and others to organize stock company to trade with Guinea.

The British established themselves in the Rio Gambia (Company of Adventurers of London).

(1619)

1619

The British introduced the first Africans (twenty) brought in
a Dutch ship into Virginia. They were not slaves. They were
stolen freemen. They were free in Africa; free by the laws
of Virginia. By force and fraud they and their children were
gradually forced to a slavery the legality of which was not
fully recognized for several decades.

1620

Introduction of women who were sold as wives to American
colonists for from 100 to 150 pounds of tobacco.

1621

Attempt by Felipe IV by legislation to reduce rebelliousness
among blacks and "mulatos" of Cartagena.

Dutch West India Company given monopoly of American slave
trade.

The private companies trading in the west were all merged into
the Dutch West India Company, which sent, in four years,
15,430 blacks to Brazil, carried on war with Spain, supplied
the British plantations, and gradually became the great slave
carrier of the day.

Royal decrees in Brazil prohibited the activity of nonwhites
in the industrial arts, the goldsmith's trade, and weaving.
These restrictive decrees were in vogue from the time of
Manoel I in Brazil. One of the orders, dated 20 October expressly stated that no Negro, mulatto, or Indian may work as
a goldsmith.

The Dutch launched the overseas slave trade as a regular institution. By this time the Dutch had captured Portugal's
various slave forts on the West Coast and they proceeded to
open sixteen forts along the coast of the Gulf of Guinea.
Ships sailed from Holland to Africa, got slaves in exchange
for their goods, carried the slaves to the West Indies or
Brazil, and returned home laden with New World produce.

1622

Virginia "imposed fines for fornication with a Negro, but did
not restrict intermarriage until 1691. According to this law,
if any free English woman should have a bastard child by a
Negro or mulatto, she should pay the sum of fifteen pounds
sterling. In default of such payment she should be taken into
the possession of the church wardens and disposed of for five
years. Such illegitimate children should be bound out as servants until they reached the age of thirty. If the woman in
question happened to be already in servitude, five years were
added to the term for which she was then bound. This same
law was further elaborated and extended by the Virginia law
of 1753" (Woodson 1939, p. 112).

1624

Prohibition of introduction of slaves from Rio de la Plata to
Peru.

"A Negro child was baptized and called William, and from that
time on in almost all, if not all, the oldest churches in the
South, the names of Negroes baptized into the church of God
can be found upon the registers" (Du Bois 1903, p. 10).

1625

The French took possession of Haiti.

Certain authors give this date for the foundation of Dahomey.
Others, as M. A. LeHerisee, would not place this event farther
back than the reign of the Prince Wagbaja, between 1650 and
1680. The map of Joannes Janssonius, published at Amsterdam
in 1627, entitled Guinea, shows the country and the city of
Dauma to the North of the Arder (Ardra) and East of the Volta
where the Dahomey that we know is situated. Moreover, Leo
the African, who lived between 1491 and 1540, and who traveled
in the Sudan around 1507, also mentioned the Kingdom of Dauma,
which he situated much to the East of Dahomey, but which might
very probably be the same as the Dauma of Joannes Janssonius.

69

(1626)

1626

First French settlement in West Africa at St. Louis on the
Senegal River.

1627

"It is true that the Spanish Jesuit Alonso de Sandoval in the
early seventeenth century made a widely circulated plea to his
brothers of the Society in the united kingdom of Spain and
Portugal asking for more human care of the Negros [sic], who
were human and equal in the sight of God, Naturaleza, policía
sagrada i profana, costumbres i ritos, disciplina i catechismo
evangélico de todos Etipoes por el P. Alonso Sandoval, natural
de Toledo, de la Compañia de Jesus, Rector del Colegio de
Cartegena de las Indias, Sevilla, 1627. But as C. R. Boxer,
who has considered the phenomenon of the Jesuits in Brazil
(enemies of Indian slavery but indifference to or approving of
Negro slavery) points out, Sandoval admitted the validity of
African slavery under canon and civil law. The Indian was
born free, but the Negro was accustomed to slavery as his
natural condition. Essentially this was the Aristotelian
position of the sixteenth-century Juan Gines de Sepulveda"
(Corwin 1957, fn., p. 167).

1628

African slaves introduced into Canada.

A decisive battle enabled the Portuguese to displace the
ruling Monomotapa with a convenient nominee of their own; a
year later this virtual puppet, Mavura, duly signed a treaty
which gave the Portuguese a free run in looking for minerals
and, if they could find any, in mining and exporting them.
This was an early example of an Afro-European treaty of the
"concession type" which was to become common in later years.

c.1630

Queen Nzinga tried in vain to save Ndongo (Angola) from dis-
integration and later organized the state of Matamba.

1630

In Virginia, Hugh Davis, a white, was whipped because he was
"guilty of defiling his body by lying with a Negro" (Woodson
1931, p. 111).

70

(1638)

1630-1697

Republic of Palmares.

1631

Charles I of England granted a second charter to Richard Young
and others giving exclusive trade to the coast of Guinea,
between Cape Blanco and the Cape of Good Hope, for a period
of thirty-one years.

Mombasa, under Yusuf bin Hasan, rebelled against Portuguese
control.

The Kamba now traded regularly with Mombasa.

Bunyoro at height of its power.

Rise of Buganda.

1637

French merchants of Dieppe constructed Fort St. Louis in
Senegal and obtained privileges of trade for ten years.

The Portuguese castle at Elmina passed into Dutch hands. Soon
after this the rent agreement for Elmina, called "the Note,"
became the possession of the King of Denkyira who had taken
the Dutch into peaceful trading partnership. This "Note" was
among the spoils acquired by Asante in its defeat of Denkyira
after 1700. After that time, the Dutch were lessees of Asante,
not Denkyira, and so came to regard Asante as their principal
trading partner.

The Portuguese possessed a clever black general, Henry Diaz,
who served with distinction in their wars against the Dutch.

1637-1638

The Dutch are substituted for the Portuguese in Arguin, Goree,
and Elmina.

1638

The first black people arrived in Boston as slaves, being
part of a cargo that also included tobacco and cotton.

(1640)

1640

Sweden entered the slave trade.

When a certain Captain Smith, about 1640, attacked an African village and brought some Africans home to Massachusetts, he was arrested and the Africans sent home at the colony's expense (Du Bois 1896, p. 30).

1641

Limitations on slavery in Massachusetts; law sanctions slave trade and the holding of blacks and Indians in bondage.

c.1642

Foundation of the French Compagnie de l'Orient for the purpose of colonizing Madagascar.

1642-1645

The French introduced African slaves in Martinique.

1642-1864

In North and South Carolina, Virginia, Louisiana, Florida, Georgia, Mississippi, and Alabama, maroon communities consisting of fugitive slaves and their descendants provided havens, served as bases for marauding expeditions against nearby plantations, and at times, supplied leadership for planned uprisings.

1645

Sweden constructed Fort Christianborg on the Gold Coast.

Slaves exported from Mozambique to Brazil.

1647

Black slave proclaimed himself King of Guinea in Santiago de Chile.

1648

Luanda fell to fifteen ships and 1500 men from Brazil.

1650

Sugar planting began in the West Indies.

Rise of new states in West Africa: Akwamu after 1650; Asante after 1690; and Dahomey after 1700.

Sugar planting began in Martinique. Within a century there were 60,000 slaves in the island and it took three revolts and a civil war to make them free.

Omani Arabs recaptured Muscat from Portuguese and began to build a new empire based on strength at sea in the Indian Ocean.

1651

The Navigation Ordinance of 1651 was aimed at the Dutch, and two wars were necessary to wrest the slave trade from the Dutch and place it in the hands of the British. The final terms of peace, among other things, surrendered New Netherlands to England and opened the way for England to become the world's greatest slave trader.

British East India Company took the island of St. Helena from the Dutch.

1652

First Omani expedition against Portuguese along Swahili coast.

Many new states in Congo grasslands. Incoming ancestors of Lozi and Bemba entered Zambia at about this time.

Angolan kingdoms of Kongo and Ndongo are thoroughly ruined by Portuguese invasions and the Atlantic slave trade.

Dutch founded small settlement at Cape of Good Hope.

Rise of Bambara on middle Niger, and of Yoruba of Oyo in southwestern Nigeria.

Perpetual slavery for whites and Africans prohibited in Rhode Island.

(1652)

Dutch expedition of three ships sent by the East India Company, under command of Jan van Riebeek, landed at Table Bay and erected a fort in Cape Town (Cape Colony).

1653–1674

British fight Dutch for supremacy at sea.

1655

Revolt of maroons in Jamaica.

Oliver Cromwell, in his zeal for God and the slave trade, sent an expedition to seize San Domingo. His fleet, driven off there, took Jamaica from Spain. The English found the mountains already infested with 1500 or more maroons, and more blacks continually joined them. Jamaica was finally captured and held by Cromwell and became the West Indian base for the slave trade.

1657

George Fox, founder of the Quakers, impressed upon his followers in America "the duty of converting the slaves, and he himself preached to them in the West Indies" (Du Bois 1903, p. 21).

The Danish took possession of Fort Christianborg on the Gold Coast.

1658

The first Hottentot Wars began as a result of runaway slaves and cattle raiding. Some West African slaves had been introduced in South Africa.

Blacks and Indians rebelled in Hartford, Connecticut.

From Togoland went the first African ambassadors to the courts of Europe: Bans, who was sent to the Court of Philip IV of Spain, and Don Matthew Lopes, who was ambassador to Louis XIV at Versailles in 1670.

1658-1659

First slaves in any numbers were two shipments from Angola and West Africa to the Cape. Many absconded and eventually nearly all were returned to the Dutch company. Some slaves in South Africa came from Bay of Bengal, Indonesia, and other Asian areas until 1767.

1660

Scheme of government for South Carolina drafted by John Locke gave every free man absolute power and authority over his black slaves.

Connecticut barred blacks from military service.

Up to this date it appeared accepted in most colonies and in the British West Indies that baptism into a Christian Church would legally free an African slave.

1660-1780

The Pashas of Spanish and African ancestry ruled at Timbuktu. After 1780 the title of Pasha disappeared and "mayors" of Timbuktu were chosen alternately by the Bambara, the Tuareg, and the Fulani.

1660-1862

Bambara, south of Timbuktu, flourished.

1661

Virginia passed a law stating that black people and their children would be slaves for life.

New Netherlands Slave Petition: Emanuel Pieterson and Reytory, free black husband and wife petitioned the Noble Right Honorable Director-General and Lords Councillors of New Netherlands to declare Anthony, born of free parents, whom they reared after his parents died, to be a free person. The petition was granted.

Act in Virginia declared all servants not being Christians brought in by sea were declared slaves for life.

(1661)

"But slavery for life was still tenuous as long as the slave
could extricate himself by baptism. The fact that Negroes
were heathens had formerly justified their bondage, since
infidels were 'perpetual' enemies of Christians" (Handlin
1957, p. 13).

1662

A British African Company chartered by Charles II built a fort
at James Island, at the mouth of the Gambia. This company,
composed of persons of high rank and distinction had the
king's brother, the duke of York, at its head. Taking advantage of the war declared against Holland, it seized and re-
tained several Dutch forts on the Gold Coast between 1665 and
1672.

Virginia law declared children should be held bond or free according to the condition of the mother.

The "Royal Adventurers," including the British king, the queen
dowager, and the duke of York, invested in the African slave
trade.

1663

Maryland declared that black slaves should serve durante vita
(for duration of life). This law gave legal recognition to
slavery in the colony of Maryland.

French slavery in the New World centered in Haiti. The French
annexed the eastern part, thus dividing the island between
France and Spain.

The freedom of the maroons of Jamaica was acknowledged, land
was given them, and their leader, Juan de Bolas, was made a
colonel in the militia. He was killed, however, the following
year, and from 1664 to 1788, 3,000 or more black maroons
fought the British in guerilla warfare. Soldiers, Indians,
and dogs were sent against them, and finally in 1738 Captain
Cudjo and other chiefs made a formal treaty of peace with
Governor Trelawney. They were granted 2,500 acres, their
freedom was recognized, and they were promised bonuses for
runaway slaves returned by them.

(1667)

First serious conspiracy involving African slaves in English America occurred in Gloucester, Virginia. There were others in 1687, 1709, 1710, 1722, 1723, 1730.

Maryland law declared that free-born English women marrying blacks shall be servants of the masters of their husbands and the children of such marriages should be slaves for life.

Charles II granted charter to the Company of Royal Adventurers which established forts and factories for engaging in slave trade.

The Italians, Grillo and Lomelin, obtained an asiento from the government of Spain for transporting 24,000 African slaves to America.

1664

Maryland law stated that Christian baptism had no effect on status of slave; similar laws passed in North Carolina, New Jersey, New York, and Virginia. Maryland law prohibited marriage between white women and black men.

1665

Duke's laws for the government of New York did not exempt non-Christian Africans and Indians from slavery.

1667

Virginia declared that killing a slave by extremity of correction should not be considered a felony.

Cabildo of Buenos Aires informed the king of the scarcity of slaves due to deaths from pestilences.

Act to regulate the Negroes on the British Plantations passed. Slaves were forbidden to leave the plantation without a pass; never permitted to leave on Sunday; forbidden to carry weapons. Punishments: severe whipping for striking a Christian; second offense branding on the face with a hot iron. Slaves forbidden to possess horns or other signaling devices. No punishment for owner who inadvertently whipped a slave to death; small fines for killing his own slave or another man's slave.

(1667–1671)

1667–1671

> In the United States a series of laws laid down the rule that
> conversion alone did not lead to a release from servitude.
> The truly vexing problem was to decide on the proper course
> when one parent was free, for it was not certain whether the
> English law that the issue followed the state of the father
> would apply. Maryland, which adopted that rule in 1664, found
> that unscrupulous masters mated black males and white females,
> which not only gave them the offspring but the service of the
> woman for the life of her husband (Handlin 1957, p. 14).

1669–1734

> There were slave uprisings in Jamaica in 1669, 1672, 1673,
> twice in 1678, 1682, 1685, 1690, 1733, and 1734. There were
> other revolts in Jamaica in 1760, 1765, and 1766, 1807, 1815,
> 1824. The Christmas Rising of 1831 is estimated to have in-
> volved possibly 20,000 slaves and maroons.

1670

> Southern Europe began to see a number of diplomatic visitors
> from Africa in the fifteenth and sixteenth centuries. In the
> seventeenth century they began to reach northern Europe. One
> of the earliest was Matteo Lopez, royal interpreter to
> Kpoyizoun, the king of Ardra (in present-day Dahomey). He was
> presented at the court of Louis XIV and was lionized briefly
> by the French aristocracy but the projected treaty of alliance
> between France and Ardra was never ratified. He was followed
> a few years later by Aniaba from the Ivory Coast. Aniaba
> succeeded in passing himself off as the son of the reigning
> king when he was only the slave of a courtier. He stayed in
> France from 1687 to 1701, serving as an officer in the French
> cavalry. He was not merely received at the French court; he
> was baptized by Bossuet himself, with Louis XIV acting as god-
> father.
>
> In the eighteenth century, the romantic view of the "noble
> savage" aroused the European interest in Africans, especially
> when they were thought to have had high status in their own
> societies. Later, in the nineteenth century, the romantic
> interest in Africa was replaced by the humanitarian concern of
> the antislavery movement. Both motives prompted Europeans to
> record slave narratives.

1671

Maryland encouraged the importation of slaves.

1672

Denmark established forts on the Gold Coast.

Attempt of fugitive slaves in Virginia to form small armed groups.

Royal African Company, formerly the British African Company, chartered by Charles II. Among the stockholders were the King, Duke of York, and others of distinction. The company carried on a growing African slave trade for a quarter of a century.

1673

Introduction of sugar cultivation in colonies increased demand for slaves.

1674-1702

Barbados developed a savage slave code and the result was attempted slave insurrections in 1674, 1692, and 1702. These were not successful but a rising in 1816 destroyed much property under the leadership of a mestizo, Washington Franklin, and the repeal of harsh laws and eventual enfranchisement of the "colored" people followed.

1675

Virginia Petition for freedom: According to the petition of Philip Corven, a black, he was to have his freedom, in keeping with his mistress's will, eight years after her death. His new owner forced him to sign an indenture for twenty years from which he sought relief. There is no indication of the decision in the case.

1676

Slavery prohibited in West New Jersey.

(1679)

1679

Revolt in Haiti. "In San Domingo itself the dangers of slave revolts were not unknown. For years runaway slaves had hidden in the mountains especially in the northeastern part of the island. There were serious slave revolts in 1679, 1691, and 1718, and in the middle of the eighteenth century a Negro, Macandel, carried out systematic poisoning which created a panic" (Du Bois 1939, p. 162).

Decree of Charles II abolished slavery in Chile.

1680

Bill passed in Virginia restraining blacks from meeting in considerable numbers, walking abroad, bearing arms, carrying clubs, staves or other offensive weapons or instruments.

New York declared that more than four slaves should at no time and at no place meet together away from their master's service or carry arms.

1680–1688

The English African Company sent 249 ships to Africa, shipped app. 60,000 black slaves, and after losing 14,000 on the middle passage, delivered 46,000 in America.

1680–1786

It is estimated that over 2 million slaves were imported into the British West Indies. Even young Irish peasants were "hunted down as men hunt down game, and were forcibly put aboard ship, and sold to the planters in Barbados" (Du Bois 1939, p. 152).

1681

Planters sometimes married white women servants to blacks in order to transform these servants and their children into slaves. This happened in the case of Irish Nell, a servant woman brought to Maryland and sold to a planter when her former owner returned to England. The proceedings to obtain freedom for her offspring by her black husband occupied the courts of Maryland for a number of years. The petition was

finally granted. This procedure was especially legislated
against in 1681 by a measure that penalized this custom by
the planters (Woodson 1931, pp. 110ff).

1682

Virginia Slave Code reduced all non-Christian bondservants to
permanent slave status, regardless of any later religious
conversions.

Dutch East India Company acquired commercial monopoly in East
Indies.

Negro serfdom recognized. The charter of the Free Society of
Traders in Pennsylvania recognized the slavery of blacks.
Slaves were to be freed after fourteen years of service, upon
condition they cultivate land allottted to them, and surrender
two-thirds of the produce annually.

1684

Portuguese gradually lost all their positions on the coasts
of Kenya and Tanzania, but remained along the coast of Mozambique.

On 6 March 1684, the General Congregation of Propaganda Fide
and the Holy Office, two of the most powerful organs of the
Papacy, handed down a set of decisions "which if they had
been implemented rigorously, would have effectively halted
almost all the worst excesses of the slave trade a century
before Wilberforce and his associates mounted their full-scale
campaign against it." The decisive initiatives leading to
these decisions were made by an African, Lorenzo de Silva e
Mendoza, Procurator General for a religious association of
Africans, "Africans of mixed ancestry," and for many other
institutions. He was of African descent and was probably
living at the time in Rome. At the request of Pope Innocent
XI, his Memorial was formerly considered 6 March 1684 (Gray
1981, p. 37).

Huge expansion of sugar and tobacco growing on Caribbean
islands and in mainland of Americas by colonists of European
stock. This demanded great increase in slave labor; the
Atlantic slave trade entered its main period. In 1713 Britain
became the largest buyer of Africans for enslavement.

(1685)

Great profits helped to make possible the British Industrial
Revolution.

1685

The French Code Noir of 1685 made baptism and religious instruction of blacks obligatory (Du Bois 1903, p. 9).

Baltasar Coyman received an asiento from the government of
Spain for transporting 10,000 African slaves to America.

The French West Indian Company gradually began to occupy San
Domingo and their right to the western part was recognized in
the Treaty Ryswick. There were so many slaves and "coloreds"
at this time that Louis XIV issued his celebrated Code Noir,
which was notable in compelling bachelor masters, fathers of
colored children, to marry their concubines. Children followed
the condition of the mother as to slavery or freedom; slaves
could have no property; harsh punishments were provided for,
but families could not be separated by sale, except in the
case of grown children; emancipation with full civil rights
was made possible for any slave twenty years of age or more.
Indigo, cocoa, and sugar cane were planted and by 1728, there
were 50,000 blacks. The number increased to 172,000 by 1710
(Du Bois 1939, p. 156).

1687

Slave conspiracy in Virginia.

Brandenburg (Prussia) settlers established themselves at
Arguin Island off the coast of French West Africa, south of
Cape Blanco; there they established a slave market.

1688

One of the first protests of the Friends was the celebrated
Germantown Protest of Mennonite Quakers against slavery drawn
up by Franz Daniel Pastorius and his associates.

c.1690

Portuguese were finally driven out of Mashonaland by Changamire
Dombo, who considerably strengthened the Rozwi state. The
Portuguese were never able to return.

1691

Virginia law prescribed that any white woman in Virginia marrying a black, bond or free, was to be banished.

1692

Virginia act declared that resisting or runaway slaves may be lawfully killed; the master was to receive from the public 4,000 pounds of tobacco for the loss of his slave. The Governor and Council of Pennsylvania approved an ordinance: "Upon the Request of some of the members of the Council, that an order be made by the Court of Quarter Sessions for the Countie of philadelphia, the 4th July instant (proceeding upon a presentment of the Grand Jurie for the bodie of the sd countie), agt the tumultous gatherings of the Negroes of the towne of philadelphia, on the first dayes of the weeke, ordering the Constables of philadelphia, or anie other person whatsoever, to have power to take up Negroes, male or female, whom they should find gadding abroad on the said first dayes of the weeke, without a ticket from their Mr. or Mris., or not in their Compa, or to carry them to gaole, there to remain that night, and that without meat or drink, and to Cause them to be publickly whipt next morning with 39 Lashes, well Laid on, on their bare backs, for which their sd. Mr. or Mris. should pay 15d. to the whipper, etc." (Du Bois 1899, pp. 235, 411).

Membo Changamire, Dombo of Urozi, acted against Portuguese in his domain. He evicted them altogether from Urozwi; they were never to return. His capital at Great Zimbabwe is now an imposing stone structure.

1694

First discovery of gold in Taubate, Brazil. Slaves were used as laborers in the gold mines.

1695

The Cachu Company (French-Portuguese) contracted with the government of Spain to transport 4,000 slaves annually to America for a determined number of years.

Republic of Os Palmares overthrown.

(1695)

Insurrection was often attempted in South America, especially
among the Mohammedan blacks around Bahia. About this time,
a group revolted and held out for a long period. In 1719 a
widespread conspiracy failed but many of the leaders fled to
the forest. In 1828 a thousand blacks rose in revolt at
Bahia and again in 1830. From 1831 to 1837 revolt was in the
air and in 1835 came the great revolt of the Mohammedans, who
attempted to enthrone a queen. The blacks fought with furious
bravery but were finally defeated.

Reverend Samuel Thomas conducted a school for Negroes in Goose
Creek Parish, South Carolina.

1696

There were already 20,000 Africans in Pondicherry, India.

Omani beseiged Mombasa and took it from Portuguese after two
years. The Omani commander was a Mazrui, the first of his
family to appear on the coast.

Deepening chaos in empire of the Mwanamutapa mainly because
of Portuguese interference and aggression.

Friends (Quakers) sought to regulate slavery in the United
States in a general way and prevent its undue growth. They
suggested in the Yearly Meeting of 1696, and for some time
thereafter, that since traders "have flocked in amongst us
and . . . increased and multiplied negroes amongst us," members ought not to encourage the further importation of slaves,
as there were enough for all purposes. In 1711 a more active
discouragement of the slave trade was suggested, and in 1716
the Yearly Meeting intimated that even the buying of imported
slaves might not be the best policy, although the Meeting
hastened to call this "caution, not censure." By 1719 the
Meeting was certain that their members ought not to engage in
the slave trade, and in 1730 they declared the buying of
slaves imported by others to be "disagreeable." At this mile-
stone they lingered thirty years for the Meeting had evidently
distanced many of its more conservative members. In 1743 the
question of importing slaves, or buying imported slaves, was
made a disciplinary query, and in 1754, spurred by the crusade
of leading Quakers Benjamin Lay, John Woolman, and Anthony
Benezet, offending members were disciplined. In 1758 the same
golden rule was laid down as that with which the Germans,

seventy years previous, had taunted them, and the institution
of slavery was categorically condemned. Here they rested
until 1775, when, after a struggle of eighty-seven years,
they decreed the exclusion of slaveholders from fellowship in
the Society (Du Bois 1899, pp. 12, 13).

1697

Osai Tutu came to the throne and founded Kumasi.

1698

The British Parliament ended the monopoly of the Royal African
Company and permitted private traders to operate after paying
a duty of ten percent because Parliament believed the slave
trade to be highly beneficial and advantageous to England,
the plantations, and the colonies. Thus the slave trade was
legally open to New England merchants. By 1700 Boston slave
traders had made the slave trade almost exclusively a Massachusetts enterprise with Boston the chief slave port supplying
all the New England colonies and Virginia. However there were
not more than a thousand blacks in all New England because
most of the trade was triangular: New England exported food
to the West Indies in exchange for rum; the rum was bartered
for slaves who were taken to the West Indies and exchanged or
sold for more rum, sugar, molasses, and cocoa. The making of
rum from molasses was the largest industry in New England at
the outbreak of the Revolutionary War; shipbuilding and seafaring, important economic enterprises in New England, were
also dependent on the slave trade (Du Bois 1896, pp. 2, 3).

"Whereas, the great number of negroes which of late have been
imported into this Collony [sic] may endanger the safety
thereof if speedy care be not taken and encouragement given
for the importation of white servants" 1. £13 are to be given
to any ship master for every male white servant (Irish ex-
cepted), between sixteen and forty years, whom he shall bring
into Ashley river; and £12 for boys between twelve and sixteen. Every servant must have at least four years to serve,
and every boy seven years. 2. Planters are to take servants
in proportion of one to every six male Negroes above sixteen
years" (Du Bois 1896, p. 203).

(1698–1707)

1698–1707

It seems probable that 25,000 blacks a year arrived in America.
After the Asiento of 1713 this number rose to 30,000 annually,
and before the Revolutionary War it reached at least 40,000
and perhaps 100,000 slaves a year. It is estimated that
nearly 900,000 slaves were brought to America in the sixteenth
century, 2.75 million in the seventeenth, 7 million in the
eighteenth, and over 4 million in the nineteenth, perhaps 15
million in all. Certainly it seems that at least 10 million
Africans were expatriated. The Mohammedan slave trade meant
that expatriation or forcible migration in Africa of millions
more. Many other millions were left dead in the wake of the
raiders. It would be conservative, then, to say that the
slave trade cost Africa from a fourth to a third of its population (Du Bois 1939, p. 142).

c.1700

Bristol became an important center of the slave trade, followed by London and Liverpool. Liverpool soon overtook both
Bristol and London. After 1700, slave codes were common in
many states. Slave codes were formal recognition that blacks
were not governed by the laws of other men (Handlin 1957,
p. 18).

"Slaves were a special kind of property, not quite like
houses or beasts of burden, but not quite like people either,
within the meaning of the law. A special set of laws was
therefore designed to protect the owners of such property and
to shield all whites against such dangers as might arise from
the presence of so many slaves. These codes began to develop
in the seventeenth century, and long before the Civil War they
were fully refined. From time to time it was necessary to
modify them, and they differed from state to state; but in
important particulars they were quite similar. Since they
were designed to achieve due subordination of the slaves,
they were frankly repressive, a fact for which the white
planters and legislators made no apologies.

"A slave had no standing in the courts. He could not be
a party to a suit at law; and he could not offer legal testimony except against another slave or a free Negro. Since he
had no legal responsibility, his oath was not binding. Thus,
he could not make a contract, and his marriage was not a legal

contract. His children were not legitimate. The ownership of
property by slaves was generally forbidden, and although some
states permitted them to possess certain types of holdings,
there was no legal basis for even this concession. A slave
could not strike a white person, even in self-defense; but
the killing of a slave, however malicious, was rarely regarded
as murder. The rape of a female slave was a misdemeanor when
it involved trespassing on the property of another person.
Slaves could not leave the plantation without the permission
of their master; and any white person encountering a slave who
was away from the plantation without permission could take him
up and turn him over to the public officials. Slaves could
not possess firearms and, in Mississippi, they could not beat
drums or blow horns. Laws generally forbade the hiring out of
slaves, but many owners ignored this proscription.

"Slaves could not purchase or sell goods or visit the
homes of whites or free Negroes. They were never to assemble
unless a white person was present; and they were never to
receive, possess, or transmit any incendiary literature cal-
culated to incite insurrections. They were not to be taught
to read or write or cipher; and any white person or free
Negro found guilty of violating this law was to be subjected
to severe punishment or fine or imprisonment or both. Slaves
guilty of petty offenses were to be punished by whipping, but
the more serious offenses drew severe punishments such as
branding, imprisonment, or death. Arson, rape of a white
woman, and conspiracy to rebel, for example, were capital
crimes in all the slaveholding states. Since slaves were
always regarded with suspicion and since they could not testify
against a white person who accused them, many of them were
found guilty of crimes they did not commit, and against which
they were unable to defend themselves.

"Despite the elaborateness of the slave codes and the
machinery of enforcement, there were numerous infractions
that went unpunished altogether. When times were quiet the
laws were disregarded, and slaves could get away with a great
deal. But when there were rumors of revolts among the slaves,
the white community became apprehensive and tended to enforce
the codes with unusual zeal. Slaveowners, moreover, did not
generally pay much heed to the slave codes where their own
slaves were concerned. The planter conceived of himself as a
valid source of law and justice and he preferred to take all
matters involving his own slaves into his own hands and mete

out justice in his own way. He was certain that he could
handle his own slaves, if only something could be done about
those on the neighboring plantation. Such an attitude was
obviously not conducive to the uniform, effective enforcement
of the slave codes" (Smythe 1976, pp. 25, 26).

1700

Founding of Ashanti with Kumasi as capital: 1700-1895.

Four bills were introduced in Pennsylvania: one regulating
slave marriages was not passed; the other three were passed,
but the Act for the Trial of Negroes--a harsh measure providing death, castration, and whipping for punishments, and
forbidding the meeting together of more than four Negroes--
was afterward disallowed. The remaining acts became laws,
and provided for a small duty on imported slaves and the
regulation of trade with slaves and servants (Du Bois 1899,
pp. 13, 411).

Francis Williams, born of free black parents in Jamaica, was
picked to be the subject of an experiment, which, it is said,
the Duke of Montagu was curious to make. The purpose of this
experiment was to discover whether by proper cultivation at
school and the university, a black might be found as capable
of literature as a white person. Williams, trained in British
grammar schools and in Cambridge, is the author of a Latin
ode, Integerrimo et fortissimo viro, Georgia Holdane [To that
most upright and valiant man, George Haldane]. It was written
on Haldane's assuming the governorship of Jamaica and printed
at least as early as 1774 when it was included in Edward
Long's History of Jamaica. Williams may have been the author
of a published ballad apparently no longer extant: Welcome,
Welcome, Brother Debtor! (Long 1774, pp. 475-80).

John Chavis was one of the last black Americans to become the
subject of a social experiment and to receive an intensive
education at the expense of sympathetic whites. Some say it
was as a result of a friendly disagreement between two
southerners. One was willing to bet that a black could not
learn Greek or Latin. The other argued with just as much
certainty that a black could learn these classics. The matter
was settled by sending Chavis to Princeton. There, Chavis
distinguished himself as a Latin and Greek scholar. He was
not able to attend classes with the other students but he was

taken as a private student of the president of Princeton who
was an outstanding classical scholar of his day. It is said
that Chavis not only attended Princeton but studied at what
is now Washington and Lee University at Lexington, Virginia.
He later conducted what might be called a portable school;
his was a classical school that prepared students for college
(Savage 1940, pp. 14ff).

His advertisement read: "John Chavis takes this method of
informing his employers and citizens of Raleigh in general
that the present quarter of his school will end the 15th of
September, and the next will commence on the 19th. He will
at that same time open an evening school for the purpose of
instructing children of color, as he intends, for the accomo-
dation of some of his employers to exclude all children of
color from his day school. The evening school will commence
at an hour by the sun. When the white children leave the
house, those of color will take their places and continue
until ten o'clock." Chavis had as his students persons who
were distinguished in the history of North Carolina:
"Priestley Mangum, a lawyer of distinction, and the brother,
W. P. Mangum, Senator of the United States, prominent during
the Administration of Andrew Jackson; Charles Manly, governor
of North Carolina; Abraham Rencher, minister to Portugal and
governor of New Mexico; and James H. Horner, founder of the
Horner School; Archibald E. and John L. Henderson, sons, or
Chief Justice Henderson, and many others of less distinction"
(Savage 1940, pp. 14ff).

1701

The Society for the Propagation of the Gospel in Foreign
Parts was founded and incorporated under William III. The
Society was "formed with the view, primarily, of supplying
the destitution of religious institutions and privileges
among the inhabitants of the North American colonies, members
of the established church of England; and, secondarily, of
extending the gospel to the Indians and Negroes" (Du Bois
1903, p. 12).

Boston town meeting favored abolition of slavery.

1701-1713

The French Royal Senegal Company held the coveted Asiento.
Owing to wars with England, the French never became great

(1702)

slave traders and their West Indian possessions were supplied
mainly by the Dutch and Portuguese in the earlier days.   On
the other hand the French developed on the island of San
Domingo a system of slavery which had great influence upon
the descendants of Africans and the economic history of the
world.

1702

The Xosa crossed the Kei River (in Cape Province, South
Africa) and came in contact with the Dutch in cattle barter.
A war broke out and the Dutch drove out the Xosas and seized
5000 cattle.

1703

Slave narratives, as a genre, began with John Saffin's Tryall
in answer to Samuel Sewell's well known antislavery tract,
The Selling of Joseph, one of the earliest appeals in the
antislavery movement, published in 1700.

South Carolina put duty on the importation of slaves.

1704

First(?) black school established in New York by Elias Neau--
as many as 200 met nightly until his death in 1722.   Mr.
Neau's school was blamed for the plot of 1712 by blacks in
New York to destroy all the English.   Two of Mr. Neau's
students were charged with the plot; one was cleared and the
other was convicted of being involved in the conspiracy but
guiltless of his master's murder (Du Bois 1903, p. 13).

1705

The Virginia slave code defined slaves as being real estate.

1706

Massachusetts enacted a law against the interbreeding of
blacks and whites.   Another act for the trial of blacks was
passed in Pennsylvania.   It differed slightly from the Act of
1700.   It provided that "Negroes should be tried for crimes
by two justices of the peace and a jury of six freeholders;
robbery and rape were punished by branding and exportation,

homicide by death, and stealing by whipping; the meeting of
Negroes without permission was prohibited. Between this time
and 1760 statutes were passed regulating the sale of liquor
to slaves and the use of firearms by them; and also the general
regulative Act of 1726 'for the Better Regulation of Negroes
in this Province.' This act was especially for the punishment
of crime, the suppression of pauperism, the prevention of
intermarriage, and the like--that is, for regulating the
social and economic status of Negroes, free and enslaved"
(Du Bois 1899, p. 13).

1708

Perpetual (for life) slavery recognized in Rhode Island.

Generally, laws in America at this time did not hinder slaves
from learning trades. However, laws against teaching slaves
severely hindered black mechanics from attaining very great
efficiency, except in rare cases. They usually had to work
by rule of thumb. North Carolina allowed slaves to learn
mathematical calculations but not reading and writing.
Georgia, in 1833, decreed that no one should permit a Negro
"to transact business for him in writing" (Du Bois 1902,
pp. 15ff). Mississippi, in 1830, debarred slaves from
printing offices and Georgia, in 1845, declared that slaves
and free Negroes could not take contracts for building and
repairing houses, as mechanics or masons. Restrictions,
however, were not always enforced, especially in the building
trades, and the slave mechanic flourished. One obstacle he
encountered for many years was the opposition of white
mechanics. In 1708 the white mechanics of Pennsylvania protested against the hiring out of Negro mechanics and were
successful in getting acts passed to restrict the further importation of slaves. These laws were disallowed, however, in
England. In 1722 they protested again and the Legislative
Assembly declared that the hiring of black mechanics was
"dangerous and injurious to the republic and not to be sanc-
tioned" (Du Bois 1899, pp. 14, 15). Opposition was fierce,
particularly in border states. In Maryland, the legislature
was urged in 1837 to forbid free Negroes from being artisans;
in 1840 a bill was reported to keep Negro labor out of tobacco
warehouses; in 1844 petitions came to the legislature urging
the prohibition of free black carpenters and taxing free
black mechanics; and finally in 1860 white mechanics urged a

(1708)

law barring free blacks "from pursuing any mechanical branch of trade" (Du Bois 1902, p. 15).

Uprising in New York. One black woman and three black men were executed in retaliation for the killing of seven whites. The men were hanged, the woman burned alive. Some of the participants, including a pregnant woman, were captured. Others, including a woman, committed suicide rather than surrender.

1709

Liverpool sent out one slaver of thirty tons; encouraged by Parliamentary subsidies which amounted to nearly a half million dollars between 1729 and 1750, the trade increased to 53 ships in 1751, 86 in 1765, and at the beginning of the nineteenth century, 185, which carried about 49,000 slaves in one year.

1710

There was a widespread slave conspiracy in Brazil; between 1828 and 1837 Mohammedan blacks revolted repeatedly.

1711

With the aid of blacks, the Portuguese penetrated the valley of the Amazon from the Parana to Guiana. Blacks helped them conquer the land, fighting against the French in Rio. Nash wrote in The Conquest of Brazil, "When gold came to dominate the economic life of Brazil, the Negro assumed the entire load. Every panful of earth from which the gold was washed, every clod of cascalho from which diamonds were gleaned, and all the millions of tons that yielded nothing at all, were moved by Negroes carrying upon their stalwart heads the loads their masters were too stupid to move on wheelbarrows. Negroes carried upon their well-muscled backs the full weight of that Portuguese Empire in the eighteenth century, as they alone carried the weight of the Brazilian Empire for the first half of the new nineteenth century" (Du Bois 1939, p. 151).

La Compania Francesa de las Indias (The French Company of the Indies) obtained an asiento for transporting slaves to Spanish America for an undetermined number of years.

Audrestoe, "mulato" leader of rebellion in Venezuela.

Blacks fought French in Brazil.

1712

William Southeby petitioned the Pennsylvania Assembly to abolish slavery; they refused but did pass an act that refused the importation of Negroes and Indians, the first such act in America.

Population of Maryland was about one fifth African slaves.

As early as 1686 the Carolina colony (North and South Carolina) forbade blacks to engage in any kind of trade or to leave their master's plantation without written authorization. In 1722 white justices were authorized to search blacks for guns, swords, and other offensive weapons and to confiscate them unless the black could produce a permit to carry such a weapon less than one month old; patrols could search blacks and whip those considered dangerous to peace and good order. After uprisings and numerous attempted uprisings, South Caroline, now separated from North Carolina, enacted one of the most stringent slave codes to be found anywhere in the New World. No more than seven blacks were permitted to be together without a white person present; between Saturday evening and Monday morning, no slaves were permitted to possess firearms or carry them; under no conditions were blacks to be taught to read and write.

African plot in New York to kill whites greatly upset the city.

New York and Massachusetts enacted law for preventing, suppressing, and punishing the conspiracy and insurrection of African and other slaves.

Great Britain obtained from Spain, by the Treaty of Utrecht, a thirty year monopoly of introducing African slaves in the Spanish American colonies at the rate of 4,800 per year (Royal African Company). England engaged to supply the colonies within that time with at least 144,000 slaves at the rate of 4,800 per year. The English counted this prize as the result of the Treaty of Utrecht, which ended the mighty struggle against the power of Louis XIV. The British held the monopoly for thirty-five years until the Treaty of Aix-la-Chapelle, although they had to go to war over it in 1739.

(1713-1733)

1713-1733

Fifteen thousand slaves were imported annually by the English.

1715

There were about 60,000 Negroes in all the British colonies in America at this time (Blake 1859, p. 378).

Royal decree permitted free introduction of blacks into Puerto Rico (Blake 1859, p. 378).

Ricardo O'Farrill established a factory in Havana for the entrance and sale of slaves.

Slave revolts in Surinam, Dutch Guiana.

Sieur Andre de Brue, who went to St. Louis in 1697 as the Governor of the French Senegal Company, established during the next eighteen years the French colony of Senegal.

North Carolina tried to put an end to amalgamation of the races by restricting "the intercourse of the two races." Clergymen officiating at mixed marriages were penalized. These precautions, however, failed to prevent amalgamation which continued in North Carolina as it had elsewhere in spite of the fact that the law of 1741 legislated against "that abominable mixture and spurious issue, which hereafter may increase in this government by white men and women inter-marrying with Indians, Negroes, Mulattoes or Mustees" (Woodson 1939, p. 113).

North Carolina passed an act that declared: "That if any master or owner of Negroes or slaves, or any other person or persons whatsoever in the government, shall permit or suffer any Negro or Negroes to build on their, or either of their, lands, or any part thereof, any house under pretense of a meeting-house upon account of worship, or upon any pretense whatsoever, and shall not suppress and hinder them, he, she, or they so offending, shall, for ever default, forfeit and pay fifty pounds, one-half toward defraying the contingent charges of the government, the other to him or them that shall sue for same" (Du Bois 1903, p. 10).

1715-1763

Fighting continued in Guiana until formal treaties between the Dutch and blacks were made.

Portuguese law declared that all slaves who set foot on the soil of Portugal were to be considered free.

In South Carolina, where Jews and blacks had been voting, they were expressly denied those rights.

There was a black militia in the French part of St. Domingo.

1716-1723

Hannibal, an African, and Pushkin's great-grandfather, spent five(?) years in France, which included service in the French army.

1719

Slave revolt in Brazil.

1720

Coffee introduced in Martinique by French.

Portuguese Crown prohibited colonial adminstrators from engaging in any aspect of the slave trade.

Slave conspiracy in South Carolina.

1720-1730

Dutch East India Company maintained a depot at Delogoa Bay for slaves from Madagascar and East African slaving centers.

1721

The French occupied the Island of Mauritius, located in the Indian Ocean, east of Madagascar. Its capital was Port Louis.

c.1721-1776

Angelo Solliman, "Friend, favorite and tutor of European

(1722)

royalty. Personal attendant of Prince Lobkowitz and later of
Prince de Lichtenstein. Still later, companion of Joseph II
of Austria, with the approval of his mother, Empress Maria
Theresa, who felt that Angelo's influence on her son would
help to make him a better king. Francis I, Emperor of the
Holy Empire, liked him so well that he invited him to enter
his personal service." Abbé Gregoire, who wrote a sketch of
him in his An Enquiry Concerning the Intellectual and Moral
Faculties and Literature of Negroes, spoke highly of him
(Rogers 1947, p. 551).

1722

Slave plot in Virginia.

1723

Coffee emerges as major product of Brazil.

No black, mulatto, or Indian was allowed to vote in Virginia.

1724

Black Code with fifty-five articles regulating the government
of slaves published in New Orleans.

1724-1728

Dahomey conquered the other two states established by three
sons of an African monarch in the seventeenth century; a
powerful kingdom was established.

1726

Terentius Afer (Terence the African) was an ex-slave in Rome.
He was the greatest of the Latin stylists, the author of six
plays. He is most famous for his "Homo sum; humani nihil a
me alienum puto"--"I am a man and nothing human is alien to
me."

The Act of 1726, for the Better Regulation of Negroes in this
Province, declared: "Whereas free Negroes are an idle and
slothful people and often prove burdensome to the neighborhood and afford ill examples to other Negroes, Therefore, be
it enacted that if any master or mistress shall discharge or

set free any Negro, he or she shall enter into recognizance with sufficient securities in the sum of £30 to indemnify the country for any charge or incumbrance they may bring upon the same, in case such Negro through sickness or otherwise be rendered incapable of self-support" (Du Bois 1899, pp. 413, 414).

An Act for the Better Regulation of Negroes in the Province: "In case of freedom by will, the executor or administrator was required to give bond, or such slaves should not be re- garded as free. Any Negro becoming free under age, 21, might be bound to service until of age. The Act further provided penalties for the harboring of Negroes by each other; for trading or dealing with each other without license--all on pain of being sold into slavery if unable to pay fine; also provided penalty of £100 for anybody who should marry a Negro and white person; £30 for Negro caught living in marriage relation with white person, in such cases Negro to be sold into slavery for life" (Du Bois 1899, pp. 413, 414).

Peter Vantrump, a free black, agreed to go to Europe with Captain Mackie. Instead he was taken to North Carolina where he found himself in slavery. His petition to the Honorable Christopher Gale, Esquire, Chief Justice of the General Court of North Carolina was denied.

1726-1727

Series of slave rebellions in Surinam.

1727

Yearly meeting of Quakers in London censured slave trade.

1728

Earliest known writing in Kiswahili: the Utendi wa Tambuka.

Asante a powerful state.

Gregorio, the slave of Don Jorge Burgues, was functioning in Montevideo as a common crier. In the creation of the Cabildo of Montevideo by order of Zabala, 20 December 1729, persons of color were mentioned in an official order of the Banda Oriental (Uruguay): Africans of mixed ancestry were excluded

(1729)

from serving as aldermen or councilmen. In 1731 records indicate the presence of other blacks, slaves of Francisco
de Acosta.

1729

Discovery of diamonds in Brazil.

Cabildo of Montevideo excluded "mulatos" from serving as
aldermen or Councilmen.

York and Talbot Decision that slaves, alone or accompanied,
reaching Great Britain or Ireland, are not free.

Ralph Sandiford, a Philadelphia Quaker, wrote A Brief Exami-
nation of the Practice of the Times, By the Foregoing and the
Present Dispensation. . . . an early Quaker antislavery tract
(Benjamin Franklin, printer).

Ignatius Sancho was an African, born on board a slave ship
bound for South America. "His Letters [edited by Joseph
Jekyll], published in London in 1782 in a two volume edition,
form a work not equalled perhaps in charm and literary merit
by any other butler, white or black, before Sancho's day or
since" (Loggins 1931, p. 7).

1729-1730

Portuguese transported large numbers of Africans to Minas de
Geraes.

1730-1812

The most brilliant figure of this artistic age in Brazil was
Antonio Francisco Lisboa, popularly called Aleijadinho, an
architect and sculptor.

1731

Royal decree ordered the destruction of the slave quilombo
of Cumbe. A quilombo was a cooperative community of fugitive
slaves (Diggs 1953, p. 63).

Slave rebellion in Santiago del Prado, Cuba.

1731-1823

Conspiracies and revolts in Guiana: Berbice revolt in 1731; revolt in Demerara in 1823. Berbice also had revolts in 1762, 1763-1764, and 1767. The Great Rebellion of 1763-1764 under Cuffy may have involved half the slaves in the colony and led to widespread slave executions. Essequibo, another territory of Guiana, remained relatively quiet after the unsuccessful revolts of 1731, 1741, and 1744. In Demerara there were two revolts in 1772; another in 1773; and two others in 1774-1775. Another revolt was staged in 1803 and another in 1823 when the slaves revolted and staged at least one major battle involving thousands from at least thirty-seven plantations. They were motivated by cruelty, unsuccessful attempts to negotiate, a desire for a shorter work week, and the belief that they had been freed by the British and were being held illegally by the planters. They imprisoned most of the whites instead of killing them, but this did not lessen the viciousness of their punishment.

1732

New colony of Georgia prohibited African slavery as fatal to the interests of the poor white settlers for whose special benefit the colony was projected.

Slave rebellion in Louisiana. A black woman and four black men were executed and their heads publicly displayed on poles.

1733

Spanish royal decree announced that all fugitive slaves reaching Florida were to be permitted to reside there as free people.

Boston Slave Petitions for freedom.

1734

Ayuba Suleiman Diallo of Bondu was known to the Europeans as Job en Solomon. He was captured by enemies during a commercial venture to the Gambia in 1731, sold as a slave to Maryland, and put to work growing tobacco. After an attempted escape, he was rescued from slavery by Thomas Bluett, who discovered his education and recognized his quality. With the assistance of English gentlemen, he was emancipated, taken to England, presented at the British court, and finally helped to return home. Bluett later wrote the memoirs of Solomon.

"Job ben Solomon was elected in 1734 to the scholarly Spalding Society whose membership had included Newton and Pope, was received at Court and presented by the Queen with a gold watch" (Edwards 1981, p. 41).

1737

Benjamin Lay was one of the earliest Quakers to condemn slavery and the slave trade; he used both nonviolent resistance and a biting pen. His tracts were printed by Benjamin Franklin.

1738

Treaty with maroons of Jamaica gave them "autonomy" from Britain.

Ignoring Britain's monopoly of the trade in Africans with Spanish territories, the Cabildo petitioned in 1738 with the support of the Military Governor, Don Domingo Santos de Uriarte, that Montevideo be permitted to use three boats for acquiring slaves in Brazil in exchange for tallow, dried beef, and wheat.

Anton Wilhelm von Amo, from Guinea, came to Europe in 1707 at the age of four. Educated under the supervision of the Prince of Brunswick, his education was completely European. He spoke Hebrew, French, Dutch, and German. Amos lectured publicly, was a Doctor at University of Wittenberg, and was made a councillor of state by the Court of Berlin. In c.1734 he wrote the dissertation "On Sensations considered as absent from the Mind, present in the Body." His published work consisted of Latin treatises on logic, psychology, and history. His metaphysical essay written in Latin, Tractatus de arte sobrie et accurate philosophandi, was published in 1738. He defended African culture against European prejudice and returned to the Gold Coast sometime between 1740 and 1758.

1738-1830

A series of inventions revolutionized the cotton industry.
These inventions had far reaching effects on the manufacture
of cotton goods. Where the cotton was coming from was soon
answered by the southern United States and the invention of
Whitney's cotton gin. The South increased its cotton culture
and became a one crop region (Du Bois 1896, pp. 151, 152).

1739-1740

A group of slaves from Charleston set out for St. Augustine
where they were told they would be free. On the way they
killed all whites they met until they were surrounded and
massacred. Twenty-one whites and forty-four blacks lost their
lives. A second insurrection at Stono River, South Carolina,
led by slave Cato resulted in the death of thirty-one whites
and a larger number of slaves. A third uprising occurred at
St. Johns Parish in Berkeley County, South Carolina.

1740

Slave insurrections in South Carolina resulted in many deaths.

Slaves in New York City accused of conspiring to kill their
masters by poisoning the water supply. "Many late horrible
and barbarous massacres have actually been committed and many
more designed on the white inhabitants of this province by
Negro slaves" (Du Bois 1896, pp. 22, 206).

South Carolina declared: "Whereas, the having of slaves
taught to write or suffering them to be employed in writing
may be attended with inconveniences, be it enacted, That all
and every person and persons whatsoever, who shall hereafter
teach or cause any slave or slaves to be taught, or shall use
or employ any slave as a scribe in any manner of writing what-
ever, hereafter taught to write, every such person or persons
shall for every such offense forfeit the sum of £100 current
money." In 1800 and 1833 the teaching of free Negroes was
restricted: "And if any free person of color or slave shall
keep any school or other place of instruction for teaching
any slave or free person of color to read or write, such free
person of color or slave shall be liable to the same fine, imprisonment and corporal punihsment as by this act are imposed
and inflicted on free persons of color and slaves for teaching
slaves to write." Other sections prohibited white persons
from teaching slaves (Du Bois 1901, pp. 18, 19).

(1740)

In Charleston, South Carolina a black woman was condemned to die for arson.

1741

New York slaves plotted to burn the city and murder the whites. A white was accused of providing the blacks with weapons and he and his family were executed. A Catholic priest was hanged as an accomplice. Thirteen blacks were burnt alive, eighteen hanged, and eighty transported.

Tomas Navarro granted asiento to supply slaves to Buenos Aires and Montevideo.

Philip Quaque (Kweku) born on the Gold Coast. He was connected with the slave trade through the merchants who carried it on--not as one of the human cargo. In 1754, at the age of thirteen, he was sent to England for education, sponsored by the Society for the Propagation of the Gospel in Foreign Parts; he was ordained as a priest of the Church of England, the first African to attain this distinction. In 1766, he returned to the Gold Coast as a missionary. Over the next half century, he wrote a series of letters to the Society for the Propagation of the Gospel in Foreign Parts in London.

1742

James Eliza John Capitein, kidnapped from Africa when he was seven or eight years of age and educated in Holland at the expense of a philanthropic Dutch merchant, published at Amsterdam a volume of sermons and a Latin treatise which is said to defend slavery as a social institution. He also published an essay in Leyden which defended the thesis that slavery per se is not contrary to Christian doctrine.

1743

Tomas Navarro exchanged a shipment of Africans for hides in the Port of Montevideo.

Toussaint L'Ouverture born.

1744

School for Negroes established in Charleston, South Carolina lasted for ten years; taught by a Negro for free Negroes only, although some slaves who hired their time were able to send their children (Du Bois 1901, p. 21).

1746

A semiliterate slave girl named Lucy Terry, in Massachusetts, commemorated an Indian raid on the town of Deerfield with a poem that she called "Bars Fight."

1749

Authorized importation and use of African slaves permitted in Georgia.

1750

British act for extending and improving the African trade; merchants were allowed to engage in the slave trade for small duties. This marked the total abolition of monopoly in the slave trade.

Two hundred twenty thousand blacks in the United States.

Coastal cities partially recovered from Portuguese ravages of seventeenth century but the Indian Ocean trade remained much smaller than in earlier times.

Bemba and Lozi had established themselves firmly in Zambia.

Muslim revival movement in Western Sudan; rise of new Muslim states.

Boer (Afrikaner) farmers gradually penetrate northwards from Cape of Good Hope.

Parliament authorized that for every four Africans in the colony of Georgia there was to be at least one white male servant of militia age; that Africans were not to be employed in any trade except agriculture nor were they to be apprenticed to artisans with the exception of carpenters.

The Royal African, or Memoirs of the young prince of Annamaboe [sic]. Comprehending a distinct account of his country and family, his elder brother's voyage to France, and reception

(1751)

there; the manner in which himself was confided by his father to the captain who sold him; his condition while a slave in Barbadoes; the true cause of his being redeemed; his voyage from thence; and reception here in England. Interspers'd throughout with several historical remarks on the commerce of the European nations, whose subjects frequent the coast of Guinea. To which is prefixed a letter from the author to a person of distinction, in reference to natural curiosities in Africa; as well as explaining the motives which induced him to compose these memoirs . . . (London: W. Reeve).

1751

Sugar cane from San Domingo introduced in Louisiana by the Jesuits.

Macandal, a leader of the maroons in Haiti, plotted to poison the whites. He raided and terrorized the plantations of the whites until he was betrayed and captured.

South Carolina enacted a law providing the death penalty, without benefit of clergy, for slaves convicted of attempting to poison a white person.

1754

French captain bought slaves in Kilwa region for transport to St. Domingue (Haiti).

A French captain bought slaves in Kilwa region both for use in the Mascarene Islands, Mauritius, and Bourbon (later re-named Reunion), and for transport to St. Domingue (afterwards Haiti).

C. Croft of Charleston, South Carolina had two of his female slaves burned alive because they set fire to his buildings (Woodson 1931, p. 92).

1755

Georgia, which had legal slavery beginning in 1755, in 1793 stopped the entry of free blacks and in 1798, under heavy penalties, prohibited the importation of all slaves. This provision was placed in the constitution of the state, poorly enforced, and never repealed (Du Bois 1896, p. 71).

Mark and Phillis, slaves of John Codman of Charlestown, Massachusetts, learned that their master had made them free by his will, and poisoned him to expedite matters. Mark was hanged and gibleted, and Phillis was burned to death. Included in Abner Cheney Goodell, The Trial and Execution, for petit treason, is an account of other punishments by burning in Massachusetts (Cambridge: J. Wilson and Son 1883 [sic]).

1756

Black Jasmin Thomassam, a St. Domingo liberated slave, established a Home for Negroes and poor colored persons, which he carried on for forty years under his own management.

1758

Protest against the African slave trade voiced in Brazil by Manoel Ribeiro da Rocha.

Francis Williams, first Negro college graduate in the United States, published Latin poems.

Quakers of England recommended that Friends carefully avoid being involved in the slave trade in any form.

1759

Paul Cuffe born free near Bedford, Massachusetts. By his efforts the Act of 1783 was passed in Massachusetts; it gave Negroes legal rights and privileges. In 1797 he built a small school house in Westport. Later in his life he was active in the movement that proposed an exodus of Negroes to Africa.

1759–1803

Between 1759 and 1803, 642,000 blacks were imported into Brazil from Angola alone (Schurz 1954, p. 163).

(1760)

1760

Jupiter Hammon, born about 1720 (some say 1711), published a
broadside of eighty-eight lines entitled An Evening Thought:
Salvation by Christ with Penetential Cries: Composed by
Jupiter Hammon, a Negro Belonging to Mr. [John] Lloud, of
Queen's Village on Long Island, the 25th of December (1760)
(Reprinted in Porter 1971, pp. 529ff). Hammon also wrote:
An Address to the Negroes in the State of New York (1787); An
Address to Miss Phillis Wheatley appeared as a broadside in
1778 (Reprinted in Porter 1971, p. 535); An Essay on the Ten
Virgins in 1779; A Winter Piece, a sermon in prose with "A
Poem for Children with Thoughts on Death" attached appeared
in pamphlet form in 1782; another prose pamphlet, An Evening's
Improvement, also included a dialogue in verse entitled "The
Kind Master and the Dutiful Servant" (published without date).
All Hammon works were published in Hartford.

Slave rebellion in Jamaica.

The first slave narratives published: A Narrative of the Un-
common Sufferings and Surprising Deliverance of Briton Hammond,
a Negro man, servant to General Winslow of Marshfield, Massachusetts, he returned to Boston after having been absent almost
thirteen years. The narrative was sold by Green & Russell in
Queen Street, Boston. There was a steady stream of slave
narratives, often in autobiographical form. In addition,
several ex-slaves wrote fictionalized accounts of the lives
of the slaves. Perhaps the most important body of Negro literature to appear at this time was that written by fugitive
slaves. Their accounts of what it had meant to be enslaved
served as important ammunition for the antislavery movement,
especially in the 1840s, a period of widespread abolitionist
activity (Porter 1971, pp. 522ff).

These narratives are among the very few personal recollections
of men who were enslaved and shipped from Africa. They give
us some notion of the feelings and attitudes of many millions
whose feelings and attitudes are unrecorded. Imperfect as
they may be, they represent the only source from which we can
view slavery form the point of view of the slave. Perhaps in
the beginning, the dealings in Africa were a partnership between African sellers and European buyers of slaves; a more
equal partnership than it was to be in the nineteenth century
when European military power made itself dominant in Africa.

The eighteenth century was also a time when some Africans
found their way to Europe as free men. Some say there were
more free Africans in Europe than Europeans in the trading
posts of Africa.

"To prevent the mischiefs that may be attended by the importation of negroes into this Province" [South Carolina] . . . "so
much larger was the influx of black slaves that the colony
[South Carolina] in 1760 totally prohibited the slave-trade"
(Du Bois 1896, p. 11). This act was immediately disallowed
by the Privy Council and the governor reprimanded. It was
thought that the best way to obviate such danger was to impose
an additional duty. A prohibitive duty of £100 was imposed
in 1764 which probably continued until the Revolutionary War.

1760-1855

> Chronological Bibliography of Anti-Slavery Tracts. "This is
> a chronological catalogue of printed antislavery pamphlets
> 1760-1855. It contains about 1,200 entries which average
> about 30 words each. It is in the form of about 300 unnumbered
> pages of typescript with emendations in ink and pencil. The
> entries are arranged alphabetically within years, by author's
> name, name of institution or, where anonymous, by the first
> word of the title. Conjectural authors are given in many
> cases for anonymous pamphlets. There is no index. It was
> compiled by the amalgamation of several lists: 37 volumes of
> Slavery Tracts in the Friends House Library; other antislavery
> pamphlets in the Friends House Library; antislavery pamphlets
> at the Anti-Slavery Society; the bibliographies of two theses
> on slavery by Patrick C. Lipscomb and Joyce Birt; and Ragatz'
> Guide for the Study of British Carribean History 1763-1834,
> Washington, D.C., 1932."

c.1761

Phillis Wheatley brought to America from Africa by a slaver.

Quakers in England excluded from membership those found "concerned" in the slave trade.

1762

Fraunces Tavern was bought by Samuel "Black Sam" Fraunces, a
West Indian of African and French extraction. In those days,

(1763)

Fraunces called his establishment Queen's Head Tavern. George Washington was a frequent visitor as were many of his senior officers. His friendship with Fraunces continued through the years. After the great parade that followed the evacuation of New York by the British on 24 November 1783, the reception and banquet were held at the tavern. It was also the place that served as the forum on 26 November for Washington's farewell address to his officers before he retired to Mount Vernon. When New York called for troops, Fraunces was one of the first to enlist. A wealthy man, he assisted the cause of the Revolution with food and money. It appears that plots against liberty as well as for it were fomented at Black Sam's for in 1776, there were men in England who saw the personality of Washington as one of the greatest dangers to England's hold upon the colonies. These men were not above removing the danger as best they could. It happened that a frequenter of Black Sam's place was a young Englishman named Hickey, who had deserted from the British army and enlisted as an American volunteer. Because he was a clever man, despite his bad record, he had become one of General Washington's body guards. This man was the leader in a plot to assassinate Washington, and the first step in the plan was for him to win the help of the general's housekeeper. This person was none other than the young and attractive West Indian girl, Phoebe Fraunces, daughter of Black Sam. The murderer first won her heart and made her his mistress. Then he let her know of his plan and the part she was to play. The plot was to poison Washington with a dish of peas. Phoebe threw them out of the window. When eaten by chickens in the yard, it caused their immediate death. There is no record of the struggle that took place in the mind of Phoebe Fraunces when she found that the man she loved was the appointed murderer of her master. But the fact remains that she revealed the plot to Washington and saw her lover hanged. Much of the tavern's original furnishings and decor are still intact at Broad and Pearl Streets, New York City. The third floor, now a museum, contains several Revolutionary War artifacts, while on the fourth floor, one can find a historical library with famous paintings and other pertinent data.

1763

Berbice slave revolt in what is now Guyana.

Quakers in England attach criminality to those who aid and abet the slave trade in any manner.

On the island of St. Vincent, Indians sought to enslave fugitive blacks, but the blacks drove the Indian men away and took
the Carib women. The black Caribs fought with the British and
others for three-quarters of a century when finally the
British took possession in 1763. Eventually the black Caribs
received a third of the island as their property. Then they
helped the French against the British and were deported to
the island of Ruatan off Honduras (Du Bois 1939, pp. 154, 155).

Kabaka Kyabuga came to power in Bugunda; opened trade with
East Coast; died in 1780.

Abbas, called "El Mahdi," black, thick-lipped, and broad-
nosed, ruled Yemen.

Western Angola reduced by the Portuguese to little more than
a reservoir of slaves for Brazil. Portuguese were unable to
penetrate the inland country of Angola because of African
opposition.

Yoruba empire of Oyo at height of its power.

Rise of overseas slave trade along the African coast in this
period; growth of slave-worked plantations in French islands
of Mauritius and Bourbon.

1764

A quarter of the shipping of Liverpool was in the African
trade; Liverpool merchants conducted one half of England's
trade with Africa. The value of all British goods sent to
Africa was 464,000 pounds sterling of which three-fourths was
of British manufacturers.

1766

In Haiti an order was given to throw into the sea a certain
kind of flour which was supposed to aid in the dissemination
of a specially fatal tertian ague at Port au Prince. Of the
sixty barrels thrown into the sea, seven belonged to Lambert,
a free black, who was the only man to come of his own accord
and offer his flour to the authorities for destruction.

(1776-1773)

1776-1773

Controversy in Massachusetts as to the justice and legality of African slavery.

1776-1842

"James Forten was Philadelphia's leading Negro and a close friend of Paul Cuffe. Orphaned at an early age, Forten came to the attention of the great Quaker abolitionist Anthony Benezet, who provided him with an education. Starting out as a humble errand boy, Forten eventually became a successful sailmaker and earned a fortune that has been estimated at nearly $100,000. Forten was a Quaker, a pacifist, a supporter of temperance and women's rights causes, and a zealous opponent of slavery" (Harris 1972, pp. 153, 154).

1767-1830

Father Jose Mauricio, a black, considered the first founder of a school of music in Brazil, was born in Rio de Janeiro. Upon ordination he was named Choir Master of the Rio de Janeiro Cathedral; his numerous pupils formed the Orchestra of the Royal Chapel. He devoted his talents as a composer primarily to sacred music. He was the author of a treatise on harmony completed shortly before his death.

1768

Coffee introduced in Cuba.

1769

Importation of slaves into Connecticut prohibited.

c.1770

The word race appeared in the Oxford dictionary.

Sālih Bilāli was born in Massina. He was captured, enslaved, and shipped from the Gold Coast in about 1790. Known as Tom, he became head driver of Hopeton Plantation, Georgia, in 1816. In the Muslim Fulbe community in which he was born, all the children were taught to read and write Arabic by the priests. The reminiscenes of Sālih Bilāli were published by

(1770–1830)

William Brown Hodgson in <u>Notes on Northern Africa, the Sahara, and the Soudan</u> (New York, 1884), pp. 68–75.

Crispus Attucks, a slave, was a leader of one of the groups involved in the Boston Massacre. He was killed by British soldiers.

1770

Anthony Benezet and the Quakers of Philadelphia established a school for blacks in Philadelphia.

Bill to prohibit introduction of slaves into Rhode Island failed.

Slavery was well established in the Cape of Good Hope by this date.

The unwritten law of the land was that Negroes should receive no instruction. Georgia fined any person who taught a slave to read or write £20 (Du Bois 1901, p. 81).

Georgia in 1770 forbade slaves "to assemble on pretense of feasting . . . and any constable, on direction of a justice, is commanded to disperse any assembly or meeting of slaves 'which may disturb the peace or endanger the safety of his Majesty's subjects; and every slave which may be found at such meeting, as aforesaid, shall and may, by order of such justice, immediately be corrected, without trial, by receiving on the bare back twenty-five stripes, with a whip, switch, or cow-skin'" (Du Bois 1903, p. 11).

1770–1830

It is extremely difficult to obtain statistics as to the number of slaves who entered the port of Montevideo. Most of the documents do not give the number of "pieces" or the provenience. Nevertheless, as Pereda Valdes says: "Without doubt the black formed a very important nucleus in the population of Montevideo from 1777 until 1830 and at times represented at least a third of the population" (Pereda Valdes 1941, p. 17).

(c.1771)

c.1771

> Phillis Wheatley, <u>To Mrs. Leonard, on the Death of Her Hus-</u><u>band</u>. Broadside (n.d.).

1771

> Bill to prohibit introduction of slaves into Massachusetts failed.

> "In 1771 the Minister of Colonies declared against granting mulattoes certificates of citizenship and said that Louis XV was determined to maintain the principle that colored people and their posterity could never be permitted the same advantages as whites. After 1777 mulattoes were refused the right to come to France" (Du Bois 1939, p. 158).

1772

> Phillis Wheatley, <u>To the Rev. Mr. Pitkin on the Death of His</u><u>Lady</u>. Broadside (Boston).

> Carlos III condemned slavery and declared free fugitive slaves who set foot on his territory while at the same time permitting slavery in his territories.

> "In 1770 there were in England itself not less than 15,000 slaves brought in by traders as attendants and servants. There was no decided check to this influx until the famous Somerset decision. Somerset had run away from his master in Virginia. When captured he was shipped to Jamaica, where he was to be sold. A writ was procured by Granville Sharp, however; and there followed a hearing which finally brought the question before Lord Mansfield. He gave the opinion that the state of a slave is so odious that it can be supported only by positive law to that effect. Such law did not exist in England. He therefore ordered the slave to be discharged." This decision declared free all slaves held in England (Woodson 1931, p. 101).

c.1773

> Scipio Morehead may have been the first American black painter. He is known only because Phillis Wheatley, a contemporary, wrote a poem to him: <u>To S. M., a Young African</u>

Painter, on Seeing His Works. She described two of his
paintings: Aurora and Damon and Pythias.

1773

In Tucamán, Argentina, all the houses had large numbers of
slaves, and in Córdoba a thousand slaves were sold from only
two plantations owned by religious orders. Among these blacks
were musicians and others skilled in all of the various crafts.

Petition for freedom of a group of Africans in the Province of
the Massachusetts Bay. They complained that they had no
property, no wives, no children, no city, no country, and
neither they nor their children to all generations would be
able to possess and enjoy anything, not even life itself,
unless they had freedom.

The black Caribs of St. Vincent fought with Indians, English,
and others for three-quarters of a century until the Indians
were exterminated. After hard fighting a treaty was signed
in 1773; the Caribs received one-third of the island as their
property.

Benjamin Rush, An Address to the Inhabitants of the British
Settlements, on the Slavery of the Negroes in America, 2d ed.
(John Dunlap: Philadelphia). One of the most important anti-
slavery documents of the eighteenth century was written by
Benjamin Rush, who was a signer of the Declaration of Independence, a pioneer American physician, and a founder of the
first antislavery society in the nation. In these talks,
Dr. Rush provided a basic understanding of the eighteenth century, white antislavery viewpoints.

The Marquis of Case Eirle obtained the privilege of introducing African slaves in Cuba.

Phillis Wheatley, Poems on Various Subjects, Religious and
Moral (London).

Phillis Wheatley formally freed.

Slavery abolished in Portugal.

Possibly the earliest request of slaves to return to Africa
and freedom was made by Peter Bestes and others of Boston in

(1773)

their petition.   There were other petitions in 1774, 1777, and 1779.

Phillis Wheatley, <u>To the Hon'ble Thomas Hubbard, Esq; on the Death of Mrs. Thankfull Leonard</u>.   Broadside (Boston).

The Baptists had black preachers for black members as early as 1773 but they were under the supervision of whites and had no voice in general church affairs (Du Bois 1903, p. 21).

Quakers in New England, at their yearly Meeting, banned members from owning slaves; by 1782 they could note that no Friend in their part of the country owned slaves. "Still, despite their antislavery stance, white Quakers were part of a racist society and displayed as much anti-Negro bias as their fellow white Americans. White Quakers failed to recognize any contradiction between their abolitionist commitment and their disdain for the black man. Thus, many local Meetings refused to admit blacks as members. Other, more tolerant Meetings permitted Negroes to join their organization, but insisted they attend services on a segregated basis. Many of these Meetings established separate 'Negro benches' for their black associates" (Harris 1972, p. 27).

1774

Importation of slaves into Connecticut prohibited because "the increase of slaves . . . is injurious to the poor and inconvenient" (Du Bois 1896, p. 37).

Convention to form provincial congress met at New Berne, North Carolina, and decided all importation of African slaves should cease.

Africans in Boston conspired for liberty and tried to get the British to help them.

A group of slave women and men were arrested in the Saint Andrews Parish, Georgia slave revolt. Before they were captured several slave owners were killed and others wounded. The slave leaders were burned to death as punishment.

Importation of slaves into Rhode Island restricted.

Free Negroes of Charleston, South Carolina, established a school for free blacks.

1774-1775

    Nearly all the American slave markets were overstocked with slaves; many of the strongest partisans of the system were bullish on the market, and desired to raise the value of slaves at least by a temporary stoppage of the slave trade (Du Bois 1896, pp. 41, 42).

c.1775

    The Xosa crossed the Fish River, which was an informal line of separation between the Africans and Dutch in South Africa.

    The Ovaherero and the Damaras came into southeast Africa. South of the empire of the Congo and along the ocean arose the state of Mataman, composed of the Herero, Damaras, and the Hottentots.

1775

    John Woolman, Some Considerations on the Keeping of Negroes, in the Works of John Woolman (two parts) (Philadelphia: Joseph Crukshank, 1776; London: T. Letchworth, 1775). Woolman was perhaps one of the most influential antislavery activists of the eighteenth century. These are his most important antislavery works.

    Bill to prohibit importation of slaves into Delaware vetoed by the governor.

    When George Washington took charge of the Continental Army he did not want slaves to serve because he was afraid that arming blacks would lead to conspiracies and insurrections. A committee made up of Benjamin Franklin and others concurred and recommended that all blacks be excluded from the army, which Washington agreed to do. Later when so many joined the British, who promised freedom, he recommended that free blacks be accepted into the Continental Army. Some black soldiers fought in integrated units and were used as spies, guerilla fighters, and navy pilots.

    Thomas Paine published his first article, African Slavery in America, in a Pennsylvania newspaper; he denounced slavery, demanded its abolition, and recommended that freedmen be given land.

(1775)

With the help of Peter Salem and other blacks, minutemen defeated the British on Concord Bridge.

The Society for the Relief of Free Negroes Unlawfully Held in
Bondage, the first abolition society, organized in Philadelphia with Benjamin Franklin as president.

Five slaves in Maryland were convicted for conspiring to
poison whites and two slaves were convicted in Virginia in
1803 for conspiracy to poison.

Continental Congress 13 October passed a resolution barring
blacks from the American Revolutionary Army. 7 November Lord
Dunmore, royal governor of Virginia, offered freedom to all
male slaves who joined the British forces. In response to
Dunmore's Proclamation, George Washington ordered recruiting
officers to accept free blacks beginning 31 December.

c.1776

John Gloucester, first black minister of the Presbyterian
Church, was born in Kentucky.

Adam Smith, The Wealth of Nations, maintained that work done
by slaves, although it may appear costs only their maintenance,
is ultimately very costly; work done by freedmen is cheaper.

1776

French made contact with Kilwa for purposes of overseas slave
trade; they concluded a treaty with the Sultan of Kilwa. This
treaty allowed the French an exclusive right to purchase
slaves from Kilwa as well as to build a fort there if they
wished. The fort was never built and the whole seaboard fell
to dominant British naval influence after the Napoleonic wars.
Early in the nineteenth century, Portuguese slave exports
from the Mozambique coast were running at the rate of about
10,000 a year, very much higher than in any previous period.

The first move against the slave trade in England came in
Parliament but it was not until thirty-one years later, in
1807, that the trade was banned through the efforts of
Clarkson, Wilberforce, Sharp, and others.

Slave woman executed in Maryland for setting fire to her
master's house, outhouses, and tobacco house.

A Baptist church for blacks was founded in Petersburg, Virginia.

Phillis Wheatley, "Letter . . . to His Excellency General Washington," Pennsylvania Magazine or American Monthly Museum 2:193.

Declaration of Independence.

When Virginia adopted a Frame of Government, it was charged that the king had perverted his high office into a "detestable and insupportable tyranny, by . . . prompting our negroes to rise in arms among us, those very negroes whom, by an inhuman use of his negative, he hath refused us permission to exclude by law." In 1778 the further legal importation of slaves into Virginia was stopped definitively (Du Bois 1896, p. 14).

In Delaware by the Constitution, and in 1787 by law, importation and exportation of slaves were prohibited.

1777

Mestizoes from Haiti were forbidden to come to France.

Spain acquired Fernando Po for the purpose of establishing there a slave "factory."

Slavery condemned and declared illegal in the Constitution of Vermont; abolished in 1786.

Chile established a semimilitary organization for persons of color.

Boston Slave Petition for Freedom. The petition against slavery presented to the Massachusetts House of Representatives called their attention to the fact that blacks were aware that they were in a Christian country, that in common with all other men they had a natural and inalienable right to freedom; that they had been unjustly brought to this country; that they had presented petition after petition to the legislature of Massachusetts and were astonished that they had never been considered in view of the difficulties the whites were having with Great Britain. There were six other petitions; the first was in 1773.

(1778)

1778

Quakers recommended education for children of freedmen.

Importation of slaves into Virginia prohibited on motion of
Thomas Jefferson (Blake 1859, p. 389; Du Bois 1869, p. 12).

Slavery (Knight case) declared repugnant to English and
Scottish law.

A black named Joseph Knight, whose Scottish owner had purchased him in Jamaica and brought him to Scotland, claimed
his freedom. He failed in the court of first instance, appealed to the Edinburgh Court of Session with its fifteen
judges, the majority aware of the Somerset decision of 1772
set him free (Usherwood 1981, pp. 40ff.).

Because his army was dwindling, George Washington asked the
Continental Congress to approve reenlistment of blacks in the
Continental Army. Congress agreed. Massachusetts law promised
freedom to enlistment of slaves as soldiers in state militia.

The census taken by order of Vertiz y Salcedo established the
population of Buenos Aires at more than 24,000 of whom 15,719
were whites; 7,269 blacks and Africans of mixed ancestry;
1,218 Indians and mestizos. In the city militia were included
eight cavalry companies composed of free Africans of mixed
ancestry and three companies of the infantry composed of free
blacks. In the Jesuit Colegio alone there were more than
300 blacks.

1779

Haitians helped the United States Revolution. (The American
Negro Academy, Occasional Papers No. 5 [Washington, D.C.,
1889]).

Slaves petitioned the New Hampshire legislature to abolish
slavery.

Emancipation of slaves in Vermont.

Slave trade restricted in Rhode Island.

War broke out in South Africa; the British colonists won in
this first war and drove the Xosa back across the Fish River,
seizing over 5000 cattle.

When the French undertook to help American independence, Comte
d'Estaing was able to raise 800 volunteers among Haitian
blacks and "coloured," including Rigaud and the great
Christophe, who at the siege of Savannah, saved the American
army from annihilation by the British. Particulars of the
battle were given to the United States Minister in Paris in
1849 and are now to be found in the collection of the Pennsylvania Historical Society.

"Many Africans in Britain learned to play musical instruments,
for pleasure and as a means to earn a living, and numbers of
them were employed throughout the country as bandsmen. One
group formed a band which played at an all-black ball, tickets
costing five shillings apiece, and no whites admitted. There
was one quite exceptional black musician of the period, George
Polgreen Bridgetower, a violinist for whom Beethoven composed
the Kreutzer sonata. Bridgetower was born in 1779 in Poland,
of an African father and a Polish or German mother. His
father, who appears to have been a great showman, brought him
to London at the age of ten, and there he soon gained a name
for his virtuoso performances. He played in several concerts
in the company of Haydn, and the Prince of Wales became his
leading patron" (Edwards 1981, p. 41).

1779-1846

There were no fewer than seven Dutch-Kafir wars in which the
Dutch were hard pressed by the Xosa, especially when the Dutch
tried to seize more land. The Dutch had guns and defeated
the Africans, who had only assagais.

1780

Ali Aisami, born in the later 1780s in Bornu and enslaved in
about 1810, was sold from one master to another until he was
finally shipped from Porto Novo (now in Dahomey) in 1818.
His father was a Kanuri teacher-scholar and he received a
good education in the Islamic tradition of his country. He
was known as William Harding. A narrative dictated by Ali
Eisami Gazirmabe of Bornu to S. W. Koelle in Sierra Leone in
about 1850 was published in Koelle's African Native Literature

(1780)

(London, 1854), (in Kanuri, pp. 115-21, and in English trans-
lation, pp. 248-56).

"After eight years of open warfare with the French and Spanish,
maroons in San Domingo completed a treaty of peace with the
French. The maroons were organized under chiefs, among whom
were Père Jean in 1679; Michel in 1713; Colas in 1720; Polydor,
1730; Macandel, 1758; Conga, 1777; and Santiague, 1782. The
great chief at the time of the slave revolt was Jean Francois,
who was soon succeeded by Biassou; after Biassou became
Toussaint L'Ouverture."

John and Paul Cuffe petitioned for the right to vote. Americans connected citizenship with the possession of property;
the right to vote and hold public office rested on property
holdings. John and Paul Cuffe and other propertied black
men were denied citizenship rights in post-revolutionary Massachusetts. The Cuffes petitioned the Commonwealth and authorities in Bristol County and the Town of Dartmouth requesting
exemption from property and poll taxes. Since blacks and
Indians were excluded from the election rolls in Massachusetts,
the petitioners requested exclusion from the tax ledgers.
They pointed out that blacks were not allowed to vote in the
town meetings nor to choose an officer; that no black had ever
been heard in the active court of the general assembly. Their
request was not granted. The Cuffe brothers persisted in
their struggle for equal rights. They refused to pay their
county property taxes and poll taxes during the years 1778,
1779, and 1780. On 15 December 1780, the authorities issued
a warrant for the arrest of John and Paul Cuffe. They were
arrested on 19 December and placed in the common jail in
Taunton. A writ of habeas corpus was served and they were
released in a few hours. Delays and postponements prevented
the trial until March 1781. The brothers conceded defeat and
paid their fine 11 June. On 12 June the Court of General
Sessions ordered that "the petition of Paul Cuffe and John
Cuffe and the proceedings thereon be dismissed" (Harris 1972,
pp. 33ff., 159, 160).

Emancipation of slaves in Massachusetts.

Slavery abolished in Pennsylvania.

Probably the earliest effort to organize for mutual benefit
occurred in Newport, Rhode Island, when Newport Gardner and
his friend met to establish the African Union Society for the
purpose of promoting the welfare of the colored community by

providing a record of births, deaths, and marriages; by
helping to apprentice Negroes; and by assisting members in
time of distress. It was absorbed in 1803 by the African
Benevolent Society which provided a school that continued in
operation until the city of Newport opened a school for Negro
children in 1842.

The Act of the Gradual Abolition of Slavery was passed. This
act, beginning with a strong condemnation of slavery, provided
that no child thereafter born in Pennsylvania would be a slave.
The children of slaves born after 1780 were to be bond servants until twenty-one years of age--that is, beginning with
the year 1808 there was to be a series of emancipations in
Pennsylvania.

c.1781

Abram Petrovich Hannibal, 1696-c.1781, was a black slave
(Moor of Peter the Great) brought to Constantinople and stolen
by the Russian envoy. Peter the Great became his godfather
and gave him an education. He studied military science and
fortification in France and took part in the War of the
Spanish Succession. After a brilliant career he died in 1781,
having attained the rank of lieutenant-general in the Engineering corps and commander-in-chief of Peter the Great's army.
Abram had several children, one of whom became an admiral and
commanded the fleet at the Battle of the Navarins in 1773.
Abram married his second wife a Livonian gentlewoman, and his
granddaughter, Nadezhda, married Sergei, son of Leo Alezan-
drovich Pushkin. Alexander Sergeyevich Pushkin was born in
Moscow 6 June 1799.

1782

"Petition of an African" presented to the Senate and House of
Representatives of Massachusetts by Belinda, reportedly
seventy years of age, to demand protection for herself and her
daughter from her owner. This, perhaps the first recorded
indictment of slavery for which a black American was responsible, was published in Matthew Carey's American Museum 1
(June, 1787).

Deborah Garnett enlisted as a regular soldier in the 4th
Massachusetts Regiment under the name Robert Shurtliff and
served for over a year.

(1782)

Gregon, a Liverpool shipping firm, sued the insurers of the
slaver Zong for nonpayment of a claim. The Zong made the
passage from Africa to Jamaica. They failed to make their
intended landfall and the captain, fearing that he would run
short of water, ordered one hundred thirty-three slaves to be
thrown overboard. The owners claimed they were entitled to
the value of the drowned slaves. The magistrates found for
the owners. The insurers appealed to Lord Mansfield's court
where their counsel argued that the drowning of the slaves was
murder. Mansfield agreed that no charge of murder could be
considered: "Though it shocks me very much to say so, the
case of the slaves was the same as if horses had been thrown
overboard." He ordered a new trial. The owners gave up the
case but Granville Sharp pursued it when it was brought to
his attention by a free black, Olaudah Equiano, whose published autobiography became very well known. Sharp appealed
to the Prime Minister, the Duke of Portland, asking that the
Royal Navy should prevent the recurrence of such atrocities
on British ships (Usherwood 1981, pp. 40ff.).

1782-1784

Louisiana was a constant target of maroon attacks. When
twenty-five of this maroon community were taken prisoners,
men and women alike were severely punished.

1783

Letters of the Late Ignatius Sancho, An African were published
in two volumes in London. Ignatius Sancho made a name for
himself as a writer after having been brought to England from
the West Indies as a child.

A Serious Address to the Rulers of America, by Anthony
Benezet, on the inconsistency of their conduct respecting
slavery; forming a contrast between the encroachments of
England on American liberty, and American injustice in tole-
rating slavery (Trenton, N.J.: printer unknown; London:
J. Phillips).

Peter Williams, Sr., a slave, was purchased by the John
Street Methodist Church of New York. Immediately liberated,
he remained in its employ as sexton until his death in 1823.

Slavery prohibited in New Hampshire.

(1786)

Friends (Quakers) in England established a society for the abolition of the slave trade.

Importation of slaves in Maryland prohibited.

1784

Phillis Wheatley Peters, An elegy, sacred to the memory of that great divine, the reverend and learned Dr. Samuel Cooper. . . . (Boston).

Phillis Wheatley Peters, "Liberty and Peace," a poem (Boston).

Partial emancipation of slaves in Connecticut.

New conflicts between Swahili cities and the Omani.

In Rhode Island slaves and all persons born after March, 1784 were declared free; participation in slave trade was forbidden in 1787.

Branding of slaves prohibited in the Rio de la Plata.

1785

John Marrant published A Narrative of the Lord's Wonderful Dealings with J. Marrant, a Black . . . Taken Down from His Own Relation; one of the first autobiographies written in English by a black.

Baptist churches for blacks existed in Williamsburg, Virginia and Savannah, Georgia and in 1790, Lexington, Kentucky.

Partial prohibition of slave trade in New York.

David Walker (1785-1830) is best known for Walker's Appeal, a pamphlet he wrote urging slaves to resort to violence in order to be freed.

1786

Proposal by Dr. Henry Smeatham of plan to found settlement for slaves who had found asylum in England from the West Indies and the United States.

(1786)

Importation of slaves into New Jersey and North Carolina prohibited.

External slave trade prohibited in Vermont.

Geoffrey L'Islet was an officer of artillery and guardian of the depot of maps and plans of the Isle of France. In 1786 he was named a correspondent of the French Academy of Sciences to which he regularly transmitted meteorological observations and hydrographical journals. In the almanac of the Isle of France, several contributions of L'Islet's were inserted. A collection of his manuscript memoirs are deposited in the archives of the Academy of Sciences. L'Islet was well versed in botany, natural philosophy, geology, and astronomy. He established a scientific society in the Isle of France of which some whites refused to become members merely because its founder was black.

The Life and Confession of Johnson Green, who is to be Executed this Day, August 17th 1786 for the Atrocious Crime of Burglary together with his Last and Dying Words; "may contribute to a better understanding of the social obstacles and frustrations of blacks which bore down upon some blacks in colonial times and after" (Porter 1971, p. 401).

1787

An Address to the Negroes in the State of New York, by Jupiter Hammon. Hammon was satisfied with his status as a slave and did not desire his freedom. He wrote "Now whether it is right, and lawful, in the sight of God, for them to make slaves of us or not, I am certain that while we are slaves, it is our duty to obey our masters, in all their lawful commands, and mind them unless we are bid to do that which we know to be sin, or forbidden in God's word" (Porter 1971, pp. 309, 313).

In Philadelphia, black Methodists organized the Free African Society for benevolent and religious purposes, largely as a result of discriminatory practices encountered as they worshipped with whites at St. George's Methodist Episcopal Church. It was under the leadership of Richard Allen and Absalom Jones. The Society later developed into St. Thomas Protestant Episcopal Church under the leadership of Absalom Jones, the

first rector, and the Bethel Church, Methodist, of which
Richard Allen was organizer.

Attabah Cugoano, liberated from slavery in Granada and placed
as a servant in homes in England, is partially responsible for
a volume published in London as his own: Thoughts and Sentiments on the Evil and Wicked Traffic of Slavery and Commerce
of the Human Species, Humbly Submitted to the Inhabitants of
Great Britain.

A committee on the abolition of slavery, with Granville Sharp
as president, is organized in Great Britain.

Exportation of slaves from Delaware prohibited.

Act and Ordinance prohibited importation of slaves into South
Carolina.

Slavery and involuntary servitude, except as punishment for
crime, were forbidden in the Northwest Territory.

Reorganization of the Pennsylvania Abolition Society.

Importation of slaves into Rhode Island prohibited.

First African settlers sailed from Portsmouth, in charge of
Captain B. Thomson, and arrived in Sierre Leone having purchased land from King Tom.

Caserio for Africans for the Royal Company of the Philippines
established in Montevideo.

Negro Masonic Order African Lodge was established through the
efforts of Prince Hall, an active member of the Boston Free
African Society. Prince Hall and others petitioned the Grand
Lodge of England for permission to establish this Masonic
Lodge.

Poems on comic, serious and moral subjects, by Phillis
Wheatley, 2d ed. (London: J. French).

Idea developed of repatriating stolen Africans on the coast
of Africa. About 400 Africans from England were sent to
Sierra Leone with 60 white prostitutes for wives.

Establishment of New York African Free School.

(1787)

Samuel Hopkins wrote, "The inhabitants of Rhode Island, especially those of Newport, have had by far the grand share in
this traffic, of all these United States. This trade in human
species has been the first wheel of commerce in Newport, on
which every other movement in business has chiefly depended.
That town has been built up, and flourished in times past, at
the expense of the blood, the liberty, and happiness of the
poor Africans; and the inhabitants have lived on this, and by
it have gotten most of their wealth and riches" (Du Bois 1896,
pp. 34ff.).

Africans in Boston petition the State Legislature for equal
educational facilities.

The private physician of San Martin, Dr. Zapata, was a black
from Lima who had fled to Mendoza because of his "patriotic
convictions" (Lanuza 1946, p. 66).

c.1787-1791

Abraham or Abram, born of slave parents in Pensacola, 1787,
fled as a lad to the Seminoles from Pensacola where he was a
slave to Dr. Sierra. Seminole slaves were rather in the position of dependents, or even proteges, of their masters. As
interpreter he accompanied a delegation of Seminoles to Washington in 1826. On his return he was liberated in consequence
of his many and faithful services and great merits, married
the widow of the former chief of the nation, and was appointed
to an office which combined the duties of private secretary,
chief counsellor, and spokesman.

Peter Peckard, Am I not a Man? And a brother? with all
humility addressed to the British legislature . . . (Cambridge: J. Archdeacon, printer to the University).

1788

During this year there were brought to San Domingo 29,500
slaves in 98 vessels. In ten years, 1782-1792, the number of
slaves employed on its plantations probably doubled.

Slave trade prohibited in New York.

Slave trade prohibited in Massachusetts.

James Ramsey, Objections to the Abolition of the Slave Trade, with Answers, 2d ed. (London: J. Phillips).

Thomas Clarkson, An Essay on the Impolicy of the African Slave Trade, in two parts (London: J. Phillips).

Slave trade prohibited in Pennsylvania by amending the Act of 1780; the amendment sought to prevent internal and foreign trade and to correct kidnapping and other abuses.

"An Essay on Negro Slavery" appeared in the November and December issues of the American Museum, pp. 414-17; 509-12 signed by the pen name "Othello" of Maryland.

Slave trade prohibited in South Carolina for five years.

Protest, under Prince Hall's leadership, against kidnapping and sale into slavery of free Negroes.

Societe des Amis des Noirs [Society of the Friends of Blacks] established in France for abolition of slave trade and slavery.

Cabildo of Buenos Aires warned of the inherent danger in the gathering of multitudes of free blacks and slaves in the city.

The African Union of Newport, Rhode Island proposed a general exodus to Africa, but the Free African Society of Philadelphia soberly replied: "With regard to the emigration to Africa you mention we have at present but little to communicate on that head, apprehending every pious man is a good citizen of the whole world" (Du Bois 1899, p. 20).

More than 700 black Americans fought side by side with the whites in the battle of Monmouth.

1789

The Society for the Free Instruction of Orderly Blacks and People of Color was organized in Philadelphia. As early as 1760 two schools for the education of Negroes existed in Philadelphia.

The memoirs of Olaudah Equiano represented a uniquely de- tailed account of an African's movement out of slavery. He was kidnapped as a boy from his home in what is now the Benin province of Nigeria. After several changes of ownership he

was sold to British slavers in 1756 and brought by them to
Barbados. From there he was taken to Virginia, where a
British naval officer bought him and took him to England as a
servant, giving him the name of Gustavus Vassa. After serving
with his master in the British navy during the Seven Year's
War, he had hopes of acquiring his freedom, but his master
returned him instead to the West Indies for resale. He bought
his freedom in 1766. In 1876 he was involved in the prepara-
tions for the expedition of the "Black Poor" which resulted
in the foundation of Freetown, Sierra Leone.

Slave trade prohibited in Delaware.

Spanish Royal Decree, having special reference to Florida,
granted land and freedom to fugitive slaves.

James Derham, black physician, practiced in Philadelphia and
New Orleans. Born a slave (1762-?) in Philadelphia he became
an assistant to his master, a doctor. He was sold to a New
Orleans doctor whom he assisted and three years later set up
his own practice.(Loggins 1931, pp. 8, 368).

Julian Raymond and Vincent Ogé went to Paris as members of a
delegation and presented a petition to the National Assembly
asking citizenship rights in San Domingo for free blacks. In
1790, the Constituent Assembly of France voted by a large
majority not to interfere with the interior government of the
colonies, or subject them to laws "incompatible with their
local establishments." They also buttressed the slave trade
by declaring that the National Assembly would not make any
innovation directly or indirectly "in any system of commerce
in which the colonies were already concerned" (Du Bois 1939,
p. 159). Bitterly disappointed with the decision of the
French Assembly, Ogé returned by way of the United States in
order to collect arms and escape observation. Landing secretly
in the north of San Domingo, he collected a force of 300 men.
They were immediately attacked by a much larger force from
Cap François and compelled to take refuge in the Spanish part
of the island. The governor surrendered them, and Ogé and
Chavannes, the two leaders, on 12 March 1791, were sentenced
"whilst alive to have their arms, legs, thighs and spines
broken; and afterward to be placed on a wheel, their faces
toward Heaven, and there to stay as long as it would please
God to preserve their lives; and when dead, their heads were
to be cut off and exposed on poles" (Du Bois 1939, pp. 160,
161).

John Marrant, A Sermon; Preached on the 24th Day of June, 1789, Being the Festival of St. John the Baptist, at the Request of the Right Worshipful the Grand Master, Prince Hall, and the Rest of the Brethren of the African Lodge of the Honourable Society of Free and Accepted Masons in Boston (Boston).

"A Letter on Slavery" by a "Free Negro" was published in the American Museum 6 (July):77-80.

1790

The Amis des Noirs [Friends of Blacks], organized by Gregoire, Robespierre, Mirabeau, Condorcet, and others, succeeded in getting the decree of 8 March 1790 supplemented 28 March by "instructions recognizing the right to vote in parishes of all free persons twenty-five years of age." The authorities of Martinique, Guadeloupe, and San Domingo all decreed that this applied only to white persons. Franklin and Thomas Paine were members; Thomas Jefferson was a corresponding member.

United States population 3.9 million including 698,000 slaves. Free Negroes 59,500 (U.S. Census).

Abu Bakr Al-Siddiq was born in Timbuktu. He claimed descent from the Prophet. His family belonged to the class of men of learning for generations. He received his early education at Jenne where he was instructed in reading and construing the Koran. In Buona, he continued his education with more advanced work on the Koran while still too young to proceed to the studies of logic and rhetoric. He was taken as a prisoner to the port of Lagos, where in about 1805, he was sold to an English ship and transported to the West Indies. In 1834, he became free. The inhabitants of Kingston donated twenty pounds to Abu Bakr by public subscription. Abu Bakr Al-Siddiq left two autobiographical fragments written in Arabic.

Proceedings of the National Assembly of France upon the proposed abolition of the slave trade in that kingdom; declared colored persons in Haiti born of free parents entitled to privileges of French citizens. White governor delayed to make this decree effective.

Gustavus Vassa presented a petition for the suppression of the slave trade to the Queen and the British Parliament.

(1790)

A "Negro's Prayer" by a "slave in the lower part of Virginia"
possibly written by a slave and appended by A. Mott to his
abridged edition of The Life and adventures of Olaudah Equiano,
or Gustavus Vassa, the African. Written by himself (New York:
S. Wood & Sons, 1829).

Benjamin Franklin, An Essay on the African Slave Trade
(Philadelphia: Daniel Humphreys, printer). Signed Historicus
but attributed to Franklin.

1791

The black slaves of Haiti, of whom there were 452,000 arose
in revolt to help the free blacks.

A black insurrection in Dominica, under Farcel, greatly dis-
turbed England in 1791 and 1794 and delayed slave trade abolition; in 1844 and 1847 further uprisings took place and these
continued from 1853-1893.

A charter granted to the Sierra Leone Company, founded by
Granville Sharp and others, for trade and aid to the colonists.

France abolished slavery; it was later reintroduced and
finally abolished in 1848.

Free Negroes of Charlestown, South Carolina protested severe
legal disabilities and requested an opportunity to exercise
their duties and responsibilities as free citizens.

Royal decree designated Montevideo, for a term of six years,
as the only port of entry for slaves in southern part of
South America.

Haitian slaves massacred Europeans; suppressed with troops
and help of "mulatos."

National Convention of France gave civil rights to mulattoes
in Haiti.

Founding of Freetown, Sierra Leone.

At the close of this year Jamaica had 767 sugar plantations with 140,000 blacks; 607 coffee plantations with 21,000 blacks; 1,047 grazing and breeding farms with 31,000 blacks; and a number of small settlements for cotton, ginger, and pimento employing 58,000 blacks (Du Bois 1939, p. 153).

Abbé Gregoire, protagonist of the blacks, wrote his famous letter to the citizens of color in the French West Indies: "You were men, you are now citizens" (Du Bois 1939, p. 161).

Toussaint L'Ouverture planned and led revolt in San Domingo.

A strong and definite pronouncement, 15 May, gave French citizenship and the right to vote and sit in colonial assemblies to free blacks in Haiti. On 24 September, just before it went out of existence, the Constituent Assembly virtually repealed the decree, which left the fate of free blacks and those of mixed ancestry in the hands of the Colonial Assembly.

Benjamin Banneker, astronomer, mechanician, surveyor, botanist, zoologist, philosopher, wit, letter writer, versifier, and almanac maker, was known as a learned man. He published almanacs that were printed in New Jersey, Pennsylvania, Maryland, Delaware, and Virginia. In 1791 he sent Thomas Jefferson, the Secretary of State, a manuscript copy of his first almanac together with a letter concerning the emancipation of the Negro. He stated that he hoped Jefferson would "embrace every opportunity to eradicate that train of absurd and false ideas and opinions which so generally prevails with respect to us; and that your sentiments are concurrent with mine. . . ." Banneker was the principal assistant to Andrew Elliot, geographer general of the United States, in the official survey of the site chosen for the new nation's capital by Washington.

1792

Denmark abolished slavery and the slave trade in her dominions after 1802.

Fifteen vessels sailed with about 1200 Negroes from Nova Scotia. An American Negro, Thomas Peters, who had served as sergeant under Sir Henry Clinton in the British army in

(1792)

America, went to England seeking an allotment of land for his fellows. The Sierra Leone Company welcomed him and offered free passage and land in Sierra Leone to the Negroes of Nova Scotia.

Importation of slaves into South Carolina prohibited until 1795.

Decree of French Commission offered freedom to all slaves in Haiti who would join their forces.

A company of freed slaves brought from Nova Scotia by Lieutenant John Clarkson arrived in Sierra Leone, founded Freetown, and later came under the protection of the Sierra Leone Company.

Virginia Revision of Acts: "An Act to reduce into one, the several acts concerning slaves, free negroes and mulattoes."

Decree of 4 April by the Legislative Assembly of France dealing with Haiti. "The persons of color, mulattoes and Negroes, free, shall be admitted, as the white colonists, to vote in all electoral assemblies, and shall be eligible to all positions when they have also the requisite qualifications" (Du Bois 1939, p. 166).

Trial of Captain John Kimber, for the murder of a Negro girl, on board the ship Recovery; by suspending her by the legs and arms, and flogging her in a most cruel and barbarous manner. Taken in shorthand, by a student of the Middle Temple (London: H. D. Symonds).

No Rum!-No Sugar! or, The Voice of Blood: being half an hour's conversation between a Negro and an English gentlemen, shewing the horrible nature of the slave trade and pointing out an easy and effectual method of terminating it by an act of the people , . . . (London: L. Wayland).

1793

Freedom of slaves in northern provinces of Haiti proclaimed.

United States Fugitive Slave Act: Permitted masters to have runaway slaves returned from another state; made it a crime to harbor a fugitive slave or prevent his arrest.

Provision made in upper Canada for gradual emancipation of
African slaves in the Province.

Importation of free Negroes into Georgia prohibited.

Invention of the cotton gin by Eli Whitney made cotton the
leading industry of the South; cotton gin patented in 1794.

The emancipation of slaves in San Domingo was announced and
confirmed; nevertheless in 1801, Napoleon, by decree, reestablished slavery.

"A Plan for a Peace Office," placed prominently in the 1793
Almanac, has been attributed to Benjamin Banneker. It proposed the establishment of a Department of Peace in the
national administration to offset the existing Department of
War.

1793-1794

Free Negroes of South Carolina protested against poll tax.

Decree suppressed slavery in Senegal.

Importation of slaves in North Carolina prohibited.

Carrying on of the slave trade from the United States to any
foreign place prohibited.

Toussaint L'Ouverture raised the flag of the Republic of
Haiti--the first independent government of blacks outside of
Africa.

Dominican and Cuban slave revolts.

Slave importation into Kentucky, except for personal use of
importer, prohibited.

In Albany, New York, three slaves, two of whom were women,
were executed for antislavery activities.

1794

A Narrative of the Proceedings of the Black People during the
Late Awful Calamity in Philadelphia; and a Refutation of Some

(1794)

Censures Thrown upon them in Some Late Publications (Philadelphia: Richard Allen and Absalom Jones). The calamity was
yellow fever.

As a result of the fear caused by the Haitian Revolution, the
first national act against the slave trade became law 22 March.
A Quaker petition for a law against the transport traffic in
slaves had been received in Congress.

1795

Toussaint L'Ouverture won his first battle in Haiti.

The Free African Society of Newport, Rhode Island sent out a
party of blacks to West Coast of Africa to explore the possibilities of establishing a black colony.

Conspiracy of French and blacks in Buenos Aires to free all
the slaves and Indians and distribute the land. They abandoned their work and went on strike.

North Carolina prohibited the importation of West Indian
slaves.

Great Britain took possession of the Cape of Good Hope.

There were in the Cape of Good Hope 16,000 Europeans, 17,000
slaves, and an unknown number of Hottentots and Bushmen.

Jamaica maroons rebelled and tried to incite a general slave
insurrection. They gave the British a severe drubbing. Bloodhounds were used by the British against the maroons. The
maroons offered to surrender on the express condition that
none of their number would be deported from the island, as
the legislature wished. General Walpole hesitated, but could
obtain peace on no other terms so he agreed. The maroons
surrendered their arms and the whites immediately seized 600
of the ringleaders and transported them to Nova Scotia. The
legislature then voted a sword worth $2,500 to General
Walpole, which he indignantly refused to accept. Eventually
many of these exiled maroons found their way to Sierra Leone,
West Africa.

At the beginning of the Napoleonic Wars, nine British war-
ships with troops landed in South Africa and after some

fighting, took possession. By this time the Hottentots were regarded as free men. Their tribal system had been broken up and most of them had been deprived of their lands.

1796

Importation of slaves into Maryland prohibited.

Mungo Park, sailing under patronage of English African Society, discovered the river Niger at Segu.

Importation of slaves into South Carolina prohibited until 1799.

St. Lucia slave revolt against the British; the blacks were induced to lay down their arms on condition that they remain free.

Boston African Society established; the purpose of the society was to care for sick and impoverished members--particularly women and children.

1797

Paul Cuffe tried to establish a school in Massachusetts but was initially unsuccessful. He finally built a school house at his own expense on his own grounds and allowed anyone who desired to attend--thus establishing a public school.

North Carolina Slave Petition. Congress refused to accept the first recorded petition to Congress by American blacks. The petition was from four illegally manumitted North Carolina blacks, asking for relief as a people, who had fled North to avoid reenslavement.

The Constitution of the Friendly Society of St. Thomas Protestant Episcopal Church in Philadelphia made provisions for loans to its members, when funds were available, to purchase lands.

An address by Abraham Johnstone was handed out on the morning of his execution and later published in Philadelphia; contained protests against slavery and injustice against blacks.

Baltimore slaves imported between 1792-1797 declared to be dangerous to the peace and welfare of the city.

(1797)

Last slave publicly sold at Montreal.

African Petition to Congress through Representative from
Pennsylvania protested a North Carolina law requesting blacks
who were freed by Quaker masters to be returned to North
Carolina and to slavery.

1797-1854

Juan Francisco Manzano was the son of the mestizo slave
Toribio Castro and the favorite slave of Marquesa Justiz de
Santa Ana, Maria del Pilar Manzano. At the death of Donna
Beatriz, the Marquesa de Santa Ana, the mother and son became
the property of the Marquesa de Prado Amemo. Juan Francisco
was twelve years of age. Until he was twenty-one he was
severely mistreated by the Marquesa de Prado Amemo. In 1818
Nicolas de Cardenas y Manzano brought him to Havana where he
began educating himself by using the books in the library of
his protector. His first poems, Poesias Liricas [Lyric poems]
were published with special permission because slaves were not
permitted to publish books. In 1835 he married the mestizo
pianist, Delia, who was the inspiration for the poem La Musica
published in 1837. The literary group before whom he read
"Mis Treinta Años" in 1836 were so touched they collected 850
pesos which the Marquesa de Prado demanded.

1797-1883

Sojourner Truth: black abolitionist and suffragette; one of
the most efficient operators of the "underground railroad."

1798

Osifekunde of Ijebu born. Enslaved and shipped from the coast
of Warri in 1820, he spent almost twenty years in Brazil. He
then came to France with his master and subsequently lived in
Paris, employed as a servant. In Paris he met Marie Armand
Pascal d'Avezac-Macaya, Vice President of the Societe Ethno-
logique of Paris and member of numerous geographical societies
and associations with interests in Africa and the Orient.
D'Avezac realized that Joaquin, as he was called in France,
came from a kingdom which had been named on maps of the seventeenth and eighteenth centuries but which Europeans had less
knowledge than of almost any other part of this coast.
D'Avezac interrogated Osifekunde for weeks on his homeland and

its language. He also arranged for Osifekunde's return to
Africa but Osifekunde preferred servitude under his former
master in Brazil where he could be with his son. He slipped
away secretly from Le Havre and disappeared from history.

A Narrative of the Life and Adventures of Venture, a Native
of Africa, but Resident About Sixty Years in the United States
of America, by Venture; reprinted in 1835 and 1896 (Porter
1971, pp. 516, 517, 538ff.).

On 1 October "Toussaint entered Mole St. Nicholas as conqueror.
The white troops saluted him. He was dined in the public
square on a silver service which was afterwards presented to
him in the name of the King of England. A treaty was signed
by which the English gave up the island, recognized Haiti as
independent, and entered into a commercial agreement. They
then tried secretly to induce Toussaint to declare himself
king, but he refused" (Du Bois 1939, p. 170).

Rebellion of blacks in Bahia.

Sayyid Said of Oman signed treaty of trade and friendship with
the British East India Company by which he made them his ally.

Slave trade in New Jersey prohibited.

Importation of slaves into Mississippi prohibited.

Importation of slaves from Africa or any foreign place into
Georgia prohibited.

Prince Hall school for blacks established in Massachusetts;
was paid for by blacks.

1799

Absalom Jones led Seventy-Three Others to address a petition
to the legislature of Pennsylvania praying for the immediate
abolition of slavery. They also petitioned Congress to repeal the fugitive slave law and emancipate all Negroes. This
latter petition created an uproar in the House of Representatives. It was charged that the petition was instigated by
the Haitian revolutionists and the Negro group was censured
for certain parts of the petition.

(1799–1804)

1799–1804

Gradual emancipation began in New York and New Jersey.

1800

Gabriel Prosser led unsuccessful slave conspiracy in Virginia.

Boston refused to support black schools.

Americans forbidden to trade in slaves from one foreign country to another or to serve on board any vessel so employed.

African slaves and free Negroes prohibited from being brought into or to enter South Carolina.

South Carolina Slave Code provided that all meetings at which slaves were present were to be open—never closed or barred; slaves were prohibited to meet together and assemble for the purpose of mental instruction or religious worship "either before the rising of the sun or after the going down of the same."

Half the population of Brazil was African.

United States population 5,308,000, including 897,000 slaves and 108,000 freemen.

Nat Turner born; Denmark Vesey bought his freedom.

African Petition to Congress against slavery, slave trade, and fugitive slave act of 1793 through representative from Pennsylvania.

Portuguese slave exports from Mozambique were about 10,000 a year.

Arrival in Freetown of 550 maroons from Jamaica. They were former slaves who had been deported to Nova Scotia from their homeland in 1796 and then sent on to Sierra Leone at their own request.

The Cabildo of Montevideo planned to set up a pillory for punishment of those audacious blacks who walked about armed with knives and clubs. The pillory was not erected and blacks

continued to plot insurrections. Slaves were known to kill
their masters and whites lived in fear. On one slave was
found a scrap of paper with the inscription "Long live Freedom" which was sufficient evidence for questioning and tor-
ture (Lanuza 1946, pp. 151ff.).

1800-1801

There were eighty-three bankruptcies in four months in Ham-
burg, where British ships sold their sugar and Parliament had
to loan the West Indian merchants of Liverpool $2½ million
because the profit in American slavery and slave trade was
decreasing (Du Bois 1939, p. 154).

1800-1850

Perhaps 2 million Africans came to Brazil.

1800-1861

Fifteen different schools were conducted in the District of
Columbia for blacks, mainly at the expense of blacks.

1801

Slave trade prohibited in New York.

Santo Domingo abolished slavery; Toussaint L'Ouverture made
Governor-General for life.

Napoleon, by decree, reestablished slavery.

On 14 December, Le Clerc, with a fleet of five squadrons,
left Europe for Haiti. Napoleon, who could not tolerate
"colored" or black men and had relieved General Dumas, son of
a French Marquis, from his command for no other reason but
color, admonished Le Clerc, "Remember that blacks are not
human beings."

1802

Slavery prohibited in Ohio.

Le Clerc, sent by Napoleon to Haiti, was refused entry by
Toussaint L'Ouverture; later L'Ouverture and Dessalines

(1802)

surrendered and eventually a peace treaty was signed by
Le Clerc and L'Ouverture.

L'Ouverture taken to France, imprisoned by Napoleon at Fort
de Joux.

The Romance of Antar, a cycle of poems published in Cairo in
thirty-two volumes, was introduced to European readers. A
Bedoueen romance translated from Arabic by Tarrick Hamilton,
the work is a companion piece to the Arabian Nights and a
standard work of Arabia. It is founded on the career of the
son of Sheik Shedad and a black woman. One of Antar's poems
was hung in the temple at Mecca and was considered to be among
the greatest poems written.

1803

Death of Toussaint L'Ouverture in prison.

Discovery of plan of group of slaves in Montevideo to escape
and fortify themselves in the forest.

Introduction of slaves into states which had forbidden slave
trade prohibited.

South Carolina legalized slave trade.

Margaret Bradley, a black woman of York, Pennsylvania, was
convicted of attempting to poison two whites; the black inhabitants of the area revolted en masse. They made several
attempts to destroy the town by fire and succeeded, within a
period of three weeks, in burning eleven buildings. A reward
of $300 was offered for the capture of the insurrectionists.

Rochambeau surrendered and white authority died in San
Domingo. The effect was far reaching. Napoleon gave up his
dream of American empire and sold Louisiana for very little.
"Praise, if you will, the work of a Robert Livingstone or a
Jefferson, but today let us not forget our debt to Toussaint
L'Ouverture, who was indirectly the means of America's expan-
sion by the Louisiana Purchase of 1803" (DeWitt Talmadge in
Christian Herald, 28 November 1906).

Dessalines and his troops captured Port-au-Prince; French
agreed to leave; Dessalines proclaimed independence of Haiti.

(1804)

1803-1807

First Ashanti war under King Osai Tutu Kwamina began with the
theft of gold and valuables from a grave--a blasphemy of death
and eternal life. The King of Ashanti demanded redress, but
his messengers to the accused Fanti were killed. This led
to a war between the Ashanti and the Fanti in which the English
governor promised to defend some of the allies of the Fanti.

1803-1874

There were six wars with the English and the Ashanti. Ostensibly they were aimed at the custom of human sacrifice in
Ashanti and to put down aggression upon the Fanti who owed
allegiance to Ashanti but became allied with the English. In
reality these wars all aimed at trade monopoly and economic
empire for the English (Du Bois 1939, pp. 58, 59).

1804

Thomas Branagan, <u>A Preliminary Essay, on the Oppression of
the Exiled Sons of Africa</u>. Branagan, a Dublin man who became
a slave trader during the eighteenth century, wrote this
scathing denunciation of the African trade (Philadelphia:
the author).

Sayyid Said became ruler of Oman and embarked on a new policy
of expansion along East African Coast. He made his main base
on Zanzibar where clove planting was introduced in 1818.

Supremacy of Nyamwezi as inland traders in central Tanzania.

Gradual expansion of ivory trade with inland countries of
Africa; little by little this gave way to trading in slaves
and firearms as well.

Gradual emancipation began in New Jersey.

Dessalines proclaimed governor of Haiti for life; he was
crowned Emperor Jacques I. He ordered the massacre of all
white persons.

The Underground Railroad may have begun when General Thomas
Boude, a Revolutionary War officer, purchased a slave, Stephen
Smith, and took him to Columbia, Pennsylvania. Smith's mother

(1804)

escaped and followed her son. The Boudes took her in and refused to return her to her mistress.

In Virginia the Act of 1804 forbade all evening meetings of slaves. This was modified in 1805 in order to permit a slave, in company with a white person, to listen to a white minister in the evening (Du Bois 1903, p. 22).

Slaves were arrested and imprisoned in Georgia, South Carolina, and Virginia for attempted arson and revolt. About twenty slaves were executed for poisoning whites.

1805

Black laws of Ohio passed. Africans prohibited from giving evidence in any court; restricted rights and movement of blacks.

Maryland law forbade free blacks to sell corn, wheat, or tobacco without a license.

Master of Arts conferred by Middlebury College on Lemuel B. Haynes.

Slave trade to Orleans Territory permitted.

The British sent sixty-one ships and seized the Cape. At that time there were 25,000 Boers, 25,000 "Hottentots," 25,000 slaves. British settlers began to come. The Xosas were now across the Fish River and claimed land. The English began to push them back and to build block houses.

1806

Assassination of Dessalines; Christophe chosen chief executive in Haiti.

Virginia required all Africans who might be manumitted in the future to leave the state unless permission to the contrary was granted by the legislature.

Free blacks built the African Meeting House in Boston.

Boston granted $200 a year to black school; black children paid 12½ cents a week tuition.

Prince Saunders, teacher of a free colored school in Col-
chester, Connecticut; Saunders was born and reared in Vermont.
He later migrated to Haiti and was minister of education under
the government of Henri Christophe.

1807

Thomas Clarkson, Three Letters to the Planters and Slave
Merchants; principally on the subject of compensation (London).

Blacks of District of Columbia, led by three free blacks--
George Bell, Nicholas Franklin, and Moses Liverpool--founded
first black school. The school was supported by blacks.

African Institution founded in London for the abolition of
the slave trade.

General Alexander Pétion defeated Christophe, and Haiti was
divided: Christophe ruled north and Pétion was President at
Port-au-Prince.

An Act of Parliament abolished the slave trade in the British
dominions.

Sierra Leone became a British colony.

Britain ended her own slave trade and began trying to per-
suade other European powers to end theirs. This did not occur
for more than seventy years.

1808

Sierra Leone and Gambia became Crown colonies.

Passed in 1807, the Congressional Act abolishing the slave
trade did not become effective until January 1808.

Slave trade was abolished in state of New York. Peter
Williams, Jr., who later became Rector of St. Philip's Church
in New York City, organized a group to improve the conditions
of the Negro. They petitioned the legislature for a Charter
of Incorporation.

The Thompson-Clarkson Collection was intended to represent the
complete source materials of Thomas Clarkson's History of the

(1808)

Rise, Progress and Accomplishment of the Abolition of the
African Slave-Trade. It was put together by Thomas Thompson
(1776-1861), a pharmaceutical and manufacturing chemist of
Liverpool, who was a lifelong member of the Society of Friends.
The Collection was in four volumes. It was handed down
through Thompson's family until 1936 when three volumes were
given the Library of the Society of Friends. Volume 4 has not
been traced. Much of the autograph material is in the form of
letters to James Phillips (1743-1799) who was in effect the
official printer for British Quakers.

An Oration on The Abolition of the Slave Trade; delivered in
The African Church in the City of New York 1 January 1808 by
Peter Williams, Jun., a Descendant of Africa (New York).

Thanksgiving Sermon, preached 1 January 1808 in St. Thomas's,
or the African Episcopal Church, Philadelphia: on account of
The Abolition of the Slave Trade, on that Day, By the Congress
of the United States, by Absalom Jones, Rector of the Said
Church; printed for use by the congregation (Philadelphia:
Fry and Kramer).

1809

The Negro Baptist Church had its definite beginnings in the
North with the organization of congregations in Boston, Philadelphia, and New York.

An Oration Commemorative of the Abolition of The Slave Trade
in the United States delivered before the Wilberforce Philan-
thropic Association, in the City of New York, on the Second of
January, 1809, by Joseph Sidney (New York: J. Seymour).
Oration on the Abolition of the Slave Trade delivered in The
African Church in the City of New York, 2 January 1809, by
Henry Sipkins (New York: John C. Totten).

Antislavery address in New York by William Hamilton, Negro
pioneer abolitionist and organizer of subsequent nationwide
Negro conventions.

Square in Buenos Aires named Plaza Fidelidad in commemoration
of the loyalty of blacks, pardos, and Indians who were volunteers against the British in 1806.

1809-1844

Placido (Gabriel de la Concepcion Valdes), Cuban poet, chiefly
remembered for his protest in verse against Spanish oppression,
was born in Mantanzas, Cuba. Son of a black barber and a
Spanish dancer, Placido was executed without any proof what-
ever that he was guilty on order of the Spanish Governor
O'Donnell in 1844 for participation in a "racial conspiracy"
of blacks and mestizos, La Escaler. He is considered one of
Cuba's greatest poets.

1810

Abstract of the Acts of Parliament for abolishing the slave
trade.

"The Hottentot Venus was brought from South Africa with
promises that she would make a fortune by putting her body,
with its prodigious buttocks, on display to the public. She
was monstrously exploited, despite the efforts of abolitionists to have her released on a writ of habeas corpus in 1810
(three years after the parliamentary bill which banned the
slave-trade); she herself declared that 'she did not wish to
go home as she liked this country, and was very kindly
treated by her Keeper, who gave her money, and took her out
riding in a coach on Sunday, which she liked very much.' But
she died an alcoholic in 1815 in Paris, where her skeleton
and a plaster cast of her body remain in the Musee de l'Homme"
(Edwards 1981, p. 42).

Although the Congress of the United States passed a law in
1807 forbidding Americans to participate in the slave trade,
they were reported by eye witnesses as carrying slaves to the
Rio de la Plata on the eve of the revolution of 1810 (Diggs
1951, pp. 286ff.).

1810-1830

Four Select Committee Reports published in England examining
the relations between white settlers, liberated Africans, and
slaves in Sierra Leone and Fernando Po (Slave Trade 1969).

1811

Delaware passed a law stating that slaves involved in

(1811)

conspiracy or poisoning would be punished by death. Poisoning
was considered a form of revolt--certainly a form of protest.

In North Carolina there was a confrontation between a maroon
community and a slave-catching posse. Local newspapers reported that the maroons refused to surrender. Two black
males were killed, one wounded, and two black women were captured.

Paul Cuffe, free Negro shipowner and navigator, firmly believed that American Negroes should return to Africa as
colonists and traders. He explored Sierra Leone for purposes
of colonization and trade and established thirty-eight blacks
in West Africa at his own expense. While in Sierra Leone,
Cuffe wrote A Brief Account of the Settlement and Present
Situation of the Colony of Sierra Leone (New York: Samuel
Wood, 1812). Cuffe died in 1817 only months after the American Colonization Society was formed.

Christophe crowned King Henry I of Haiti.

Children of slaves in Chile born free.

Uprising in St. Charles and St. John the Baptist parishes
near New Orleans. Some sixty-six slaves were killed or executed; sixteen were captured and seventeen reported missing.
Those tried in the city were decapitated and their heads
strung at intervals from New Orleans to Major Andry's plantation.

Practical Rules for the Management: And Medical Treatment of
Negro Slaves, in the Sugar Colonies, by a Professional Planter
(Dr. Robert Collins) (2d ed., Boston: Eastburn's Press, 1853
with different title: Essay on the Treatment and Management
of Slaves).

"On the first of the present month of August, 1811, a vessel
arrived at Liverpool, with a cargo from Sierra Leone, the
owner, master, mate, and whole crew of which are free Negroes.
The master, who is also owner, is the son of an American
slave, and is said to be very well skilled both in trade and
navigation, as well as to be of a very pious and moral character. It must have been a strange and animating spectacle to
see this free and enlightened African entering as an independent trader, with his black crew, into that port which was so

lately the <u>nidus</u> of the Slave Trade" (Loggins 1931, p. 48).

A proclamation was issued in Brazil stating that all soldiers for the militia would be drawn from whites whose great-grand-parents were whites and whose parents were born free.

1811-1877

There were six Kafir-English wars. The one in 1818 grew out of the interference of the English with the Kafir family system. A war between 1834 and 1835 was followed by the annexation of all the country as far as the Kei River. Intratribal fighting among the Xosa concerning the paramount chieftainship. The British began to offer land for new settlers and Parliament voted money. Some 5,000 British came between 1820 and 1821.

1812

Boston helped pay the expenses of a black school.

Louisiana authorized the enrollment of regiments of free persons of color.

Georgia declared inciting, or attempting to incite, rebellion, a capital crime.

John Jasper, son of Philip and Tina Jasper, was born 4 July.

<u>Early Recollections and Life of Dr. James Still</u> (Philadelphia: Lippincott); Still was a black physician. This self-taught Maryland country doctor began making and selling medicines in 1843. He practiced thirty years spurred on by the belief that all diseases were curable.

General insurrection of slaves in Venezuela. Slave rebellions in Havana, Trinidad, Byan, Puerto Principe, Holguin.

The legislature of the Illinois Territory forbade the immigration of free blacks and required registration of free blacks in the territory.

Martin Robison Delany born free in Charlestown, Virginia. Was interested in inventing and in a colonization scheme for blacks in Central America. He lived for a time in a black

(1813)

colony in Canada. He led a party of black explorers, who
were interested in finding a place for a black colony in the
Niger Valley region of Africa. He rose to the rank of major
in the United States Army during the years immediately following the Civil War. He died in 1881.

1813

George Lawrence, Oration on the Abolition of the Slave Trade,
delivered on the First Day of January 1813 in the African
Methodist Church (New York: Hardcastle and Van Pelt).

Letters from a Man of Color, attributed to James Forten, was
published anonymously in Philadelphia. The author argued
against a bill introduced into the Legislature of Pennsylvania
in 1813 prohibiting further immigration of free persons of
color. After this protest the bill was never considered again.
Forten also protested against the proposed registration of
Negroes.

Sweden abolished the slave trade.

Lott Carey organized the African Mission Society.

1814

Congress of Vienna declared slave trade contrary to human
principles.

Holland abolished the slave trade.

Slave trade abolished by France.

Cape Colony ceded by Holland to Great Britain.

James Forten (educated by Benezet), Absalom Jones, Richard
Allen, and others were asked, in the midst of the alarm felt
at the approach of the British, to raise "colored troops." A
meeting was called and 2,500 volunteers were secured, or three-
fourths of the adult male population of Philadelphia; they
marched to Gray's Ferry and threw up fortifications. A
battalion for service in the field was formed but the war
closed before they reached the front.

Narrative of the Most Remarkable Particulars in the Life of
James Albert Ukawsaw Gronniosaw, an African Prince (Leeds,
England). A former slave in New York, Gronniosaw lived in
England in 1814 under the guardianship of the Countess
Huntingdon's Calvinistic Methodist Circle.

Oration of the Abolition of the Slave Trade, by Russell
Parrott, delivered on the first of January at the African
Church of St. Thomas (Philadelphia: Thomas Stiles).

The Treaty of Ghent ending the War of 1812 included a provision for the restoration of slaves who had taken sanctuary
with the British. In 1826 the United States minister to the
Court of St. James (Albert Gallatin of Pennsylvania) obtained
$1,204,960 from the British for slaves not returned in spite
of the treaty.

1815

Joseph Wright, who belonged to the Egba subgroup of the
Yoruba, was born. He was enslaved and shipped from Lagos in
1826 or 1827. "The Life of Joseph Wright: A Native of Ackoo,"
the original title of a manuscript, was found in a small bound
notebook in a box labeled "Sierra Leone, 1835-1840," in the
Archives of the Methodist Missionary Society, London. Apparently in the author's hand, with grammar and punctuation un-
corrected, it is dated June, 1839. A printed version was included in John Beecham, Ashantee and the Gold Coast (London:
1841), pp. 349-58.

An Oration on the Abolition of the Slave Trade delivered in
The Episcopal Asbury African Church, New York, 2 January 1815
by William Hamilton, a descendant of Africa (New York: C. W.
Bruce).

The Narrative of Bethany Veney, A Slave Woman, by Bethany
Veney, born 1815 (Worcester, Mass.: George Ellis, 1889).

Fifty Years of Slavery in the United States of America, by
Harry Smith, born 1815 (1891). Relates Smith's life as a
slave (Grand Rapids, Michigan: West Michigan Printing Co.).

Decree by Napoleaon Bonaparte abolished slavery in French
territory; confirmed by Louis XVIII, 8 January 1817 and by
the law of 15 April 1818.

(1815)

Five hundred thousand square miles of Africa were under
European claims and partial control; a million square miles
in 1880.

One thousand blacks manned a former British port in Georgia
and resisted the power of the United States.

John Baptist Philip, a native of Trinidad, awarded Doctor of
Medicine from Edinburgh University (Edwards 1981, p. 41).

1815-1830

Spain and Portugal gradually abolished the slave trade; illicit slave trade continued.

1816

Under the leadership of Washington Franklin much property in
Barbados was destroyed during a slave insurrection.

American philanthropists decided that whether slavery persisted
or died out, the main problem was getting rid of the useless,
pernicious, if not dangerous free Negroes, of which there
were then 200,000 in the United States. Accordingly the
American Colonization Society was proposed and founded 1 January 1817 with Bushrod Washington as president.

South Carolina forbade the importation of slaves from any
part of the United States.

William Wells Brown, author, lecturer, historian, traveler,
medical doctor was born of slave parents.

George Bourne, The Book and Slavery Irreconcilable. One of
the most famous of all abolitionist works. Written by a
Presbyterian minister in Virginia, the volume cost him his
job in the South and led to his being charged with heresy.
Bourne became a founder of the American Anti-Slavery Society;
an outspoken and militant abolitionist, and perhaps the first
white American to demand immediate emancipation (Philadelphia:
J. M. Sanderson & Co., 1816).

Prohibition of exportation of slaves from Argentina.

In Great Britain, a slave registry was instituted for the

purpose of checking the importation of new slaves or the enslavement of free blacks.

It was discovered that a community of 300 escaped slaves--
men, women, and children--had occupied a fort in Florida.
After the United States Army was dispatched with instructions
to destroy the community, a ten day seige terminated with all
but forty of the 300 dead.

Prince Saunders published his Haytian Papers (London), translated excerpts from the Code Henri and other Haytian Laws;
the American edition was published in Boston in 1818.

African Methodist Episcopal Church established as an independent national organization; Richard Allen was its first bishop.

Various Methodist African Societies met in Philadelphia.
These Methodist Societies of Free Africans felt the need to
consolidate themselves into a strong organization and to extend the work of the A.M.E. Church.

Henry Clay, at the first meeting of the American Colonization
Society, founded in Washington, praised the society's aim to
rid the United States of a useless and pernicious, if not
dangerous, portion of its population, the free blacks.

Remarks on the Insurrection in Barbadoes, and the bill for the
registration of slaves (London: Ellerton and Henderson).

1817

Founding of American Colonization Society to encourage the
emancipation of slaves by providing a place outside the United
States to which they might emigrate.

Two Seminole wars (the other in 1835) were raids to make
Indians give up black slaves and their children by Indian
women (Du Bois 1939, p. 202).

Spain abolished the slave trade north of the equator for a
compensation from England of 400,000 pounds sterling.

New York law prohibiting slavery took effect.

(1817)

Auguste Lacaussade, one of France's most gifted black poets,
was born in Ile de la Reunion. Lacaussade repeatedly protested
against slavery (Du Bois 1939, p. 202).

The first response to the establishment of the American Colonization Society was articulated at a public meeting of free
people of color in Richmond. They interpreted the American
Colonization Society as a conspiracy to rid America of free
blacks whose presence, in the eyes of the slaveholders, presented a threat to slavery. James Forten and Russell Parrott
called a general meeting in Philadelphia at which they charged
that the American Colonization Society had issued false and
damaging propaganda against the free black population in order
to justify sending them all to Africa. James Forten's meeting
declared blacks would never leave the United States.

1817–1895

Frederick Douglass, former slave and abolitionist wrote of his
years as a slave in Maryland; his escape to Massachusetts in
1838; his travels and lectures in England; his editorship and
publication of the North Star in Rochester, New York; his
civil rights activities after the Civil War; his work for the
Freedman's bank; his participation on the Commission to Santo
Domingo; his duties for the Federal Government in Washington.
The 1892 edition reported his European and Middle Eastern
journeys of 1886–1887 and his service as Minister to Haiti.

1818

Prince Saunders, A Memoir presented to The American Convention
for Promoting the Abolition of Slavery and Improving the Condition of the African Race 11 December 1818 (Philadelphia:
Dennis Heartt).

Georgia required incoming free Negroes to register and give
full details concerning themselves and reasons for entering
the state; they were neither to own slaves nor real estate;
manumission forbidden.

Shaka of the Zulu defeated the Ndwandwe. Beginning of the
wars of wandering, named because of the migrations which they
set in motion.

Pennsylvania Augustine Society for the education of people of
color established by prominent Philadelphia free Negroes.

1819

France abolished the slave trade.

President authorized to return to Africa any Africans illegally imported and seized within the United States and to
grant a premium of $50 to informers.

Virginia forbade "all meetings or assemblages of slaves or
free Negroes or mulattoes, mixing and associating with such
slaves, . . . at any school or schools for teaching them
reading and writing, either in the day or night." Nevertheless free Negroes kept school for themselves until the Nat
Turner insurrection in 1831.

Act of 1819 provided for an African depot for recaptured
slaves taken in the contraband slave trade. An agent of the
American Colonization Society was sent to Africa to form a
settlement. This settlement eventually became Liberia.

1819-1829

Julian Froumontaine, from San Domingo, openly conducted a free
Negro school in Savannah (and secretly for some time after)
(Du Bois 1921, p. 21).

1820

Blacks in Cincinnati opened school of their own.

Missouri Compromise: slavery prohibited west of the Mississippi
(Du Bois 1921, p. 20).

The Northward stream of blacks increased, occasioning bitterness on the part of the South and leading to the Fugitive
Slave Act of 1820 and the counter acts of Pennsylvania in
1826 and 1827. These laws were especially directed against
kidnapping, and were designed to protect free blacks. The
law of 1826 was declared unconstitutional in 1842 by the
United States Supreme Court.

Slavery forced north of Mason-Dixon Line.

Christophe of Haiti committed suicide.

(1820)

United States statute made slave trade piracy.

Establishment of Liberia Colony for American Africans.

The brig Elizabeth (Mayflower of Liberia) with the first
American African colonists (86) from American left New York.
Arriving at Sierra Leone, they proceeded to Sherbro Islands
where promises to sell land had been reconsidered and broken.
The colonists returned to Sierra Leone.

Spain abolished the slave trade south of the equator.

The New York African Society for Mutual Relief was formed.
This Society served as a model for the Union Society, The
Clarkson Association, The Wilberforce Benevolent Society, and
the Woolman Society of Brooklyn.

Mohammed Ali (Ottoman viceroy of Egypt) sent his son with
Turks and Arabs to conquer Nubia. He defeated the Mameluk
Beys at Dongola and then marched through Ethiopia, but was
killed in 1822 just after he had founded Khartoum.

Daniel Coker, Journal of Daniel Coker, a Descendant of Africa,
from the Time of Leaving New York in the Ship Elizabeth, Capt.
Sebor, for . . . Africa, in Company with Three Agents and
about Ninety Persons of Color. . . . (Baltimore).

Britain now the greatest naval power. Increasing British
interest in East African Coast partly stimulated by drive to
end the slave trade.

Expansion of Bemba power under Chitimukulu and other chieftainships. They formed a confederacy but did not unite into
a single government under one ruler.

A Review of the Colonial Slave Registration Acts: In a Report of a Committee on the Board of Directors of the African
Institution, London, made on the 22 February. Registration of
slaves would, it was claimed, prevent illegal importation.

The History of Prince Lee Boo: To Which is Added, the Life of
Paul Cuffee, a Man of Colour; also, Some Account of John
Sackhouse, the Esquimaux (Dublin: C. Crookes, printer).

1820-1830

Slave insurrections in Martinique, Puerto Rico, Cuba, Antigua, Tortola, Demerara, Jamaica.

In Ohio white Mechanics' Societies combined against blacks. One master mechanic, President of the Mechanical Association of Cincinnati, was publicly tried by the Society for assisting a young black to learn a trade. One black cabinet maker who had purchased his freedom in Kentucky came to Cincinnati and for a long time, he could get no work; one Englishman employed him but the white workmen struck. He was compelled to become a laborer until by saving he could take small contracts and hire black mechanics to help him. In Philadelphia, Washington, D.C., New York, and other cities, riots and disorder on the part of white mechanics, aimed against blacks, occurred several times (Du Bois 1902, pp. 15, 16).

1820-1833

A total of about 1500 blacks were sent to Africa by the American Colonization Society. Colonization became more popular in 1832 when conditions of suppression were intensified after the Nat Turner Insurrection.

1821

The Anti-Slavery Society, with Wilberforce as president, was organized in Great Britain.

The African Company terminated by Act of Parliament and all property transferred to the Crown.

Peru declared that all children born of slaves after 28 July were free.

A group of free blacks established a theater known as the African Grove in New York's Greenwich Village, where they performed plays by Shakespeare.

South Carolina repealed its law of 1740 which provided a fine of £700 for willful murder of a slave, £350 for murder in sudden heat and passion, and £100 for cutting out the tongue, putting out the eye, castrating, or scalding of a slave.

(1821)

    Maine law declared void marriages between a white and a black, an Indian, or a black with white ancestry.

1821-1913

    Harriet Tubman was born a slave on the eastern shore of Maryland. In 1849 she became a fugitive slave and one of the most effective leaders of the Underground Railroad. She worked with John Brown and other abolitionists; was a spy, cook, guide, and nurse during the Civil War.

1822

    Liberia founded by Negro slaves liberated by philanthropic societies.

    Negro Plot. An account of the late intended insurrection among a portion of the blacks of the city. . . . Prepared by J. Hamilton at the request of the City Council of Charleston (Charleston: A. B. Miller, printer).

    Denmark Vesey was born in Santo Domingo. "With some money which he won in a lottery in 1800 he purchased himself from his owner, Captain Vesey, who had brought him to Charleston. He thereafter successfully established himself as a carpenter, and accumulated property to the amount of $8,000. From Santo Domingo he brought new ideas as to freedom. He easily won the confidence of the slaves and for the next generation endeavored to inculcate in their minds discontent with their lot. Operating here in Charleston where free Negroes were to some extent a privileged class, many of them able to read and write, Vesey and his co-workers stirred up a considerable number. . . . On the second Monday in July, 1822, when most of the master class would be absent for the summer vacation, the attack was to be made. Lists of thousands of recruits were drawn up, money raised to purchase arms, and a blacksmith was engaged to make pikes and bayonets for the incipient attack. The conspirators hoped, however, to obtain a larger supply by raiding the arsenal in the city. Here again the history of Negro insurrections repeated itself. A slave hearing about it, told his master. Officials, at first, could hardly believe all that which was divulged. Some of those implicated were exonerated when first examined. By the day set for the rising, however, the plans had all been disclosed. The city then ran wild with excitement. And well might this be so, for by this

time the authorities had learned that some of the most respectable free Negroes and slaves enjoying the highest confidence of the public were deliberately planning to kill all
of the whites of the city. Denmark Vesey, Peter Poyas, Ned
Bennett, Rolla Bennett, Ballean Bennett, Jesse Blackwood,
Gullah Jack, and others, thirty-five in all, were hanged;
forty-three were banished" (Woodson 1939, pp. 179ff.; Du Bois
1903, p. 22).

The first public school for blacks opened in Philadelphia.

1823

Shadow and Light: An Autobiography, with Reminiscences of the
Last and Present Century (1902) by Mifflin Winstar Gibbs
(1823–1918). Introduction by Booker T. Washington. Gibbs
was a lawyer, judge, U.S. consul to Madagascar, and a civil
rights advocate.

The first of a long series of classified correspondence with
the Foreign Office relating to the slave trade was presented
to the British Parliament.

A proclamation was issued designed to facilitate the admission
of slaves in the British colonies to the Christian Church. It
allowed their marriage by Christian rites, validated the oath
of a Christian slave in a court of law, ensured proper food
and clothing, limited working hours, restricted the severity
and frequency of punishment, and protected the slave from mal-
treatment and the master from unfounded or frivolous complaint.

Abolition of African slavery in Chile.

Rules for the care and education of slaves in Cape Colony.
From 1826–1834 there was much negotiation as to methods of
emancipation. Some of the Dutch farmers threatened rebellion.
It was arranged that the former slaves were to be apprenticed
to their former masters for four years after 1834. A modest
compensation was to be paid.

1823–1864

Antonio Goncalves Dias, born in Maranhao, was a well known
pantheistic poet of Brazil. In his work, the feeling for
nature, the landscape, the rivers, forests, vegetation, and

(1824)

birds attained an extraordinary lyrical intensity. He wrote
of the races that made up Brazilian nationality: the black
slaves and the Indians. He taught Latin and Brazilian history at the Colegio Dom Pedro II.

1824

Great Britain made slave trade piracy.

Abolition of slavery in Central America proclaimed by a Central
American Congress.

An Appeal and a caution to the British Nation: with proposals
for the immediate or gradual emancipation of the slaves. In-
demnity must precede emancipation. By a member of the Dominican legislature (London: J. Richardson).

Elizabeth (Coltman) Heyrick of Leicester, England, Immediate,
not gradual abolition, or, An Inquiry into the shortest,
safest, and most effectual means of getting rid of West Indian
slavery (Philadelphia: J. Radestraw). First printed in
London.

1825

Thomas Fisher, The Negro's Memorial, or, Abolitionist's Cate-
chism, by an abolitionist (London, sold by Hatchard).

Maryland reenacted a law providing for the banishment of free
blacks who could not give security for proper behavior. Any
free black in Maryland or traveling through the state without
a job had to provide security for good behavior or leave the
state within fifteen days. The law carried a punishment of a
$50 fine or being sold into slavery for up to six months.

John Mosely, a wealthy black man, willed $1000 to the American
Colonization Society.

Beginning of the foundation of Basutoland by Mosheshwe.

Venezuelians found engaged in the slave trade to be declared
pirates.

Abolition of slavery in Argentine, Peru, Chile, Bolivia, and
Paraguay.

A Narrative of Some Remarkable Incidents in the Life of Solomon
Bayley, formerly A Slave in the State of Delaware, North America written by himself and published for his Benefit to which
are prefixed a few remarks by Robert Hurnard, second edition
(London: Harvey and Darton).

Alexander Pushkin (1799-1837), accorded first place among
Russia's poets, published his Boris Godunov in 1825 and his
Eugene Onegin in 1832. He was the great-grandson of Hannibal
and his second wife who was a Russian noblewoman.

1825-1826

Correspondence with British Commissioners and Foreign Powers
relating to slave trade presented to British Parliament. The
correspondence consisted of detailed information on various
aspects of the slave trade and British efforts to abolish it
in Sierra Leone, Cuba, Brazil, and Surinam. Topics covered
related to slave vessels captured, legal developments connected with the slave trade, reports from Mixed Commission
Courts, treaty negotiations, contraventions of treaties, and
the extent of the slave trade in particular areas. These
papers reveal the gradual alignment of British policies with
those of other colonial powers as a result of British diplo-
macy and pressure (Slave Trade 10:969).

The United States and Great Britain recognized the independence of Haiti.

c.1825-1897

Peter Randolph, From Slave Cabin to the Pulpit: The Autobiography of Rev. Peter Randolph: The Southern Question
Illustrated and Sketches of Slave Life (Boston: James H.
Earle, 1893). Born into slavery in Virginia, Randolph was
freed in 1847 and moved to Boston. He relates his life as a
slave, his religious life as a Baptist minister in Massachusetts, Connecticut, New York, Rhode Island, and Richmond,
Virginia, and his study of law and responsibilities as a
Justice of the Peace in Boston.

1826

Convention with Great Britian and United States regarding in-
demnity for slaves under Treaty of 1822.

(1826)

John B. Russwurm graduated from Bowdoin College (Brunswick, Maine); Edward Jones graduated from Amherst.

J. Ashmun, History of the American Colony in Liberia, from Dec. 1821 to 1823 (Washington City: Way & Gideon).

Burgher Senate of Cape Colony refused to publish, until threatened, Slave Ordinance of 1826.

Confrontation between maroons and a militia group in South Carolina; a black woman and child were killed.

Insurrection in La Guayra.

Convention with Great Britain and Brazil provided for total abolition of slave trade at end of three years.

Abolition of slave trade in Brazil, north of the equator.

South Carolina prohibited blacks from gathering for religious purposes even with whites present.

1827

First number of Freedom's Journal, a weekly, edited by Samuel E. Cornish and John B. Russwurm. Cornish withdrew from the paper in September 1827. In February 1829 Russwurm gave up the editorship and Cornish took it over independently under the name, Rights For All.

Introduction of slaves in Texas prohibited.

Slavery in New York officially abolished.

Oration delivered in the African Zion Church 4 July, "In Commemoration of the Abolition of Domestic Slavery in this State of New York," by William Hamilton (New York: Gray & Bunce).

Richard Allen, "Letter on Colonization," Freedom's Journal, 2 November. Statement of Allen's opposition to colonization in Africa.

Freedom's Journal published letter of black woman on women's rights, signed Matilda (10 August).

Rena Caillie left Senegal on the west coast of Africa to find
Timbuktu; he reached it in 1828.

The Missionary Pioneer; or, A Brief Memoir of the Life,
Labours, and Death of John Stewart, (Man of Colour,) Founder
under God of the Mission among the Wyandotts at Upper Sandusky,
Ohio, author unknown (New York).

c.1828

From Darkness Cometh the Light; or, Struggles for Freedom
(1891), by Lucy A. Berry Delaney, born 1828 (St. Louis: F. T.
Smith).

1828

The postmaster general of the United States, John McLean,
ruled that blacks might be used to carry mail bags from stage
coaches to post offices, provided that a responsible white
person supervised. Since 1810 blacks had been forbidden by
Congress to be letter carriers.

Slavery was abolished in Mexico and American pressure forced
the reinstitution in Texas, which then belonged to Mexico.

New Haven, Connecticut, had 800 resident blacks and two schools
for them. Boston had three schools for its 2000 blacks.
Portland, Maine, had 900 blacks and one school. Philadelphia
had 20,000 blacks and three schools, and New York, with 15,000
blacks, had two schools. Some of these schools were supported
by bequests. One in New Haven for sixty students was supported
by public school money for six months of the year and by
parents of students for the rest of the year. In Pennsylvania
education of blacks was at public expense under provisions for
the education of poor children.

Alexander Barclay, A Practical View of the Present State of
Slavery in the West Indies: Or, an Examination of Mr.
Stephen's "Slavery in the British West Indies Colonies" (Lon-
don: Smith, Elder & Co.).

Essay, 1828 by Isaiah G. DeGrass aged fifteen years. New York
African Free School, appeared in the Minutes of the Adjourned
Session of the Twentieth Biennial American Convention for
Promoting the Abolition of Slavery and Improving the Conditions

(1828)

of the African Race, Held in Baltimore, November (Philadelphia: Samuel Parker, printer).

Ohio blacks excluded from white schools.

Theodore S. Wright completed a theological course at Princeton
where he was a student between 1825 and 1828.

Essay to the American Convention for Promoting the Abolition
of Slavery and Improving the Condition of the African Race,
by George R. Allen; Poem on Slavery, by George R. Allen; Poem
on Freedom, by Thomas S. Sidney. This essay and poems were
in the minutes of the American Convention for Promoting the
Abolition of Slavery and Improving the Condition of the African
Race, held at Baltimore.

William Whipper led a group of free men of color to organize
the Colored Reading Society of Philadelphia for Mental Improvement. The Reading Society acquired a library under the
care of a librarian who circulated books once a week.

Morris Brown ordained a bishop in Charleston, South Carolina.
He had helped numerous slaves to purchase their freedom. Because of his sympathy for them he was forced to flee Charleston and seek refuge in Philadelphia.

Hottentots, Bushmen, and other colored persons were given
rights to own land; the freeing of slaves was imminent.

1828-1837

Black Mohamedan slaves revolted repeatedly in Brazil.

1829

David Walker's Appeal, in Four Articles; together with a Pre-
amble, to the Coloured Citizens of the World, but in Particular
and very Expressly to Those of the United States of America,
Written in Boston, State of Massachusetts, Sept. 28, 1829,
third and last edition with additional notes, corrections
(Boston: D. Walker, 1830). The appeal was considered radical
and revolutionary, even by liberal abolitionists. The governors of North Carolina and Virginia protested the appeal to

the Mass. Legislature; the governor of Georgia asked the mayor
of Boston to suppress it.

Birth of John Mercer Langston, author of From the Virginia
Plantation to the National Capitol (Hartford, Conn.: American
Publishing Co., 1894). Langston was the first and only Negro
representative in Congress from the Old Dominion.

A group of slaves, being led from Maryland to be sold in the
South, had apparently planned to kill the traders and make
their way to freedom. One of the traders was killed but
eventually a posse captured all the slaves. Of the six
leaders sentenced to death, one was a woman. She was first
permitted to give birth to her child and soon afterwards she
was publicly hanged.

St. Francis Academy for blacks established in Baltimore by the
Roman Catholics. The sisters were black.

Abolition of slavery in Mexico.

Occupation of Island of Fernando Po by British Slave Trade
Commissioners (continued until 1833).

Georgia enacted: "If any slave, Negro or free person of color,
or any white person shall teach any other slave, Negro or free
person of color to read or write, either written or printed
characters, the same free person of color or slave shall be
punished by fine and whipping, or fine or whipping, at the
discretion of the court; and if a white person so offend, he,
she, or they shall be punished with a fine not exceeding $500
and imprisonment in the common jail at the discretion of the
Court." In 1833 this law was put into the penal code, with
additional penalties for using slaves in printing offices to
set type (Du Bois 1901, p. 18).

Ohio decreed that "the attendance of black or mulatto persons
be specifically prohibited, but all taxes assessed upon the
property of colored persons for school purposes should be
appropriated to their instruction and for no other purpose."
This prohibition was enforced, but the second clause was
ignored for twenty years (Du Bois 1901, p. 19).

A black woman, convicted of having been among those who had
been the cause of a devastating fire in Augusta, Georgia, was

(1829–1849)

executed, dissected, and exposed. The execution of another
woman, about to give birth, was pending.

1829–1849

In Philadelphia, six mobs murdered and maltreated blacks. In
the Middle West harsh black laws which had been enacted earlier
were put into effect. No black was allowed to settle in Ohio
unless he gave bond within twenty days to the amount of $5000
to guarantee his good behavior and support. Harboring or con-
cealing fugitives was heavily fined and no black could give
evidence in any case where a white man was party. These laws
began to be enforced in 1829 and for three days white workers
in Cincinnati shot and killed free blacks and slaves, and
destroyed property. Aroused, the blacks sent a deputation to
Canada where they were offered asylum. At least 2000 fled the
city and trekked to Canada. Later, large numbers from other
parts of the United States joined them.

1830

Louisiana declared that "All persons who shall teach, or permit or cause to be taught, any slave to read or write shall be
imprisoned not less than one month nor more than twelve
months" (Du Bois 1901, p. 18).

Discourse Delivered in St. Phillips Church for the Benefit of
the Coloured Community of Wilberforce, in Upper Canada, by
Peter Williams, Jr. (New York: G. F. Bunce). Protested
abuses of race prejudice; presented plans for a black colony
in Canada.

Luiz Gama, one of the greatest black abolitionist leaders of
Brazil, was born free in Bahia in 1830 but in 1840 was sold
into slavery by his father and sent to São Paulo. He was the
son of a Portuguese aristocrat and a free black woman, Luiza
Mahin, who participated in the Hausa uprising in Bahia. In
his ceaseless apostolate, he retrieved some 500 unfortunates
from servitude. He combated every political movement that did
not face the slavery question squarely. He wrote several
social satires. He ridiculed those who considered themselves
pure white (even when black characteristics were plainly
visible) and others who confused cultural values with race.

Free Produce Society was organized in Philadelphia during
First National Negro Convention when 230 persons pledged not
to use slave-produced products.

Three years before the founding of the American Anti-Slavery
Society, The American Society of Free Persons of Colour, for
Improving their Condition in the United States; for Purchasing
Lands; and for the Establishment of a Settlement in Upper
Canada--the First National Negro Convention--met 20 September
in Philadelphia. The convention was in response to riots and
discriminatory laws in Pennsylvania and Ohio. Present were
black antislavery agitators from seven northern states.

Portugal and Brazil abolished the slave trade south of the
equator.

Mississippi debarred slaves from printing offices.

Four thousand five hundred blacks owned slaves. Usually the
ownership was a matter of philanthropy and meant owning members of their own family.

United States population about 13 million: 10.6 million
whites; 2 million slaves; 320,000 free blacks.

Slave trade declared piracy in Brazil. The Brothers Lander,
sent out by the British government, traced the Niger from Busa
to the sea and established its outlet in the Gulf of Guinea.

1830-1850

Race riots frequent throughout the United States.

1831

"Nat Turner was born the slave of Benjamin Turner, October 2,
1800. He learned to read and made progress in the study of
the Bible and religious literature; he also learned how to
make paper, gunpowder, and pottery. He spent much time fasting
and praying and believed voices spoke to him. It was these
divine forces, he said, that told him to go about murdering
the masters of nearby plantations. He and his followers succeeded in doing this for three nights in October of 1831. He
hid himself for six weeks and evaded his pursuers. On October
30, he surrendered. He was convicted on the fifth of November

and executed on the eleventh. This uprising caused a reign of
terror in Virginia. In less than two days 120 Negroes were
killed, most of them by ordinary man hunters who shot them as
persons in pursuit of game. One individual rejoiced that he
had been instrumental in killing between ten and fifteen.
Sixty-one white persons were killed by the conspirators.
After the general slaughter fifty-three Negroes were arraigned,
seventeen of them were convicted and executed, twelve convicted and transported, and ten acquitted. Three of the four
free Negroes subsequently tried were executed and one discharged" (Woodson 1931, pp. 181ff; Du Bois 1903, p. 24).

Virginia declared that slaves or free blacks could not preach,
attend religious services at night without permission, or be
taught reading or writing. These meetings were considered unlawful assembly. The law was carefully enforced.

In North Carolina slaves and free blacks were forbidden to
preach, exhort, or teach "in any prayer meeting or other
association for worship where slaves of different families
are collected together" on penalty of not more than thirty-
nine lashes. Maryland, Georgia, and other states had similar
laws (Woodson 1939, p. 186; Du Bois 1903, p. 25).

The Liberator began publication 1 January in Boston. William
L. Garrison was the publisher. Garrison advocated the immediate and unconditional emancipation of Africans. He later
wrote that he struggled through the first year of the existence
of The Liberator with about 50 white and 400 black subscribers.
Of its first four agents three were blacks: Messrs. Philip A.
Bell of New York City, Joseph Cassey of Philadelphia, and
William Watkins of Baltimore. A circular issued in 1834 by
Garrison and Knapp stated that only one-fourth of the total
number of subscribers were white. They added "the paper then
belongs especially to the people of color--it is their organ--
and to them its appeal will come with peculiar force." About
one-half of the $624.50 collected for the mission of Garrison
to England was contributed by blacks. Towards the expenses
of his return trip, Garrison was loaned £200 by Nathaniel
Paul, a black clergyman, then in England. It is not clear
that the loan was ever repaid. The Liberator ceased publishing
in 1861.

A large number of Phillis Wheatley's poems and several poems
by John Boyd, a self-taught Bahaman black, appeared in The
Liberator.

A high school was established by black men in New York for the
pursuance of the classics and Henry Highland Garnet was one of
the first pupils.

"Autobiography of Omar ibn Said, Slave in North Carolina,
1831," American Historical Review 30 (1924):787-95.

The Mississippi law of 1831 said: it is "unlawful for any
slave, free Negro, or mulatto to preach the gospel" upon pain
of receiving thirty-nine lashes upon the naked back of the
presumptuous preacher. "If a Negro received written permission from his master he might preach to the Negroes in his
immediate neighborhood, providing six respectable white men,
owners of slaves, were present. In Alabama the law of 1832
prohibited the assembling of more than five male slaves at
any place off the plantation to which they belonged, but
nothing in the act was to be considered as forbidding attendance at places of public worship held by white persons. No
slave or free person of color was permitted to 'preach, exhort, or harrangue any slave or slaves, or free persons of
color, except in the presence of five respectable slaveholders
or unless the person preaching was licensed by some regular
body of professing Christians in the neighborhood, to whose
society or church the Negroes addressed properly belonged'"
(Du Bois 1903, pp. 25, 26).

In Philadelphia a general convention of the free blacks of the
country assembled representing five to eight states. Among
other things, they sought to interest philanthropists of the
city in the establishment of an industrial school for blacks.
The school was to be situated in New Haven, but the New Haven
authorities, by town meeting, protested so vehemently that
the project had to be given up. The convention also met in
1833 (Du Bois 1899, p. 33). This was probably the first
attempt by blacks at industrial education.

Black women in Philadelphia organized the Female Literary
Society; the members wrote literary pieces and the group
criticized them.

Brazil passed law providing for abolition of African slave
trade.

(1831)

Negro newspaper, The African Sentinel and Journal of Liberty, established in Albany, New York, John B. Stewart, ed. At least two issues were published.

Great Britain and France entered into treaty for the suppression of the slave trade.

Many more Boer farmers settled in interior of South Africa. Foundations of Orange Free State, Transvaal, and Natal.

Religion and the Pure Principles of Morality--The Sure Foundation on which we must Build. Productions from the Pen of Mrs. Maria W. Steward. Maria W. Steward was one of the earliest, if not the first black woman lecturer whose published speeches stressed the necessity for self-improvement, education, and moral resistance to the oppressor. Her name has been spelled as Steward and Stewart (Porter 1971, pp. 460ff.).

John B. Russwurm, "Letter to the United States Gazette," Liberator, 30 April. Russwurm was considered a traitor because of his work with the American Colonization Society. He established the Liberia Herald. He was generally denounced in the United States antislavery press.

Law in Senegal prohibited slave trade.

Slave rebellion in Jamaica destroyed nearly $3\frac{1}{2}$ million worth of property and brought widespread ruin to the planters (Du Bois 1939, p. 154).

Anonymous, Minutes and Proceedings of the First Annual Convention of the People of Colour, Held by Adjournment in the City of Philadelphia, from the Sixth to the Eleventh of June, Inclusive (Philadelphia).

James Forten, a veteran of the Revolutionary War, manufactured sails in Philadelphia and amassed a fortune estimated at $100,000. He was a substantial contributor to the Liberator.

Among the famous "Treinta y Tres" (The Twenty-Three) who accompanied Captain Lavalleya in the campaign for Uruguayan independence were two black slaves: Joaquín Artigas and Dionisio Oribe. Blacks took part in the war of Uruguay with Brazil. . . . Manuel Antonio Ledesma (Ansina), the ultimo soldado artiguista (the last soldier of Artigas), inseparable from the Father of his Country in loyalty and spirit of sacrifice, in exile, is now inseparable from him in their country's gratitude (Diggs 1951, pp. 281-301).

Petition: white artisans claimed unfair competition from free blacks. The petition claimed the state did not benefit from the presence of free blacks; that their behavior was not beneficial to slaves because they encouraged insubordination by precept and example. They feared that eventually only blacks would be carpenters, painters, blacksmiths et cetera. Signed by William J. Grayson, James R. Verdier, and sixty-two other citizens of St. Helena Parish to the Senate of South Carolina.

Mary Prince, The History of Mary Prince, A West Indian Slave, Related by Herself, With a Supplement by the Editor, to Which is Added the Narrative of Asa-Asa, a Captured African (London: F. Westley and A. H. Davis).

1831-1832

Report from the Select Committee on the Extinction of slavery throughout the British Dominions at the earliest period compatible with the safety of all classes in the colonies (Slave Trade).

1831-1860

In nearly every one of the dozen or more Negro Conventions from 1831 to 1860 there was strong advocacy of trade schools for black youths. Arthur Tappan, the philanthropist, bought several acres in the southern part of New Haven, Connecticut, and completed arrangements for erecting a building, fully equipped for the purpose. But the people of New Haven and of Connecticut were bitterly opposed to the location of the

(c.1832)

institution. The commonwealth subsequently passed a law
prohibiting the establishment of any institution of learning
"for the instruction of persons of color of other states"
(Du Bois 1902, p. 29).

c.1832

The Brotherly Union Society was organized in Philadelphia
"for relieving the wants and distress of each other" and provided that funds remaining after relief were given to its
members to be invested in real estate, bonds and mortgages
not "to exceed a yearly value of 500 pounds" (Porter 1971,
pp. 51, 54).

1832

New England Anti-Slavery Society formed.

"A Colored Female in Philadelphia" expressed her support 2
January 1832 of emigration to Mexico where "all men are born
free and equal" where "the climate is healthy and Warm" and
where "the soil is rich and fertile" and where the country
"would afford us a large field of speculation, were we to re-
move thither" (Liberator 2, no. 4 [28 January]:14) (Porter
1971, p. 292).

William Lloyd Garrison, Thoughts on African Colonization . . .
Part I and Part II (Boston: Garrison & Knapp Lloyd). Con-
tains doctrines, principles, and purposes of the American
Colonization Society.

The Afro-Americas [sic] Female Intelligence Society was
organized by a group of black women in Boston.

The unwritten law of the United States was that blacks should
not receive instruction. In 1832 Alabama declared "any person
or persons who shall attempt to teach any free person of color
or slave to spell, read or write, shall, upon conviction
thereof by indictment, be fined in a sum not less than $250,
nor more than $500." Individual exception to this law in the
case of Creoles was made in Mobile in 1833 in accordance with
the treaty of 1803 with France (Du Bois 1901, p. 18).

The second convention of blacks met in Benezet Hall in Philadelphia, 4 June. They resolved to establish a society to

170

purchase land in Canada for blacks obliged to flee from the
United States and to raise money to aid the project. The con-
vention opposed national aid to the American Colonization
Society and urged the abolition of slavery in Washington, D.C.

1832-1835

Karagwe strong under King Ndagara.

1833

Reverend Nathaniel Paul, minister of the First African Baptist
Society in Albany, New York (1820-1830), had gone to England
to raise money for the Wilberforce Settlement in Upper Canada.
He delivered a speech at the Anti-Colonization Meeting held
in Exeter Hall, London, in which he launched a scathing two-
pronged attack against the Colonization Society, deeming it
cruel because it sought to expel an innocent and patriotic
element "who contributed blood, sweat and tears to the development of the United States" primarily because they were of a
"different complexion." Letters by Nathaniel Paul were published in the Liberator in 1832, 1833, and 1834. The un-
pleasantness experienced in the United States by Mrs. Nathaniel
Paul, an English woman, were revealed in the Liberator in
1841 and 1853 issues.

Prudence Crandall was arrested and imprisoned for admitting a
black-girl, Sarah Harris, to her academy for girls in Canter-
bury, Ct. The School was vandalized and demolished.

Oberlin College was founded in Ohio as an institution admitting students of all colors on equal terms.

First convention of the American Anti-Slavery Society. The
Society advocated immediate and total abolition of slavery in
the United States. "The American Anti-Slavery Society, organized in 1833, functioned chiefly as a clearinghouse for a
huge propaganda campaign mounted by agents and agitators who
looked to moral suasion for their power. Its program, however
variously interpreted in later years, originally called for
moral agitation directed at individual citizens in both
sections of the country to make them see and feel the sinful-
ness of slavery. Change people's hearts, they believed, and
the people would change their habits. The years immediately
following the organization of the American Anti-Slavery Society

saw a furious burst of abolitionist energy. Thousands of
petitions with hundreds of thousands of signatures deluged
Congress. Hundreds of antislavery agents swept over New
England, New York, and the Ohio Valley lecturing and dis-
tributing tracts. A dozen state auxiliaries and twice as
many abolitionist newspapers sprang up in the North. By 1836
the crusade against slavery had succeeded in turning the
course of American politics" (Thomas 1965, p. 2).

Libraries, reading rooms, and debating societies, intended
primarily for blacks, were reported in Philadelphia. Because
blacks were not given free privileges in the libraries of New
York in 1838, David Ruggles, black secretary of the Committee
of Vigilance of New York, opened a reading room for the exclusive use of blacks (Loggins 1931, p. 53).

Act passed by British Parliament for the abolition of slavery
throughout the colonies, the promotion of industry among the
manumitted slaves, and the compensation to the persons previously entitled to the services of such slaves by the grant
from Parliament of twenty million pound sterling. By this
Act 770,280 slaves became free. Slavery ended legally in 1838
in the British Islands, but actually continued in some other
West Indies islands until 1870. It was accompanied by widespread unrest.

In the Northern states few actual prohibitory laws were
enacted, but in Connecticut, New York, Pennsylvania, Ohio,
and elsewhere, mob violence frequently arose against Negro
schools. In Connecticut the teaching of Negroes was restricted
as follows in 1833: "No person shall set up or establish in
this state any school, academy or other literary institution
for the instruction or education of colored persons who are
not inhabitants of this State, or harbor or board, for the
purpose of attending or being taught or instructed in any such
school, academy or literary instituition any colored person
who is not an inhabitant of any town in this State without
consent, in writing, first obtained, of a majority of the
civil authority, and also of the selectmen of the town in
which each school, academy or literary institution is
situated." This was especially directed against the famous
Prudence Crandall School and was repealed in 1838 (Du Bois
1901, p. 15).

Theodore S. Wright, rights advocate, introduced a resolution
to the American Anti-Slavery Society on 10 May which recommended that the Society provide equal opportunities for blacks
to learn trades.

Ira Aldridge, black international actor, opened at Covent
Garden, London as Othello opposite Ellen Terry, one of England's
foremost actresses, as Desdemona. There is an Ira Aldridge
Chair in the Shakespeare Theatre at Stratford-on-Avon.

John Rankin, Letters on American Slavery; addressed to Mr.
John Rankin, Merchant at Middlebrook, Augusta County, Va. A
Tennessee abolitionist who was forced to flee because of his
antislavery preaching, this Presbyterian minister had a pro-
found influence on the antislavery wing of his church. His
book went through five editions in five years and soon became
a manual for antislavery speakers (Boston).

The law of 1829 in Georgia was put into the penal code, with
additional penalties for using slaves in printing offices to
set type. These laws were violated sometimes by individual
masters and clandestine schools were opened for blacks in some
of the cities before the war. In 1850 and thereafter there
was some agitation to repeal these laws and a bill to that
effect failed in the senate of Georgia by two or three votes
(Du Bois 1901, p. 18).

David L. Child, The Despotism of Freedom--Or The Tyranny and
Cruelty of American Republican Slavemasters, shown to be the
worst in the world; in a speech delivered at the first anniversary of The New England Anti-Slavery Society (Boston:
Boston Young Men's Anti-Slavery Assoc., 1833).

William Innes, comp., Liberia: Or, The Early History and
Signal Preservation of the American Colony of Free Negroes on
the Coast of Africa. Compiled from American Documents. 2d
ed. (Edinburgh: Waugh & Innes; Glasgow: M. Ogle).

Anti-Slavery Society, Suggestions . . . respecting the apprenticeship of Negro Children.

1833-1834

Philadelphia riots. Others took place in 1835 and 1838. A
two day riot in 1842 necessitated the calling out of the
militia with artillery.

(1834)

1834

Garrison Literary and Benevolent Association of New York established Negro Youth Society.

First school for Negroes (paid for by Negroes) in Cincinnati established.

Blacks in Philadelphia received passports stating they were citizens of the United States.

Conference of the African Methodist Episcopal Church held the first Negro meeting in the capital of the United States. Hundreds of whites and persons of color attended. The city officials offered their protection "should any evil designed persons attempt" to interrupt the proceedings and the President of the United States wished the Conference success (Porter 1971, p. 188).

The Origins, Horrors and Results of Slavery Faithfully and Minutely Described in a Series of Facts and its Advocates Pathetically Addressed, by Rev. W. Paul Quinn (Porter 1971).

Anon. Anecdotes and Memoirs of William Boen, a Coloured Man, Who Lived and Died near Mount Holly, New Jersey. To Which Is Added the Testimony of Friends of Mount Holly Monthly Meeting concerning Him (Philadelphia: J. Richards). Boen, a black New Jersey Quaker, related his religious experiences.

The Colored Female Anti-Slavery Society of Middletown, Connecticut, was organized on 2 April as an antislavery society and for mutual improvement and increased intellectual and moral happiness.

Anti-Slavery Reporter, a periodical containing extracts from Clarkson's thoughts on the practicability, the safety, and the advantage to all concerned of the emancipation of the slaves. There was also the Anti-Slavery Reporter under the sanction of the British and Foreign Anti-Slavery Society (London: Peter Jones Bolton, 1853).

Memoirs of Phillis Wheatley, by Margaretta Matilda Odell and B. B. Thatcher (Boston: George W. Light).

Autobiography of Bishop Isaac Lane, L.L.D. . . . Lane was
born in 1834 and died in 1937. The book contains a short
history of the C.M.E. Church in America (Nashville: M. E.
Church South, 1916).

The "Extinguisher" Extinguished, by David Ruggles, black
abolitionist, Secretary of the Committee of Vigilance, and
the "first promoter of the Underground Railroad." Among the
fugitive slaves he assisted was Frederick Douglass (New York:
Heman Howlett, 1834). "Among the early Antislavery orators,
pamphleteers and publicists there was none more uncompromis-
ingly opposed to slavery than David Ruggles. Abrogation of
the Seventh Commandment by American Churches is an example of
his power to use biblical arguments (more usually resorted to
by the slaver on behalf of slavery) quite tellingly against
'the enemy'. His appeal to virtuous or would-be American
womanhood has an unmistakable bite of irony since it challenges
individual conscience and church policy at the same time as
it acknowledges and demands the abolition of a moral double
standard applied by slavers to black women" (Porter 1971,
p. 404). "The Extinguisher" was a reply to two publications:
A Brief Review of the First Annual Report of the American
Anti-Slavery Society, by Dr. David M. Reese and An Address on
Slavery and against Immediate Emancipation, by Heran Howlett.
In his reply to Reese's claims that the Abolitionists approve
intermarriage between blacks and whites Ruggles asked "What of
it? It is certainly not repugnant to nature." And he asked
Howlett "Where are the pious Indians that can refer to the
Puritans as their spiritual fathers in Christ Jesus? The Soil
that was once peaceably pressed with their footsteps, has been
drenched with their blood: they are hunted down and driven
from mount to mount like the wild beasts of the forest"
(Loggins 1931, p. 80).

1834-1840

"Trekking" of the Boers away from Cape Colony to Orange Free
State. "There was a great deal of dissatisfaction and finally,
in 1837, numbers of Boer farmers sold their farms and some
2,000 of them crossed the Orange River on the Great Trek.
This was a quickening of a steady drift of Europeans and
mulattoes beyond the frontiers which the colony had tried to
proclaim. The Kafirs had stopped migration across the Fish
River in 1779 but in 1832 new generations of Boers were de-
manding land. The Boers regarded the colony as too small and

(1835)

were seeking expansion. The Kafir war cut across the projected
trek and when the fighting was finished, the first two organized parties of Boers crossed the Orange in 1835. Then came
a severe drought and the Great Trek got into full movement in
1836. The trek was a demand for land and the control of labor"
(Du Bois 1939, pp. 86, 87). Dingaan, the Zulu king, became
alarmed by the Trek and killed the Dutch leader, Retief, his
companions, and his Hottentot retainers. He permitted the
British missionaries to flee but attacked the Boer settlement,
and was soon attacked and defeated. The river, near which
3,000 dead were left in a field, has since been known as Blood
River, and Dingaan's Day [now Covenant Day] is the great Boer
holiday. The Boers became established in Natal and began to
push northward into Zululand. They set the Zulus to fighting
each other; this led to the flight and death of Dingaan in
1840 (Du Bois 1939, p. 87). The Zulu army, some 10,000 strong,
spent itself in repeated charges. Cannon fire combined with
musket fire wrought havoc in their ranks and eventually mounted
Voortrekkers routed the exhausted Zulu. In the entire engage-
ment no white people were killed, and only three, including
Pretorius, were wounded. However 3,000 Zulu died--a classic
example of the devastating superiority of controlled fire from
men in good defensive positions over brave and numerous Africans
armed with assagais and spears.

1835

Antislavery propaganda pamphlets taken from mails at Charleston, South Carolina and burned publicly.

Free Negroes in North Carolina disenfranchised--several hundred
free Negroes up to this date were entitled to vote.

James Bradley, "Letter on the Conditions of the Coloured
People of Cincinnati," Herald of Freedom, 7 March.

North Carolina had schools supported by free Negroes until
1835 when they were abolished by law (Du Bois 1901, p. 19).

Slave insurrections in Jaruco, Havana, Matanzas.

Anti-Slavery Record (New York: American Anti-Slavery Society,
1835-1837).

Human Rights (New York: American Anti-Slavery Society, 1835-
1839).

William Ellery Channing, Slavery, 4th ed., rev., (Boston: J. Munroe & Co.), 1836; 1st ed., 1835. This is Channing's most famous work on the subject. In it, he points out that the most essential property right of the individual is the right to the fruits of his own abilities. Since slavery deprived its victims of this right, it was, according to Channing, robbery.

Ada, "The Slave Girl's Farewell," Liberator, 27 June.

Associates of Doctor Thomas Bray for founding clerical libraries and supporting schools for blacks. Account of the institution established by the late Rev. Dr. Bray and his Associates, for founding clerical Libraries in England and Wales, and schools for blacks in British America with an abstract of their proceedings for 1834. (London: Gilbert and Rivington, printers).

By a majority vote of one in the Board of Trustees, blacks were admitted to Oberlin College.

Approximately 300 blacks came close to seizing Bahia, Brazil.

1836

The case of a black denied the right to vote came before the Pennsylvania Supreme Court. The court decided that free Negroes were not "freemen" in the language of the constitution and, therefore, that Negroes could not vote. In the constitution of 1837 the word white was inserted in the qualifications (Du Bois 1899, pp. 30, 416).

First edition of antislavery newspaper, Alton Observer, published in Alton, Illinois.

African slave trade prohibited and made piracy in Texas.

Export of slaves from a Portuguese possession forbidden.

Memorial presented in Senate asked for abolition of slavery in the District of Columbia. It was one of many antislavery petitions.

Gag Resolution adopted by the U.S. House of Representatives ruled that all petitions that had any relation to slavery

(1836)

should be laid on the table without being debated, printed, or referred.

Report from the Select Committe on the apprenticeship system in the British colonies (also in 1837).

A Narrative of Travels, etc. of John Ismael Agustus James, An African of the Mandingo Tribe, who was Captured, sold into Slavery, and subsequently liberated by a Benevolent English Gentlemen [sic] (Truro, England); said to be a "pious hoax" in the antislavery cause.

The New Man. Twenty-Nine Years a Slave: Twenty-Nine Years a Free Man (York, Penn.: P. Anstadt & Sons, 1895).

An open letter addressed to Dr. Alexander of the Princeton Theological Seminary by Theodore S. Wright was published in the Emancipator, 27 October. Wright received his training for the ministry at Princeton and was brutally attacked and kicked out of the chapel when he returned as an alumnus to the Princeton commencement.

Lydia Maria Child, An Appeal in Favor of that Class of Americans Called Africans. An early defense of Negro rights by one of the leading Abolitionists (New York: J. S. Taylor).

R. G. Williams, The Slave's Friend (New York: American Anti-Slavery Society, 1836-1838).

Angelina Emily Grimke, "Appeal to the Christian Women of the South," Anti-Slavery Examiner 1 (September 1888).

Henry Blair patented cotton planter, 31 August.

1836-1839

Incidents in the Life of Solomon Bayley, a slave who bought himself, became a Quaker, and lived in Haiti and Liberia (Philadelphia).

c.1837

Allen Parker, Recollections of Slavery Times (Worcester, Mass.: Charles W. Burbank & Co., 1895).

1837

Henry B. Stanton, <u>Remarks of Henry Brewster Stanton in the
Representatives Hall, on the 23rd and 24th of February, 1837</u>.
It went through at least five editions in one year and for a
quarter of a century set the pattern for abolitionist argu-
ments on the issue of abolishing slavery in the District of
Columbia.

<u>Out of the Briars: An Autobiography and Sketch of the Twenty-
Ninth Regiment, Connecticut Volunteers</u>, by Alexander Herritage
Newton (1910). Newton's early days as a freeman in North
Carolina; he was born in 1837.

Amanda Berry Smith, <u>The Story of the Lord's Dealings with Mrs.
Amanda Smith . . .</u> (1893); Smith was born in 1837.

William Whipper, "An Address on Non-Resistance to Offensive
Aggression," <u>Colored American</u>, 9, 16, 23, and 30 September.

A third Negro newspaper appeared, the <u>Colored American</u>, called
originally the <u>Weekly Advocate</u>. Samuel Cornish was the editor.
Later editors were C. P. Bell, James McCune Smith, and Charles
B. Ray.

The Fifth Annual Convention for the Improvement of the Free
People of Colour established the American Moral Reform Society
which held its First Annual Meeting in Philadelphia 14-19
August. Its purpose was to extend the principles of universal
peace and good will to all mankind, by promoting sound moral-
ity, by the influence of education, temperance, economy and
all those virtues that alone can render man acceptable in the
eyes of God or the civilized world.

James Williams, <u>A Narrative of Events Since the First of
August, 1834</u> (Jamaica, London). The author of this deceptive
narrative was John Greenleaf Whittier who unwittingly recorded
it as true but later found that the story of James Williams
was false. Williams's story was so valuable as propaganda
that it was written down by Whittier and published by the
American Anti-Slavery Society but Whittier was not named as
the author. A copy was sent to each member of Congress. In
October 1838, the circulation of the <u>Narrative</u> was ordered
suppressed by the Society. The controversy over Williams was
the sensation of the year in the antislavery press. Williams

(1837)

was sent to England for protection against being captured as a fugitive slave (Loggins 1931, pp. 100ff.).

Leicester A. Sawyer, A Dissertation on Servitude: Embracing an Examination of the Scripture Doctrines on the Subject, and an Inquiry into the Character and Relations of Slavery (New Haven: Durrie & Peck).

The "Negro Pew": Being an Inquiry Concerning the Propriety of Distinctions in the House of God, on Account of Color (Boston: I. Knapp).

George Bourne, Slavery Illustrated in Its Effects Upon Women and Domestic Society (Boston: I. Knapp).

Narrative of the Adventures and Escape of Moses Roper, From American Slavery (London). Roper, born in Caswell County, North Carolina claimed his father was his mother's master. Soon after his birth, his mistress, jealous of his mother, attempted to stab him in order to get revenge. His master sold him and his mother to one master and then another; he became separated from his mother. He made many attempts to escape, finally got to Savannah, New York, and Boston and arrived in Liverpool in 1835. He was sent to school in England to be trained as a missionary among blacks in the West Indies (Loggins 1931, pp. 103ff.).

James McCune Smith received a degree of Doctor of Medicine from the University of Glasgow. James McCune Smith (1813–1865) born in New York City a slave became free with the Emancipation Act of the State of New York. He was educated in the African Free School, entered the University of Glasgow in Scotland in 1832; received his M.D. in 1837. He returned to New York and practiced medicine; opened a pharmacy; served for twenty-three years on the medical staff of the Free Negro Orphan Asylum. He was active in the New York Underground Railroad and an opponent of the American Colonization Society. He was editor of the Colored American and the author of various articles and pamphlets.

The Life of Jim Crow, written by himself. Jim Crow was a dance which was said to have originated in Cincinnati. The life of the Louisville black who claimed to have been called Jim Crow was published in Philadelphia in 1837 (Loggins 1931, pp. 355, 418).

A Treatise on the Intellectual Character and Civil and Political Condition of the Coloured People of the United States, and the Prejudice Exercised Towards Them, with a sermon on the duty of the church to them, by Hosea Easton, a black man (Boston: I. Knapp). In this treatise, Hosea Easton, a minister in Hartford, answered the question why blacks did not attend church by saying that white churches made blacks feel different. He concluded that the treatment of blacks by whites was caused by public sentiment fostered by undemocratic education and not because of his color and his condition of servitude. He defended the intellectual capacity of blacks by reference to the black man's cultural past in Egypt and Ethiopia and the part blacks had played in ancient cultures. He declared "From the fourth up to the sixteenth century, they [Europeans] were in the deepest state of heathenish barbarity. Their spread over different countries caused almost an entire extinction of all civil and religious governments, and of the liberal arts and sciences. And ever since that period, all Europe and America have been little else than one great universal battlefield. . . . It is true that there is a great advance in the arts and sciences from where they once were: but whether they are anywhere near its standard, as they once existed in Africa, is a matter of doubt. . . . The Egyptians have done more to cultivate such improvements as comport to the happiness of mankind than of the descendants of Japhet put together" (Loggins 1931, p. 92).

Disenfranchisement of blacks in Pennsylvania.

"In Maryland the legislature was urged in 1837 to forbid free Negro labor out of tobacco ware-houses; in 1844 petitions came to the legislature urging the prohibition of free black carpenters and taxing free black mechanics; and finally in 1860 white mechanics urged a law barring free blacks 'from pursuing any mechanical branch of trade'" (Du Bois 1902, p. 15).

Samuel E. Cornish, "My Friends Will Please Notice," Colored American, 12 August.

Theodore S. Wright, "Address, Before the Convention of New York Anti-Slavery Society, on the Acceptance of the Annual Report, Held at Utica, 20 September 1837," Colored American, 14 October. A condemnation of the colonization scheme.

(1837)

George Moses Horton, Poems by a Slave (Philadelphia). A reprint of Hope of Liberty (Boston, 1838).

Samuel Ajayi Crowther's account of his capture and travels was
originally prepared in 1837 after his unusual abilities attracted the attention of missionaries in Sierra Leone. In response to their request he produced a letter which was first
published, with very little editing, in the Church Missionary
Record 8 (October):217-23; reprinted as an appendix to the
Journals of Rev. James Frederick Schon and Mr. Samuel Crowther
(London, 1842): pp. 371-85; and appeared, somewhat condensed
in the 1910 edition of Jesse Page, The Black Bishop (London),
pp. 9-17. Crowther prepared an account of his early life in
1841 at the request of Commander Bird Allen, on whose ship,
H.M.S. Soudan, Crowther travelled as a member of the Niger
Expedition.

Minutes and Proceedings of the First Annual Meeting of the
American Moral Reform Society held at Philadelphia in the
Presbyterian Church in Seventh Street, below Shippen, from
the 14th to the 19th of August. Philadelphia: Merrihew &
Gun, 1837. (Reprinted in Porter 1971, pp. 200ff.).

A second decree declared slavery abolished in Mexico with
compensation to owners.

Blacks denounced prejudice within the Abolitionist movement.

Elijah P. Lovejoy, publisher of Alton Observer, killed by mob.

"Nothing apparently provoked more the opposition of New York
colored men of independent mind than the idea of African
colonization. James Forten's declaration in Philadelphia in
1817 that the Negroes 'would never leave the land' became a
rousing slogan for those fighting against the colonization
movement. All of the New York leaders, with the exception of
the compromising Peter Williams and the outspoken protagonist
for colonization, John B. Russwurm, were to be classed among
the anti-Colonizationists. No one of them wrote more strongly
on the question than Theodore S. Wright, a Presbyterian minister in charge of a colored congregation in New York. His
'Address', delivered at a meeting of the New York State Anti-
Slavery Society held at Utica on September 20, 1837, is a
clear and vigorous arraignment of the whole colonization plan"
(Loggins 1931, p. 76).

(1838)

Arkansas admitted as a state with constitution that made slavery perpetual.

Indian chiefs required to surrender all slaves belonging to white persons. Chiefs notified that slaves would be tracked by blood hounds. Twenty dollars per head offered for captured slaves.

Maroon community in Mobile, Alabama, attacked; men and women resisted fiercely.

Political and civil rights meeting by blacks held in New York City.

John Quincy Adams presented petition from twenty-two slaves for abolition of slavery in the District of Columbia. The petition was tabled 9 February and Adams censured for dis-respect to the House.

Resolutions against slavery from the Legislature of Vermont presented. Pronouncement against the annexation of Texas or admission to Union of any state whose constitution included slavery. Abolition of slavery in the District of Columbia and national territories urged.

Uruguay prohibited importation of slaves.

1838

Abolition of slavery in the dominions of Great Britain.

The Atherton gag resolutions: Congress of the United States declared that petitions praying for the abolition of slavery in the District of Columbia or against the interslave trade should be tabled without being debated, referred, or printed. Similar resolutions were proposed in 1836 and 1839.

Blacks in Philadelphia had 100 small beneficial societies; Ohio blacks had 10,000 acres of land.

Charles Lenox Remond, a Massachusetts black, began his long career as an abolition agent for various New England societies.

Edward Beecher, Narrative of the Riots at Alton: In Connec-tion with the Death of Elijah P. Lovejoy (Alton, Ill.: G. Holton).

(1838)

John Gabriel Stedman, Narrative of Joanna: an Emancipated Slave of Surinam (Boston: I. Knapp).

An Appeal to the Women of the Nominally Free States: Issued by the Anti-Slavery Convention of American Women . . . (New York: W. S. Dorr).

James Gillespie Birney, Correspondence between the Hon. F. H. Elmore . . . and James G. Birney (New York: American Anti-Slavery Society). Birney was one of the secretaries of the American Anti-Slavery Society. His correspondence provided a superb ideological and statistical profile of the society at the peak of its growth.

W. Wilberforce and S. Wilberforce, Strictures on a Life of William Wilberforce, Thomas Clarkson, ed. (London: Longman, Orme, Brown, Green & Longman).

Angelina Emily Grimke, Letters to Catherine E. Beecher, in Reply to an Essay on Slavery and Abolitionism (Boston: I. Knapp).

James A. Thome and J. Horace Kimball, Emancipation in the West Indies. This important work sold hundreds of thousands of copies. It proved emancipation could work without major social dislocations (New York: The American Anti-Slavery Society).

William Yates, Rights of Colored Men to Suffrage, Citizenship, and Trial by Jury: Being a Book of Facts, Arguments and Authorities, Historical Notices and Sketches of Debates, with Notes (Philadelphia: Merrihew and Gunn).

S. B. Treadwell, American Liberties and American Slavery: Morally and Politically Illustrated (Boston: Weeks, Jordan & Company).

John Fowler Trow, Alton Trials: Of Winthrop S. Gilman (and Others) . . . Account of Trials Held at Alton, Illinois in connection with the Great Riots of 7 November 1837 (New York: J. F. Trow). Trow examines the trial of John Solomon, Levi Palmer, James Jennings, Solomon Morgan, Frederick Bruchy, and others, for a riot committed in Alton, on the night of 7 November. They were accused of unlawfully and forcibly entering the warehouse of Godfrey, Gilman & Co., and breaking up

184

and destroying a printing press. Trow used notes taken at the
time of the trial by William S. Lincoln, a member of the bar
of the Alton Municipal Court.

"Recollections of Slavery," by a "runaway slave" published as
a serial in the Advocate for Freedom and reprinted in the
Emancipator, 23 August–18 October. Presented the life of a
slave on a plantation in South Carolina and a fugitive's adventures while escaping to freedom (Loggins 1931, p. 98).

First issue of a magazine, the Mirror of Liberty, edited and
published in New York by David Ruggles.

First issue of the National Reformer, edited by William
Whipper and published in Philadelphia by the American Moral
Reform Society.

Francis Whipple Green, Memoirs of Eleanor Eldridge (Providence). Eldridge complains she had been cheated out of her
fortune because of her color.

Appeal of Forty Thousand Citizens Threatened with Disenfranchisement to the People of Pennsylvania, by Robert Purvis, son-
in-law of James Forten (Philadelphia). Legislative action
threatened to deprive blacks in Pennsylvania of the right to
vote. A convention of blacks to protest was convened and the
Appeal drawn up by Purvis as chairman of the committee selected
for the purpose; circulated widely (Loggins 1931, pp. 68, 377).
Reprinted in Pennsylvania Freeman, 29 March; Emancipator, 14
April. Another publication of Purvis's was his Letters and
Speeches, an incomplete collection published without date; it
contained a reply to a claim made by Bayard Taylor that the
Egyptians were not Negroid.

A notable black abolitionist was Andre Reboucas, who struggled
in Rio de Janeiro at the side of Jose de Patrocinio, Joaquim
Nabuco, Joaquim Serra, and other abolitionists, both white and
black. Reboucas was born in the province of Bahia 13 January
1838. He studied civil engineering and became one of Brazil's
foremost figures in engineering. A mathematician of talent,
he worked out the plans for a number of important projects.
He was in charge of the construction of the Rio de Janeiro
customs house and drew up the plans for the Rio docks. In
collaboration with his brother, he worked out the details of
the organization of the Rio water works. He became one of the

foremost authorities in Brazil on water power and utilization. All of this activity did not prevent him from devoting much time to abolition. Reboucas was not only the publicist of abolition but engaged in rural improvement, immigration of free workers to Brazil, rural prison camps, and the education of freemen. He was the author of a law concerning the education, guidance, and moral improvement of freemen. He collaborated with Jose de Patrocinio, then serving as alderman of Rio de Janeiro, in the presentation of resolutions on urban housing, public baths, and other matters of municipal interest. He also cooperated on such questions as the redistribution of parliamentary seats, marriage laws, and civil register.

1839

Samuel Ringold Ward was ordained minister of the Congregational Church and appointed an agent of the American Anti-Slavery Society.

James H. Magee, The Night of Affliction and Morning of Recovery: An Autobiography (Cincinnati: the author, 1873). Relates his travels in England after the Civil War, his early life in Illinois, his religious works as a Baptist Minister in Toronto, Illinois, Nashville, and Cincinnati.

Noyes Academy, at Canaan, New Hampshire, where a number of black boys were in attendance, was broken up by mob violence. The main building was wheeled away and dumped into a swamp, and the black students given a limited time in which to get out of the town. Alexander Crummell and Henry Highland Garnet were students there at the time (Loggins 1931, p. 128).

Tobias Barreto was a poet, jurist, and philosopher. Born in Sergipe, Brazil in 1839, he obtained a degree in law and became a Professor in the Law School in Recife. An avowed admirer of German science and thought, Barreto translated and annotated many important philosophical texts, especially the monistic doctrines of Haeckel.

Harriet Martineau, The Martyr Age of the United States. A famous foreign visitor had paeans of praises for the courage and conviction of the United States abolitionists. Her analysis of the movement in the mid-1830s included accounts of the violence they faced and the perceptive evaluation of their strength (Boston: Weeks, Jordan & Co.; New York: J. S. Taylor).

William and Samuel Williams Nesbit, Two Black Views of Liberia: Four Months in Liberia, or African Colonization Exposed; Four Years in Liberia, a Sketch of the Life of Rev. Samuel Williams.

A Letter on the Political Obligations for Abolitionists, by James G. Birney with a reply by William Lloyd Garrison. The abolitionist movement split on the issue of political action to achieve an end to bondage. William Lloyd Garrison was the outspoken voice opposing political action and James G. Birney was the most well-known advocate of political action.

Theodore Dwight Weld, American Slavery As It Is. A carefully documented collection that a quarter of a century before emancipation revealed without doubt the brutality of slavery (New York).

By this time Zanzibar was already the greatest slaving port on the whole East Coast, far eclipsing any in Mozambique. A British estimate put the total number of slaves who were sold there every year at between 40,000 and 45,000. Sayyid Said placed it higher.

The National Reformer was published monthly in Philadelphia by the Board of Managers of the American Moral Reform Society.

An Inquiry into the Condition and Prospects of the African Race, In the United States; and the Means of Bettering Its Fortunes, by an American of the District of Columbia, June, 1839 (Philadelphia: Haswell, Barrington, and Haswell).

Lemuel B. Haynes, "Letters, Sayings, and Extracts from Sermons and Addresses," in Timothy Mather Cooley, Sketches of the Life and Character of the Rev. Lemuel Haynes, A.M., . . . (New York: J. S. Taylor; New York: Harper & Brothers, 1837).

Charles Lenox Remond, "Letter," Pennsylvania Freeman, 14 November.

British and Foreign Anti-Slavery Society for the universal abolition of slavery and slave trade established.

Jeremiah Asher fought against the Negro pew in a Hartford, Connecticut, Baptist Church.

Abolition of African slave trade by Venezuela.

(1839)

The Spanish slave ship <u>Amistad</u> set sail from Havana, Cuba, to
the island of Principe with thirty-eight slaves aboard, including Cinque, an African prince. Cinque plotted an escape
and with other slaves seized the ship. Lt. Gedney of the
United States Navy captured the ship and brought it under the
jurisdiction of the Connecticut courts. The Spanish minister
demanded the return of the ship and the slaves. In Hartford,
Connecticut, Judge Thompson made the first decision in the
case: the ship, cargo, and slaves should be surrendered to
the judicial decision of the United States. The case made
headlines in newspapers across the country as the slaves were
tried from court to court for murder and mutiny. The high
point of the trial was the defense of the slaves by John
Quincy Adams, returned to a court of law after a thirty year
absence. After appeals through each succeeding court, Cinque
and his followers were freed. The friends of the crew of the
<u>Amistad</u> immediately began raising funds for their return to
Africa. In the meantime they were taught to read and write,
and the principles of Christianity were instilled in them.
Finally a vessel was found in New York harbor bound for Sierra
Leone, and passage was secured for them.

Rev. James W. C. Penington, pastor of a colored Congregational
church in Hartford, Connecticut, made an effort at this time
to send the gospel to Africa, and this was said to be the
origin of Mendi Mission which was in 1846 combined with other
societies, and became the American Missionary Association
(Jocelyn 1915, pp. 138ff.).

British estimated Zanzibar sold between 40,000 and 45,000
slaves every year.

Law in Haiti suppressed the slave trade.

c.1840

Mohammed Ali's Sudan included all the territory formerly
belonging to Napata and Meroe and from c.1840–1880 Ethiopia
was reduced to a state of ruin and misery by the Arab masters
of the Egyptians.

1840

London World Anti-Slavery Conference.

Chaga strong under Horombo.

Strongest states in Congo grasslands are those of Mwata Yamvo in Kasai river region and Kazembe in Katanga. Kazembe trades with East Coast through Nyamwezi and Swahili merchants.

Early Ngoni states in Malawi established.

Ndebele (Matabele) established in country of Urozwi and exercised overlordship over neighbors. Former Urozwi state totally destroyed.

A convention of New York State blacks declared that the splendid naval achievements on Lakes Erie and Champlain in the War of 1812 were owing mostly to the skill and prowess of colored men.

Juan Manzano, Poems by a Slave in the Island of Cuba Recently Liberated (London: T. Ward). History of the early life of the poet and descriptions of Cuban slavery and the slave traffic.

Charles Lenox Remond, "Letter to the Rev. C. B. Ray," Liberator, 16 October 1840; "Letter, from Manchester, England," Liberator, 25 September 1840; "Letter from Edinburgh," Liberator, 30 October.

Henry Highland Garnet, "Speech of H. H. Garnet, a Colored Young Man, and a Member of the Oneida Institute, at the Late Anniversary of the A. A. S. S.," Liberator, 22 May.

John Warner Barber, A History of the Amistad Captives: Being a Circumstantial Account of the Capture of the Spanish Schooner Amistad, by the Africans on Board . . . With Biographical Sketches of Each of the Surviving Africans. . . . (New Haven, Conn.: E. L. & J. W. Barber).

William H. Brisbane, Speech of the Rev. William H. Brisbane, Lately a Slaveholder in South Carolina, delivered before the Ladies' Anti-Slavery Society in Cincinnati, 12 February 1840 (Hartford: S. C. Cowles). Contained an account of the changes in his views on the subject of slavery.

Samuel E. Cornish, The Colonization Scheme Considered, in its Rejection by the Colored People; in its Unfitness for

(1840)

Christianizing and Civilizing the Aborigines of Africa, and
for Putting a Stop to the African Slave Trade, in a letter to
the Hon. Theodore Frelinghuysen and the Hon. Benjamin F. Butler,
by Samuel E. Cornish and Theodore S. Wright, pastors of the
colored Presbyterian churches in the cities of Newark and New
York (Newark: A. Guen).

Charles Lenox Remond, by 1840, had so impressed the American
Anti-Slavery Society, he was chosen to go as a delegate to a
World Abolition Convention held in London the following year.

William Ellery Channing, Emancipation. A moderate antislavery
spokesman of tremendous influence among the uncommitted,
Channing was of great importance to the antislavery movement.
He argued that since emancipation of the slaves had worked
well in the West Indies, it could work in the United States
(New York: American Anti-Slavery Society).

William Wilberforce, The Correspondence of William Wilberforce,
Robert Isaac Wilberforce and Samuel Wilberforce, editors
(Philadelphia: H. Perkins; Boston: Ives & Dennet, 1841).

Edwin H. Hatfield, compiler, Freedom's Lyre: Or, Psalms,
Hymns, and Sacred Songs, for the Slave and His Friends.

Richard Hildredth, Despotism in America: Or, An Inquiry into
the Nature and Results of the Slave-holding System in the
United States (Boston: Massachusetts Anti-Slavery Society).

National Anti-Slavery Standard (New York: American Anti-
Slavery Society, 1840-1850).

United States population 17 million; 14.2 million whites;
2.5 million slaves; 400,000 free Negroes.

Elijah Preston Marrs, Life and History of the Rev. Elijah P.
Marrs (Louisville: Bradley & Gilbert, 1885). Born a slave
in Kentucky, Marrs relates his life as a teacher, educational
administrator, Baptist minister, and his combat experiences
in the Union Army during the Civil War.

James Curry, "Narrative of James Curry, a Fugitive Slave,"
Liberator, 10 January.

"By 1837 the American Anti-Slavery Society consisted of a

loose web of semi-autonomous state and local auxiliaries,
each more concerned with converting its own section than with
supporting the national organization. . . . One phalanx, led
by James G. Birney, Joshua Leavitt, and Myron Holley turned to
politics. . . . A smaller but more militant group of abolitionists, led by William Lloyd Garrison and Wendell Phillips,
took another and--so they believed--a higher route to emancipation. . . . By 1840 . . . the abolitionists were engaged in
a civil war of their own, with both political abolitionists
and Garrisonians struggling for control of the nearly moribund
national society. When Garrison imported a boatload of women
delegates from Massachusetts for the annual meeting in New
York that year and won control, his opponents seceded, some of
them to form the rival American and Foreign Anti-Slavery
Society, others to enter the political arena with the Liberal
Party" (Thomas 1965, pp. 3, 4).

"Narrative of James Curry, A Fugitive Slave," Liberator, 10
January.

Henry Highland Garnet addressed the anniversary meeting of
the American Anti-Slavery Society; reported in the Liberator,
22 May.

Memories of a Monticello Slave; as Dictated to Charles
Campbell, by Isaac, edited by Rayford W. Logan (Charlottes-
ville, Va.: Univ. of Virginia Press, 1951). Isaac was one of
Thomas Jefferson's slaves.

Jeff Hamilton, My Master, the inside story of Sam Houston and
his times by his former slave as told to Lenoir Hunt. . . .
(Dallas, Tex.: Manfred, Van Mort & Co.).

1840-1845

Gradual abolition of slavery in Colombia, Venezuela, and
Ecuador.

1840-1850

Central College of McGrawville, New York, employed during the
late forties and early fifties at least three black profes-
sors: Charles L. Reason, George B. Vashon, and William G.
Allen.

(1841)

1841

James McCune Smith, <u>Lecture on the Haytien Revolutions, with a Sketch of . . . Toussaint L'Ouverture</u> (New York).

<u>Sketches of the Higher Classes of the Colored Society in Philadelphia</u>, by one who called himself "A Southerner" (Philadelphia).

<u>African Methodist Episcopal Magazine</u> established, George Hogarth, editor, 1, nos. 1-5 (Brooklyn, N.Y., September 1841–December 1842).

Frederick Douglass made his first speech and thereafter became one of the most prominent figures in the abolition crusade.

Daniel Alexander Payne, "An Original Poem composed for the Soiree of the Vigilant Committee of Philadelphia, May 7, 1841," <u>Liberator</u>, 28 May.

Peter Williamson, <u>The Life and Curious Adventures of Peter Williamson; Who Was Carried Off from Aberdeen and Sold for a Slave . . .</u> (L. Smith).

Charles Lenox Remond, "Remarks before the Massachusetts House of Representatives," <u>Liberator</u>, 25 February.

Charles Lenox Remond, "Letter, from New-Castle-on-Tyne," <u>Liberator</u>, 21 May.

Nancy Prince, "Letter to William Lloyd Garrison," <u>Liberator</u>, 17 September.

Thomas Paul, "Speech of Thomas Paul, a Colored Student of Dartmouth College," <u>Liberator</u>, 19 February. Thomas Paul, a black, was graduated from Dartmouth.

Charles Lenox Remond, "Speech before the Hibernian Anti-Slavery Society Held in Abbey Hall, Dublin," <u>Liberator</u>, 19 November.

James W. C. Pennington, <u>A Text Book of the Origin and History . . . of the Colored People</u> (Hartford: L. Skinner).

James Forten, "Letter to William Lloyd Garrison," Liberator,
17 September.

Ann Plato, Essays; Including Biographies and Miscellaneous
Pieces in Prose and Poetry. With an introduction by the Rev.
James W. C. Pennington (Hartford). Discusses religion, educa-
tion, benevolence, obedience, and death.

A Niger expedition, with Captain H. D. Trotter in command,
sought to start a colony in Central Africa (for which Parliament voted 60,000 pounds sterling); consisted of the Albert,
Wilberforce, and Soudan steamships.

Pennsylvania State Convention of Negroes.

Association of Colored Teachers published New York Journal of
Education and Weekly Messenger.

Slave rebellion aboard the slave trader Creole enroute from
Virginia to Louisiana; Negroes sailed to Nassau and became
free.

The white governor of Liberia died and was succeeded by the
first black governor, Joseph J. Roberts, a Virginian.

Livingstone went to Africa; he died there in 1873.

Argument of John Quincy Adams. Before the Supreme Court of
the United States, in the Case of the United States, Appel-
lants, vs. Cinque and other Africans, Captured in the Schooner
Amistad, by Lieut. Gedney, Delivered on the 24th of February
and the 1st of March, 1841; with a Review of the Case of the
Antelope, Reported in the 10th, 11th and 12th Volumes of
Wheaton's Reports. Adams's argument is a classic, and a land-
mark in the legal history of the antislavery movement
Signed: A colored American. (New York: S. W. Benedict,
printer).

Theodore Dwight Weld, Slavery and the Internal Slave Trade in
the United States of North America (British and Foreign Anti-
Slavery Society).

1842

Protest to Legislative Committee of the Massachusetts House
of Representatives against segregation in travelling.

(1842)

Decision given by Supreme Court in case of <u>Prigg vs. Penn-sylvania</u> nullified state laws granting trial by jury in case of arrest of fugitive slaves which had rendered nugatory the provisions of the federal fugitive slave law.

Frederick Douglass, "Frederick Douglass in Behalf of George Latimer," <u>Liberator</u>, 18 November.

Charles Lenox Remond, "Letter to William Lloyd Garrison," <u>Liberator</u>, 11 March.

James Gillespie Birney, <u>The American Churches, the Bulwarks of American Slavery</u>. Birney was outspoken in his criticism of the churches and their policies of maintaining discriminatory practices. This work presents his scathing indictment of the church's indifference to the slavery issue (Newburyport: C. Whipple).

Joshua Gidding presented a series of resolutions against slavery in the U.S. House; resolution of censure against him adopted; he resigned; reelected from Ohio with large majority.

Negroes massacred in Philadelphia.

South Carolina forbade free Negro seamen to leave their vessels when in port.

Slavery partially abolished in Uruguay.

Slavery to be abolished in Paraguay after 1843.

<u>The Narrative of Lunsford Lane . . . His Early Life, the Re-demption by Purchase of Himself and Family from Slavery, and His Banishment from the Place of His Birth For the Crime of Wearing a Colored Skin</u>, by Lunsford Lane (Boston: J. G. Torrey).

The earliest open letter by Frederick Douglass appeared in the <u>Liberator</u>, 18 November.

Charles C. Jones, <u>The Religious Instruction of the Negroes in the United States</u> (Savannah: T. Purse).

James W. C. Pennington, <u>Covenants Involving Moral Wrong are not Obligatory upon Man: A Sermon</u>.

1842-1847

William G. Allen was employed by Central College, McGrawville, New York as a professor of the Greek and German languages and of Rhetoric and Belles Lettres. Following his marriage to one of his white students, he went to England and in 1853 published his American Prejudice against Color; an Authentic Narrative, Showing How Easily the Nation Got into an Uproar. His marriage led to mob violence in Phillipsville, New York and was commented upon in the press in all sections of the United States (Loggins 1931, p. 187).

1843

Henry Highland Garnet was an antislavery orator and lecturer throughout the North and in England. He was a Presbyterian minister, a teacher, an operator of the Underground Railroad, an agent of Gerrit Smith in making land grants to black families, a traveler in Europe, a missionary to Jamaica, a promotor of African colonization, a college president, a United States Minister and Consul General to Liberia. Between 1839 and 1848 he published for a time in Troy, New York a newspaper, the Clarion, of which no issue seems to have been found. He was associated with the National Watchman, and the Anglo-African (Loggins 1931, p. 194). Henry Highland Garnet delivered an address before a Negro Anti-Slavery Convention in Buffalo, N.Y. which was considered so revolutionary and dangerous that its adoption was voted down because "it was war-like and encouraged insurrection and that should the convention adopt it the delegates who live near the borders of the slave states would not dare return to their homes" (Loggins 1931, p. 192). In 1848 it was printed in a volume including a reprint of Walker's Appeal and Garnet's biographical sketch on Walker. It is entitled An Address--to the Slaves of the United States of America; Garnet called for a general strike by slaves. Death is regarded for blacks of the south as better for them than slavery. They are encouraged to "cease to labor for tyrants who will not remunerate you. Let every slave throughout the land do this, and the days of slavery are numbered. You cannot be more oppressed than you have been--you cannot suffer greater cruelties than you have already. Rather die Freemen, than live to be Slaves. Remember that you are Three Millions" (Loggins 1931, pp. 192ff.).

Minutes of the National Convention of Colored Citizens, held

(1843)

at Buffalo 15, 16, 17, and 18 August. For the purpose of considering their moral and political condition as American citizens (New York: Piercy & Reed).

Charles Lenox Remond, "Letter from Buffalo," Liberator, 22 September.

Christopher Rush, with "the aid of George Collins," Short Account of the Rise and Progress of the African Methodist Episcopal Church in America (New York).

The Mystery, newspaper in Pittsburgh, published by Martin R. Delany; issued regularly until 1847 when Delany became associated with the North Star.

From Slavery to Affluence: Memoirs of Robert Anderson (Hemingford, Neb.: Hemingford Ledger, 1927).

Natal became a British Colony.

Agitation in Maryland for the outlawing of all secret Negro organizations, especially Negro Masonic Lodges.

Henry Highland Garnet, "Letter," Liberator, 8 December 1943.

S. H. Gloucester, A Discourse Delivered on the Occasion of the Death of James Forten, Sr. . . . 17 April 1842 (Philadelphia).

A Colored Convention held in Detroit took note of the War of 1812 in which black men had shown themselves to be valiant soldiers at the Battle of New Orleans.

Gold Coast organized as a Crown Colony.

Insurrection on the sugar plantation Alcancia, Cuba.

Michigan Negro Convention.

Josiah Priest, Slavery, As It Relates to the Negro, or African Race. Examined in the light of Circumstances, History and the Holy Scriptures. In defending slavery a number of authors promoted the development of a particular stereotype of blacks. Josiah Priest's Slavery summarized these stereotypes, many of which would be used by antiblack writers well after the abolition of slavery and would permeate discussion of racial questions well into the twentieth century (Albany: C. van Benthuysen & Co.).

Stephen Symonds Foster, The Brotherhood of Thieves. This work went through five editions, kept the churches in an uproar and focused national attention on the churches "soft" attitude toward slavery (New London: W. Bolles).

Theodore Parker, A Letter to the People of the United States: Touching the Matter of Slavery (Boston: J. Munroe & Company).

Report of Mr. Kennedy of Maryland . . . On the Memorial of the Friends of African Colonization, Assembled in Convention in the City of Washington, May, 1842 . . . (House Report No. 283).

John Flude Johnson, Proceedings of the General Anti-Slavery Convention; called by the Committee of the British and Foreign Anti-Slavery Society, and held in London, from Tuesday, 13 June to Tuesday, 20 June (London, 1841-1843).

United States Attorney General Hugh Legare declared that blacks were neither aliens nor citizens but were somewhere in between. However, blacks might apply for benefits under the land preemption act.

Slave population of Cuba estimated at 436,000.

In Venezuela and Colombia slave revolts occured in the mining centers and cities such as the gold mining districts along the Cauca River.

1843-1845

In Louisiana, Negroes published an anthology of their poetry.

1844

George W. Clark, The Liberty Minstrel, a collection of anti-slavery songs (New York: Saxton and Miles; Boston: Leavitt & Alden).

Light and Truth, Collected from the Bible and Ancient and Modern History, Containing the Universal History of the Colored and Indian Races, from the Creation of the World to the Present

Time, by R. B. Lewis. Represented the first extensive effort of an American black to dig into the story of his past (Boston: A Committee of Colored Gentlemen, 1836).

James McCune Smith, "Freedom and Slavery for Africans," New York Tribune.

James McCune Smith, "Freedom and Slavery for Africans," Liberator, 16, 23 February 1844; (reprinted from the New York Tribune).

George Thompson, Narrative of the Life of Moses Gandy, Late a Slave in the United States of America, 1st American Ed. (Boston).

The Liberty Almanac (New York: American and Foreign Anti-Slavery Society, 1844-1852).

The Legion of Liberty and Force of Truth (American Anti-Slavery Society). This compendium included many major anti-slavery opinions, some dating as far back as the founding fathers. The anthology went through ten editions in three years.

Alexander Glennie, Sermons Preached on Plantations to Congregations of Negroes (Charleston, South Carolina: A. E. Miller).

Instructions for the Guidance of Her Majesty's Naval Officers Employed in the Suppression of the Slave Trade Together with Appendices. The instructions included in this paper are in eight sections, each section being directed to a certain category of ship, for example, ships employed in the suppression of the slave trade and ships whose officers negotiated with African chiefs. The instructions relate to the conduct of the commanding officer in such situations as the bringing to of vessels, detention and adjudication, and the use of force. Copies of treaties and agreements made between Great Britain and various other countries for the suppression of the slave trade are included, Slave Trade 8 (1969).

In Cuba, a massacre of blacks was decreed by General O'Donnell.

John Quincy Adams carried the repeal of the gag rule against discussions of slavery.

(1845)

Alleged that in this year more slaves carried away from Africa in ships than in 1744.

School Committee of Boston denied petition of blacks to de-segregate Boston schools; Negroes sent resolutions to the committee requesting them to reconsider.

Frederick Douglass, "Milton Clark--Liberty Party--George Bradburn," Liberator, 1 November.

Samuel Laing, Slaveholding Missionaries, Correspondence of Mr. S. Laing, with the secretary of the Edinburgh Association in aid of the United Brethern's (Moravian) missions, on their holding slaves at their missionary stations in the Danish West India Islands (Edinburgh: W. Forrester, printer).

1844-1893

Series of slave revolts in Santo Domingo.

1845

In New Orleans, Les Cenelles, the first anthology of poetry written by blacks in the United States, was published. It was written by an educated group of Negroes who had studied in France. It differed in both form and content from the poetry of the slaves and other free Negroes of the time. Two other Negro poets, George Moses Horton of Chapel Hill, North Carolina, and Frances Ellen Harper, published several volumes of poetry. It is estimated that, altogether, some thirty volumes of poetry were published by Negroes between Phillis Wheatley's collection and the first volume published by Paul Laurence Dunbar in 1893.

The Narrative of the Life of Frederick Douglass, an American Slave, written by Douglass; first edition appeared in 1845. It was perhaps the most important of the slave narratives (Boston: Anti-Slavery Office).

Chile and Portugal denounced slave trade as piracy.

Jose Ferreira de Menezes, a black Brazilian who won high dis-tinction in the abolitionist campaign, was born in Rio de Janeiro. He studied law and social sciences in the School of Law. His career in law opened the way for activity in writing,

(1845)

speaking, and politics. His contribution in the fields of poetry, the novel, and the essay was enormous.

Frederick Douglass carried the message of abolition to Ireland and England.

Macon B. Allen and Robert Morris, Jr. were the first blacks to pass the Massachusetts bar and practice law in the United States.

Negroes of New England form the Freedom Association.

A Slave's Adventures Toward Freedom: Not Fiction, but the True Story of a Struggle, by Peter Bruner, 1845-1938 (Reprint. Oxford, Ohio: the author, 1925).

Recollections of the Inhabitants, Localities, Superstitions, Kuk Lux [sic] Outrages of the Carolinas, by John Peterson Green, 1845-1940 (Cleveland: the author, 1880).

Fact Stranger Than Fiction . . . by John Paterson Green (Cleveland: Riehl Printing Co., 1920). Born free, reared in South Carolina, moved to Cleveland in 1857; became a lawyer, businessman, politician; attended Union Law School, served as a Republican in the Ohio State Legislature, Justice of the Peace in Cleveland, appointed a minor official in the United States Post Office Department. Made three trips to Europe.

Frederick Douglass, "Letter I," Liberator, 26 September.

Frederick Douglass, "Letter II," Liberator, 10 October.

Frederick Douglass, "Letter III," Liberator, 24 October.

Frederick Douglass, "Letter IV," Liberator, 26 November.

Frederick Douglass, "The Folly of Our Opponents," Liberty Bell, ed. Chapman, pp. 166-173.

William Wells Brown, "Letter," National Anti-Slavery Standard, 30 January.

Charles Lenox Remond, "Letter," Liberator, 18 April.

James W. C. Pennington, "A Two Years' Absence; or, A Farewell

(1846)

Sermon Preached in the Fifth Congregational Church," Hartford,
2 November.

Aaron, The Light and Truth of Slavery. Aaron's History (Worcester, Mass.).

The Man with The Branded Hand, by Frank Edward Kettridge. In
1844, Captain Jonathan Walker attempted to help four slaves
escape from Florida to the Bahamas on his ship. After the
boat was seized by a United States revenue cutter, the slaves
were returned to their masters and Walker was imprisoned for
one year in solitary confinement before he was brought to
trial. Walker's own story of his ordeals went through at
least three editions and became a cause celebre for the abolitionist movement (Rochester, N.Y.: H. L. Wilson, 1899).

Charles Lenox Remond, "New Age of Anti-Slavery," Liberty Bell,
ed. Chapman, pp. 187-91.

Georgia prohibited slaves and free blacks from taking contracts for building and repairing houses as mechanics or
masons. Restrictions, however, were not always enforced,
especially in the building trades, and the slave mechanic
flourished (Du Bois 1902, p. 15).

Patents issued to Black Americans: Hawkins, J., Gridiron,
26 March, Pat. No. 3,973.

1846

John B. Meachum, An Address to All the Colored Citizens of the
United States; a plea for education (Philadelphia).

The first of Douglass's pamphlet publications: Correspondence
between the Rev. Samuel H. Cox, D.D., of Brooklyn, L.I.. and
Frederick Douglass, a Fugitive Slave (New York: American
Anti-Slavery Society).

An Address to 3000 Colored Citizens of New York, by Theodore
S. Wright. Plea to the blacks settled on land donated to them
by Gerrit Smith to prove themselves worthy of their benefactor
(New York).

Twelve Knights of Tabor, secret organization for freedom,
organized in St. Louis.

(1846)

Slavery prohibited in Iowa.

War of the Ax broke out on the eastern frontier between the British and the Kafirs. It lasted two or three months and cost £1 million.

American Missionary Association established to organize churches and schools in the south on avowed antislavery basis.

Correspondence with the British Commissioners on the Slave Trade. British expeditions against African chiefs who sold their subjects into slavery and efforts to negotiate treaties with the chiefs for the prevention of slavery, Slave Trade 29 [1969]).

William Hayden, Narrative of William Hayden Containing a Faithful Account of his Travels for a Number of Years Whilst a Slave in the South (Cincinnati).

Interesting Memoirs and Documents: Relating to American Slavery, and the Glorious Struggle Now Making for Complete Emancipation (London: Chapman Brothers).

Jonathan Blanchard, A Debate on Slavery Held in the City of Cincinnati, on the First, Second, Third, and Sixth Days of October, 1845. This debate over slavery between the abolitionist president of Knox College and a Southern apologist attracted national attention and laid bare all the important pro and antislavery arguments (New York: M. H. Newman; Cincinnati: W. H. Moore & Co.).

Lewis Garrard Clarke, Narratives of the Sufferings of Lewis and Milton Clarke. Lewis and Milton Clarke (sons of a soldier of the Revolution) were slaves who escaped from their Kentucky masters and became leading figures in the Northern resistance to Southern slave catchers. Slave catchers roamed the countryside searching for black men and women they could kidnap and take South as slaves (Boston: B. Marsh, 1854).

Frederick Douglass, "Letter V," Liberator, 30 January.

Frederick Douglass, "Letter," New York Tribune, 14 May.

Frederick Douglass, "Speech Delivered in Belfast, Ireland," Liberator, 6 February.

(1847)

Frederick Douglass, "Speech Delivered in Glasgow," Liberator, 29 May.

A posse of slave owners ambushed a community of maroons in St. Landry Parish, Louisiana, killing one woman and wounding two others. A black man was also assassinated.

Eliza Lee (Cabot) Follen, The Liberty Cap: Am I not a man and a brother?--Pic-nic at Dedham--Lines on hearing of the terror of the children of the slaves at the thought of being sold--Dialogue (juvenile literature).

1846-1908

Jacob Stroyer, Sketches of My Life in the South (Salem, Mass.: Salem Press, 1879). An African Methodist Episcopal minister narrated the conditions of his life in South Carolina.

1847

In 1820 an African Agency was authorized by President Monroe "to form an establishment on the island of Sherbro, or else-where on the coast of Africa and to build barracks for three hundred persons." However he warned "not to connect your agency with the views or plans of the Colonization Society, with which, under the law, the Government of the United States has no concern." The agent, after 1822, was Jehudi Ashmun, who became virtual head of the colony, fortified and enlarged it, and laid the foundations of an independent community. The agents who succeeded him came to be merely official representa-tives of the United States, and the distribution of free rations or liberated Africans ceased in 1827. About 1840 the appointment of an agent ceased, and the colony became self-supporting and independent. It was proclaimed the Republic of Liberia in 1847 (Du Bois 1896, pp. 157, 158). Liberia be-came an independent republic with a constitution copied from that of the United States and was recognized by all the powers of Europe and America. Those of American provenience, number-

(1847)

ing about 15,000, were given 700,000 Africans as subjects by treaties concluded with France and Great Britain.

George B. Vashon was the first black admitted to the bar of New York Supreme Court.

Wendell Phillips, Review of Lysander Spooner's Essay on the Unconstitutionality of Slavery: reprint from the "Anti-Slavery Standard" with additions. This exposition by the Boston lawyer, Wendell Phillips, held that the Constitution is a proslavery document. He advocated breaking up the union as the way to end human bondage.

Thomas Earle, The Life, Travels, and Opinions of Benjamin Lundy. Lundy was a Quaker who organized the Union Humane Society, and produced one of the earliest antislavery publications, The Genius of the Universal Emancipation.

Zamba, The Life and Adventures of Zamba, An African Negro King: And His Experiences of Slavery in South Carolina, Peter Neilson, editor. Said to be a blatant forgery (London).

Loring Moody, Facts For the People: Showing the Relations of the United States Government to Slavery. Compiled from official and other authentic documents (Boston: Anti-Slavery Office).

Narrative and Writings of Andrew Jackson, of Kentucky: Containing an Account of His Birth, and 26 Years of His Life While a Slave; His Escape; Five Years of Freedom, together with Anecdotes Relating to Slavery; Journal of One Year's Travels; Sketches, etc. (Miami, Fla.: Mnemosyne Publishing Co., 1969).

Meetings of the Ethnological Society of Paris were agitated by the question of slavery. There was an effort to determine the distinctive characteristics of the white and black races, "but it was in vain that the naturalists and anatomists, too few in number, tried to restrain the discussion within the limits of nature history. . . . The debate became more lively at each meeting; the outside world began to be interested; . . . and the public willingly believed that ethnology, of which it then heard for the first time, was not a science, but something between politics and philanthropy. . . . This absorbing controversy lasted nearly a year" when it was ended by the abolition of slavery. "But the Ethnological Society had been so completely absorbed by this question that, deprived of it, its chief motive to action seemed no longer to exist." The enfeebled society died (Tax 1964, p. 17).

Missouri passed an act saying that "No person shall keep or teach any school for the instruction of Negroes or mulattoes in reading or writing in this state" (Du Bois 1901, p. 18).

Dred Scott sued for freedom.

All the Spanish slave "factories" on the coast of Sierra Leone and Liberia were destroyed.

"Freedom," a poem by Charles L. Reason, occupied eight pages in Alexander Crummell's A Eulogy on the Life and Character of Thomas Clarkson: surveyed the struggle for freedom beginning with the ancient Greeks (New York).

William Wells Brown, "A Lecture Delivered before the Female Anti-Slavery Society of Salem," at Lyceum Hall, 14 November; reported by Henry M. Parkhurst (Boston: Anti-Slavery Society).

Frederick Douglass, Abolition Fanaticism in New York. Speech by a Runaway Slave from Baltimore, at an Abolition Meeting in New York, 11 May 1847 (Baltimore).

Life and Opinions of Julius Melbourn; with Sketches of the Lives and Characters of Thomas Jefferson, John Quincy Adams, John Randolph, and Several Other Eminent American Statesmen, Jabez D. Hammond, ed. (Syracuse). The authorship by Julius Melbourne has been questioned.

Leonard Black, The Life and Sufferings of Leonard Black, a Fugitive from Slavery (New Bedford: B. Lindsay).

M. M. Clark, Tract on Slavery, by . . . a Coloured Man Now on a Visit to England from the United States of America (Bradford: H. Wardman).

Narrative of William W. Brown, Fugitive Slave, by William Wells Brown. After serving less important abolition organizations, Brown was appointed agent for Massachusetts Society, possibly to replace Douglass (Boston).

(1847)

Frederick Douglass's <u>North Star</u> established with the motto: "Right is of no sex--Truth is of no color--God is Father of us all, and all we are brethern." Known as <u>Frederick Douglass' Paper</u> after 1850; as <u>Douglass' Monthly</u> after 1858. Douglass's chief associates were Martin R. Delany and William C. Nell.

<u>Reminiscences of an Active Life: The Autobiography of John Roy Lynch</u>. A Chicago lawyer and realtor and the first black elected into the United States House of Representatives from Mississippi, Lynch writes of his slave life in Louisiana and Mississippi, his political activities for the Republican party in Mississippi, his experiences in the Mississippi legislature, his duties as a United States Army officer during and after the Spanish American War, and his business and legal activities in Mississippi and Chicago (Chicago: Univ. of Chicago Press, 1970).

"At the Colored National Convention of 1847, the demand for a colored college, led by so talented and able a controversialist as the late Alexander Crummel, . . . was offset by a firm and powerful constituency that successfully insisted on industrial training having the prior claim. But it was at Rochester, N.Y., in 1853 at the most influential of all the conventions in the history of the Negro race, that their approval of industrial education was [sic] most emphatically given. At a time when 'Uncle Tom's Cabin' and the name of its authoress, Harriet Beecher Stowe, were on every tongue, she, at the urgent request of friends in Great Britain, was planning a trip to Europe. The convention, following the lead of Frederick Douglass, commissioned her by an overwhelming voice to solicit funds in their name for the establishment of an industrial and agricalatural institution. . . . The enemies of the Negro in this country severely criticized her course, but after a defence by Frederick Douglass in his paper, 'The North Star,' copied in 'The Independent,' then edited by Rev. Henry Ward Beecher, the attacks ceased. When Mrs. Stowe returned to America she had changed her mind respecting the industrial education school, and the second attempt of the colored people to found in the North what has since succeeded so well in the South, came to naught" (Du Bois 1902, p. 29).

<u>The National Era</u>, published by Gamaliel Bailey, Washington, D.C., 1847-1860.

1847-1848

Reports from the British Select Committee on the Slave Trade.
These reports deal with the effectiveness and shortcomings of
British efforts to suppress the slave trade. The committee
noted that, although the strength of the preventive naval
force was at its highest, British cruisers liberated only four
percent of the slaves carried out of Africa. It was felt that
the extent and activity of the slave traffic was governed by
European demands for the products of slave labor. Other
points covered by the inquiry included the problems of liberated Africans, the general welfare of slaves and efforts of the
Brazilian government to suppress the Trade; (Slave Trade 4
[1969]).

1847-1871

Castro Alves, acclaimed as the poet of the Brazilian abolition
movement, was born in Bahia 14 March 1847. He pursued the
humanities, studied in the law school in Recife, and later
took up residence in São Paulo. His principal work is Espumas
Fluctuantes, a book of verse, the first edition of which
appeared in 1870. He was the creator of a genre in national
verse called condoreirismo, by analogy with the flight of the
majestic condor. He flayed the evils of his times and cried
out against human injustice--especially the institution of
slavery. Among the most powerful and touching contributions
of the "poet of the slaves" are Poema dos escravos Vozes
d'Africa and Navio negreiro.

1848

The Anti-Slavery Harp, a collection of songs for antislavery
meetings by William Wells Brown, included "Jefferson's
Daughter." A note appended, ascribed to Tait's Edinburgh
Magazine, asserted that the daughter of Thomas Jefferson was
sold at New Orleans for $1000 (Boston: B. Marsh).

Henry Highland Garnet, An Address--to the Slaves of the United
States of America, printed at the instigation and expense of
John Brown in a volume including a reprint of Walker's Appeal
(New York: J. H. Tobit).

Observations of Persons and Things in South Africa . . . , by
Levi Jenkins (1848-1924). Described Jenkins's travels and

(1848)

religious works in South Africa (Philadelphia: A.M.E. Book Concern).

Susie King Taylor, Reminiscences of My Life in Camp with the 33rd United States Colored Troops. Taylor was born in 1848. In this work, she relates her life as a slave in Georgia, her activities with the First South Carolina Volunteers, her life in Boston as a teacher, laundress, and nurse (Boston: the author, 1902).

Unwritten History, by Levi Jenkins. Essayist, school teacher, and bishop of the African Methodist Episcopal Church (Philadelphia: A.M.E. Book Concern, 1919).

Autobiography and Work of Bishop M. F. Jamison. Jamison was bishop of the Colored Methodist Episcopal Church (Nashville: the author, 1912).

The French established the free Negro colony of Libreville, West Africa with Negroes freed from a captured slave ship.

William H. Robinson, From Log Cabin to Pulpit: or Fifteen Years in Slavery (Eau Claire, Wisc.: James H. Tifft, 1913). A former slave in North Carolina and Virginia, Robinson fought for the Confederate and Union Armies during the Civil War and was a fireman in Nashville after the War. He was a singer and banjo player and performed in England. Educated at Central Tennessee College, he taught school in Tennessee, worked as a railroad porter, served on a Great Lakes steamship, and as a cook in Chicago. His religious life included evangelical work in the midwest as a Baptist and an African Methodist Episcopal preacher and circuit pastor.

Railroads of Massachusetts desegregated.

William Wells Brown, "The American Slave Trade," Liberty Bell, ed. Chapman, pp. 231-38.

Frederick Douglass, "Bibles for the Slaves," Liberty Bell, ed. Chapman, pp. 121-27.

Henry Watson, Narrative of Henry Watson, a Fugitive Slave (Boston: Bela Marsh).

(1848)

William Armistead, A Tribute for the Negro: Being a Vindication of the Moral, Intellectual and Religious Capabilities of
the Colored Portion of Mankind with Particular Reference to
the African Race, Illustrated by Numerous Biographical Sketches
(Manchester and London).

Edward Needles, An Historical Memoir of the Pennsylvania
Society for Promoting the Abolition of Slavery. This invaluable history of the first antislavery society in the United
States also describes its part in easing the transition from
bondage to liberty for Pennsylvania's black population (Philadelphia: Merrihew and Thompson).

John Gregg Fee, An Anti-Slavery Manual, was the founder of
Berea College and antislavery churches, but was finally forced
to flee to Kentucky.

Horace Greeley, ed., Letters of Cassius Marcellus Clay: Including Speeches and Addresses. One of the few antislavery
Southerners to battle for abolition in the South, Clay founded
an antislavery newspaper in 1845 and ran for Governor four
years later on an antislavery platform (New York: Greeley &
McEleath).

Henry Highland Garnet, ed., Walker's Appeal (New York).

Henry Highland Garnet, The Past and Present Condition and the
Destiny of the Colored Race; a discourse delivered at the
fifteenth anniversary of the Female Benevolent Society of Troy,
N.Y., 14 February 1848 (Troy: J. C. Kneeland & Co.).

Frederick Douglass, North Star (Rochester). 3 December 1847,
1, no. 1--29 December 1848, 2, no. 1.

Frederick Douglass, "To My Old Master. Letter to Thomas Auld,"
Liberator, 22 December.

Tunis G. Campbell, Hotel Keepers', Head Waiters', and House-
keepers' Guide (Boston). Many blacks were employed in these
occupations.

William Cooper Nell, "Progress of Justice and Equality,"
Liberator, 11 February 1848.

Slavery prohibited in Wisconsin.

(1848)

Decree in Senegal abolished slavery.

The president of Harvard, Edward Everett, announced that a
black applicant would be judged only by his qualifying exam-
inations, and if the white students chose to withdraw, all
the income of the college would be devoted to the black
students.

Lewis Temple, a slave, invented the Temple Toggle Harpoon,
which was important in the whaling industry.

1849

State Convention of Connecticut Negroes.

Slavery prohibited in California.

American Anti-Slavery Almanac (Boston: 1837, 1840, 1849).

Ephraim Peabody, "Narratives of Fugitive Slaves," Christian
Examiner 47 (July):61-93.

Slavery abolished in France.

Barth explored the Sudan (also 1851).

Henry Bibb, Narrative of the Life and Adventures of Henry
Bibb, An American Slave (New York). Bibb edited Voice of
Freedom, a newspaper, after he settled permanently in Canada.

The Fugitive Blacksmith; or Events in the History of James
W. C. Pennington, . . . Formerly a Slave in the State of
Maryland. . . , by James W. C. Pennington (London: C. Gilpin).

Jarena Lee, Religious Experience and Journal of Mrs. Jarena
Lee, Giving an Account of Her Call to Preach the Gospel. Revised and corrected from the original manuscript. In spite of
regulations and her sex, she became a preacher in the African
Methodist Episcopal Church (Philadelphia).

William G. Allen, Wheatley, Banneker, and Horton: with Selec-
tions from the Poetical Works of Wheatley and Horton, and the
Letter of Washington to Wheatley, and of Jefferson to Banneker
(Boston).

William Wells Brown, "Fling Out the Anti-Slavery Flag"
appeared in the 1849 edition of the Narrative of William Wells
Brown (London).

Narrative of Henry Box Brown, Who Escaped from Slavery Enclosed in a Box 3 Feet Long and 2 Feet Wide, by Henry Box
Brown. The narrative gave him great publicity and made him a
lecturer on the abolition platform (Boston: Brown and Stearns).

William S. White, The African Preacher, An Authentic Narrative
by the Rev. William S. White, Pastor of Presbyterian Church,
Lexington, Virginia (Philadelphia: Presbyterian Board of
Publication).

William Wells Brown represented the American Peace Society at
the International Convention of Pacifists held in Paris.

"An Appeal to Enoch Price My Old Master," by William Wells
Brown, who was the first American black to attempt to write a
novel, a drama, and travel literature, was published in the
Liberator, 14 December 1849. Price was Wells's last master
in slavery and at the time of composition, still his legal
owner. He relates his genetic relationship with slaveholders
and his desire to destroy the institution of slavery.

Josiah Henson, The Life of Josiah Henson, Formerly a Slave,
Now an Inhabitant of Canada, as Narrated by Himself to Samuel
Eliot (Boston). Harriet Beecher Stowe probably interviewed
Henson while writing Uncle Tom's Cabin and may have developed
Uncle Tom from his autobiography.

Remarks Upon the Remedy for Slavery, by Charles Stearns
(Boston: Brown & Stearns, 1849).

John Van Surly de Grasse of Oneida and Clinton, New York, and
Thomas J. White of Brooklyn were graduated from the medical
course at Bowdoin.

Slavery Illustrated; in the histories of Zangara and Maquama,
two Africans stolen from Africa, and sold into slavery. Related by themselves (Mancester [sic]: W. Irwin; London:
Simpkin, Marshall). Introductory remarks signed W. A.

"Thomas Carlyle came forward as the extreme protagonist of the
planters with his Discourse on Niggers in 1849: 'You are not
slaves now; nor do I wish, if it can be avoided, to see you
slaves again; but decidedly you have to be servants to those

(1849)

that are born wiser than you; . . . servants to the whites, if
they are (as what mortal man can doubt they are?) born wiser
than you! That, you may depend upon, my obscure black friends!
Is and was always the Law of the world for you and all men.'"
(Du Bois 1939, p. 187). Discourse on Niggers published first
in Frazer's Magazine (London), December 1849.

Free Soil Association of the District of Columbia. Address of
the Free Soil Association of the District to the people of the
United States; together with a memorial to Congress, of 1,060
inhabitants of the District, praying for the gradual abolition
of slavery (Washington: Buell & Blanchard, printers).

c.1850

Arab-Swahili pioneers had pushed their way far inland from
the coast of Tanzania, and had come into contact with other
slaving agents who had walked eastward from Angola on the
other side of the continent. Slaving caused local wars through
Tanzania and Kenya into Uganda and the eastern Congo.

1850

A Narrative of the Life and Travels of Mrs. Nancy Prince,
Written by Herself (Boston: A. D. Phelps). Mrs. Prince
traveled to Russia and Jamaica and lectured in New England on
the "manners and customs of Russia." Her open letter was
published in the Liberator, 17 September 1841.

The Fugitive Slave Law passed; the law made it very difficult
for certain blacks who were before the public as antislavery
fighters. Those who were abroad when the law went into
effect, did not dare return to the United States until their
manumission had been assured.

"To the Public," reply to an attack by the New York Tribune,
by William Wells Brown, published in the Liberator, 12 July.

Echoes from a Pioneer Life (1922), by Jared Maurice Arter,
born 1850. Arter was a former slave who became an educator,
academic administrator, and Baptist minister.

From Slavery to the Bishopric in the A.M.E. Church (1924), by
William Henry Heard, born 1850 (Philadelphia: AME Book Concern).

The Works of Francis J. Grimke, . . . 1850-1937, edited by

Carter G. Woodson: speeches, sermons, thoughts, meditations
(Associated Publishers, 1942).

By 1850 in every Northern city there was a black colony with
its churches, schools, lodges, probably its shopping district,
physicians, lawyers, and newspaper (Loggins 1931, pp. 176,
177).

William Wells Brown, "Letter From Darlington, England,"
Liberator, 8 February 1850.

M. Stuart, Conscience and the Constitution: With Remarks in
the Recent Speech of the Hon. Daniel Webster in the Senate of
the United States on the Subject of Slavery (Boston: Crocker
& Brewster).

Daniel Webster, Speeches in the U.S. Senate on Slavery
(Philadelphia: T. B. Peterson & Bros.).

Incidents in the Life of the Rev. J. Asher, By Jeremiah Asher
(Reprinted Freeport, N.Y.: Books for Libraries Press, 1971).

Anon., Narrative of Sojourner Truth, Northern Slave, Emancipated from Bodily Servitude by the State of New York, in 1828
(Boston).

Reports from the Lord's Select Committee on the Final Extinction of the African Slave Trade. These reports examined in
detail the means adopted up to 1849 by Great Britain for the
extinction of the African Slave Trade. The four principal
means were: treaties with states; treaties with African
chiefs; the maintenance of forts on the African coast; and the
maintenance of armed cruisers along the coast. Many recom-
mendations are made for more speedy and effective implementa-
tion of British policy; (Slave Trade 6 [1969]).

Expedition of James Richardson, Dr. Heinrich Barth, and Dr.
Overweg to explore Central Africa. Richardson died in 1851;
Overweg in 1852. Barth crossed the country from Lake Chad to
the Niger river and arrived at Timbuktu. Barth visited Bornu,
Kano, Nupe, Sokoto, and Gando. He is the author of Travels
and Discoveries in North and Central Africa, 5 vols., 1857-
1858.

Brazil declared the slave trade piracy.

(1850)

William Wells Brown, "To the Public," Liberator, 12 July.

Charles L. Reason, "Caste Schools," Liberator, 4 January.

Samuel Ringgold Ward, "Speech on the Fugitive Slave Bill," Liberator, 5 April.

A. R. Green, The Life of the Rev. Dandridge F. Davis, of the African M.E. Church, with an Account of His Conversion and Ministerial Labors, from August, 1834, till March, 1847. Also a Brief Sketch of the Life of the Rev. David Canyon, of the A.M.E.C. and His Ministerial Labors. To Which Is Annexed the Funeral Discourse Delivered at the Ohio Conference, in Zanesville, on the Decease of the Rev. D. F. Davis (Pittsburgh: Order of the Ohio Conference).

Denmark ceded her Gold Coast forts, property, and rights to England for 10,000 pounds.

Northern legislatures passed personal liberty laws to protect free blacks liable to false accusation under the fugitive slave law.

Fugitive Slave Act of 1793 amended: imposed fine and imprisonment on any person harboring a fugitive slave or aiding him to escape, ordered marshals and deputy-marshals to obey and execute warrants, forbade trial by jury of a fugitive slave on the question of his freedom, and a fee of ten dollars was assessed if the commissioner issued a certificate of arrest to the claimant of the fugitive. It was set at five dollars in discharged cases.

United States population app. 23.2 million; 19.5 million whites; 435,000 free Negroes; 3.2 million slaves all in the South except 260.

The "Kaffir" rebellion in South Africa; Sir Harry Smith, the governor, proclaimed martial law.

Thomas Jones, The Experience of Thomas Jones who was a Slave for Forty-three Years (Boston: D. Laing).

Henry Watson, Narratives of Henry Watson, A Fugitive Slave, 3rd ed. (Boston).

(1851)

The Late Contemplated Insurrection in Charleston, S.C. with
the Execution of Thirty-Six of the Patriots by one who called
himself a "Colored American." New York. The death of William
Irving, the provoked husband; and Joe Devaul, for refusing to
be the slave of Mr. Roach; with the capture of the American
slaver trading between the seat of government and New Orleans;
together with an account of the capture of the Spanish
schooner Amistad.

1850-1860

Increase of illicit trade and actual importations amounted to
a virtual reopening of the slave trade.

1851

William Wells Brown, "Letter from Glasgow," Liberator, 7
February.

Frederick Douglass, Lectures on American Slavery. . . .
delivered at Corinthian Hall, Rochester, N.Y. (Buffalo: G.
Reese & Co.).

James W. C. Pennington, while still legally a slave, received
the degree of Doctor of Divinity from the University of
Heidelberg, at the conference of which it was said, "You are
the first African who has received this dignity from a European university, and it is the University of Heidelberg that
thus pronounces the universal brotherhood of humanity."
    Yale University refused to admit Pennington as a regular
student but did not object when he stood outside the class-
room doors and listened to the lectures.
    Pennington discharged his pastoral duties by walking
great distances in New York because blacks were not permitted
to ride in public conveyances.

Martin R. Delany was accepted as a medical student at Harvard
after having been refused admission by the University of
Pennsylvania, Jefferson College, and the medical schools of
Albany and Geneva, New York.

It is interesting to note the impact that slavery in the
United States had on science and scientific organizations.
"In Paris in 1800 was founded the Society of the Observers of
Man 'by a union of naturalists and of medical men' to promote

(1851)

the study of natural history mainly by providing guidance to travelers and explorers of far places. The Society was deprived of new data by the long series of Napoleonic Wars which interrupted commerce and foreign travel and 'turned its attention to questions of ethnology, historical and psychological. Natural history was neglected for philosophy, politics and philanthropy.' This abortive experiment had long been forgotten when some English philanthropists founded in London, in 1838, the 'Society for the Protection of Aborigines.' Eminent scholars were among its members, but 'its aims were rather political and social than scientific.' Most of their meetings became concerned with slavery, abolition of slavery and the distinctive characteristics of blacks and whites" (Tax 1964, pp. 16, 17).

Jamie Parker, Jamie Parker, The Fugitive by Mrs. Emily Catherine Pierson (Hartford).

Voice of Freedom, published in Sandwich, Canada by Henry Bibb, 1851-1852.

John Campbell, Negro-Mania: Being an Examination of the Falsely Assumed Equality of the Various Races of Men: Demonstrated by the Investigations of Champollion (and Others); comparative statement of the conditions of slaves in the West Indies before and after emancipation (Philadelphia: Campbell & Power).

An Exposition of the African Slave Trade: From the Year 1840 to 1850, Inclusive. Prepared from Official Documents, and Published by Direction of the Representatives of the Religious Society of Friends in Pennsylvania, New Jersey and Delaware (Philadelphia, 1857).

Lewis W. Paine, Six years in a Georgia prison. Narrative of Paine, who suffered imprisonment six years in Georgia, for the crime of aiding the escape of a fellow man from that state, after he had fled from slavery (New York: printed for the author).

John Fletcher, Studies on Slavery in Easy Lessons; compiled into eight studies and subdivided into short lessons for the convenience of the reader (Natchez: J. Warner, 1852).

Negroes in Canada approx. 2,100.

Black Chronology

Black Chronology

(1851–1856)

One of the first works devoted to history of the American
Negro, William C. Nell, Services of Colored Americans in the
Wars of 1776 and 1812 (Boston).

A group of Boston blacks, led by William C. Nell, unsuccess-
ully petitioned the state legislature to appropriate money
for a monument to Crispus Attucks, martyr of the Boston
massacre.

Proclamation of President Filmore called on officers and
citizens to aid in recapture of Shadrach, arrested in Boston
as a fugitive slave and rescued by a group of colored men.
Message of the President reviewed the Shadrach case and asked
in view of resistance in Massachusetts to the fugitive slave
law that the President be confirmed in the use of the army and
navy to suppress violence and execute the laws.

Colombia enacted law that all slaves should be free after 1852.

First Women's Rights Convention held with Sojourner Truth pre-
siding on 28 May.

Slave trade in District of Columbia abolished.

Horace Mann, Slavery, Letters and Speeches by Horace Mann;
from 1848-1851 (Boston: B. B. Mussey & Co., 1853).

William Johnson's Natchez: The Ante-Bellum Diary of a Free
Negro, 1831-1851 (Baton Rouge: Louisiana State Univ. Press,
1951).

Jeter's Twenty-Five Years' Experience with the Shiloh Baptist
Church (1901), by Henry Norval Jeter, 1851-1938.

1851-1856

Frederick Douglass, Frederick Douglass' Paper (Rochester).
The dates of writing by Douglass are as follows: 26 June 1851
(4, no. 27)--18 December 1851 (4, no. 52); 24 December 1852
(6, no. 1)--16 December 1853 (6, no. 52); 23 December 1853
(7, no. 1)--15 December 1854 (7, no. 52); 11 January 1856 (9,
no. 4)--5 December 1856 (9, no. 51). (Incomplete).

(1852)

1852

Harriet Beecher Stowe, Uncle Tom's Cabin, first published as
serial in the National Era (5 June 1851–1 April 1852), an
antislavery paper, Washington, D.C. Published in two volumes
by John P. Jewell, Boston, 20 March.

While in London, William Wells Brown sponsored an exhibition
of waxworks picturing the horror of slavery. The undated
catalog was entitled "A Description of William Wells Brown's
Original Panoramic Views of the Scenes in the Life of an American Slave, from His Birth in Slavery to His Death, or His
Escape to His First Home of Freedom on British Soil" (Loggins
1931, p. 164).

The law passed by the Argentine Constituent Congress convened
in Santa Fe was explicit and decisive: in the Argentine
nation there shall be no slaves. What few slaves remained
became free with the adoption of the constitution. The owners
were to be indemnified. The buying and selling of persons
became a crime; both the parties to the sale and the escribano
or functionary who authorized the sale. But in the houses, in
the estancias, blacks remained in slavery.

William Wells Brown, Three Years in Europe: or, Places I Have
Seen and People I Have Met . . . With a Memoir of the Author
(London: C. Gilpin; Edinburgh: Oliver and Boyd). Brown's
story of experiences and impressions in Europe while a fugitive
and unable to return to the United States because of the new
fugitive slave law. He met Victor Hugo, Alexandre Dumas, Ira
Aldridge, and others.

John W. Lewis, The Life, Labors, and Travels of Elder Charles
Bowles, of the Free Will Baptist Denomination . . . Together
with an Essay on the Character and Condition of the African
Race. . . . (Watertown).

Martin Robinson Delany, "Letter to Garrison," Liberator, 21
May.

Joshua McSimpson, "Away to Canada," Liberator, 10 December.
Anti-Slavery Advocate, 1852–1863 (London).

Theodore Parker, The Boston Kidnapping: A Discourse to Com-
memorate the Rendition of Thomas Simms, delivered on the first

anniversary, 12 April 1852, before the Committee on Vigilance
at the Melodeon in Boston. In April of 1851, a young fugitive
slave of seventeen was found in Boston by his Georgia master.
Despite the efforts of abolitionists to save him, Thomas Simms
was sentenced to be returned, whereupon he begged for a knife
to stab himself to death in court. Three hundred armed constables were needed to escort Simms to the ship as church
bells tolled for him.

William Hosmer, The Higher Law, in its Relations to Civil
Government: With Particular Reference to Slavery, and the
Fugitive Slave Law (Auburn, N.Y.: Derby & Miller).

Caroline E. Rush, The North and South: Or Slavery and Its
Contrasts; a Tale of Real Life (Philadelphia: Crissy &
Marley).

J. Thornton Randolph, The Cabin and Parlor: Or, Slaves and
Masters (Philadelphia: T. B. Peterson). Written to counter-
act the influence of Uncle Tom's Cabin.

William Lloyd Garrison, Sydney Howard Gay, and Wendell Phillips,
A Letter to Louis Kossuth, Concerning Freedom and Slavery in
the United States, in Behalf of the American Anti-Slavery
Society. When Hungarian Freedom Fighter Louis Kossuth came to
America in 1852 to rouse support for his embattled countrymen,
American abolitionists hoped he would endorse their struggle.
When he failed to do so, they wrote this eloquent depiction of
the international aspects of the antislavery crusade (Boston:
R. F. Wallcut).

Oration, Delivered in Corinthian Hall, Rochester, Fourth of
July, by Frederick Douglass (Rochester: Leo, Mann & Co.).
This Oration is interesting for its irony as indicated by the
following quotation: "What, to the American slave, is your
Fourth of July? I answer: a day more than all other days in
the years, the gross injustice and cruelty to which he is the
constant victim."

"Hope and Confidence," by Charles L. Reason, in Autographs for
Freedom 2:221-29.

Free-Soil Convention met in Washington, D.C., and denounced
slavery as a sin against God and a crime against man.

(1852)

Condition, Elevation, Emigration and Destiny of the Colored
People of the United States Politically Considered, published
by Martin R. Delany (Philadelphia), who concluded eight
treaties with African kings and brought evidence of land concessions and welcome. Delany's purpose in writing the book
was to encourage free blacks to migrate to Central America.
Chastised by abolitionists, Delany confessed his mistake and
withdrew it from circulation.

Dahomey coast blockaded by British in operations to suppress
the slave trade.

Slavery abolished in Ecuador.

Slavery abolished in Argentina.

1852-1871

Report from the Select Committe on the Slave Trade. The report considered treaties and engagements between Great Britain,
Spain, and Portugal, investigating the extent to which these
countries had implemented the agreements, with special regard
to slave trade to Brazil and Cuba from Mozambique, Loanda, and
Angola. The report viewed the current terms of treaties, considered briefly the greatly reduced slave trade on the West
Coast of Africa, recommending the appointment of British
agents in Spanish and Portuguese colonies while the Cuban
slave market still flourished. The report also considered the
problems of abolishing the slave trade on the East African
coast, being principally concerned with the Zanzibar and Kilwa
slave markets, and the trade with Arabia, Persia, and Madagascar; (Slave Trade 7 [1969]).

1853

Samuel Ringgold Ward, a leading black abolitionist, was not
permitted to take his meals in the public dining saloon of the
Cunard on his way to England but William Makepeace Thackeray
called on him each day for a conversation.

James M. Whitfield, America, and Other Poems. The poems were
dedicated to Martin R. Delany, leader of Central American
colonization scheme of which Whitfield was later the chief
promoter. One of the poems, "The Misanthropist," was one of
the earliest attempts by a black in the United States to

portray the pathos of social isolation (Loggins 1931, pp. 242ff.).

Robert Purvis, "Letter on Frederick Douglass," Liberator, 16 September.

Blacks like Purvis and Barbadoes helped in the formation of the American Anti-Slavery Society. For a while black men co-operated with John Brown--six or seven of his twenty-two followers were blacks. John Brown had a program for the liberation of the slaves and the establishment of a free republic in the South. The original headquarters for his scheme were in Chatham, Canada. He planned to establish himself at some strategic point to which slaves would come in sufficient numbers to defend themselves and maintain an independent government. He began by taking possession of the arsenal at Harper's Ferry in October 1859. The state of Virginia and the United States government immediately dispatched troops to capture him and his followers and bring them to justice. John Brown and his followers made a heroic defense but were overwhelmed. Those who were not killed were captured or imprisoned. On 2 December 1859 John Brown was hanged. Five blacks figured conspicuously in the Raid at Harper's Ferry. Two of the ten killed were a free black and a former slave. One of the five who escaped was a printer who served with distinction in the Civil War and later wrote an account of the raid entitled A Voice from Harper's Ferry.

The Rochester Colored National Convention pronounced against migration to other countries but nevertheless emissaries were sent in various directions to see what inducements could be offered. One went to the Niger Valley, one to Central America, and one to Haiti. The Haitian trip was successful and about two thousand black emigrants eventually settled in Haiti.

Victor Sejour presented his play, Richard III, at the Porte Saint Martin Theatre in Paris. He said he did not think he had done an inferior job in writing the play; it was the second link of a vigorous chain which he had been carrying around in his head. Sejour was born in New Orleans, Louisiana, a free man, in 1817. His first play, Diégarias, was presented in the Theatre Francais in 1844. After his play, la Chute de Sejan, was presented in 1848, he abandoned the verse form for prose.

(1853)

Frederick Douglass, "The Heroic Slave; a Thrilling Narrative of the Adventures of Madison Washington, in Pursuit of Liberty," Autographs for Freedom 1:174-239.

Anon., Twelve Years a Slave; Narrative of Solomon Northrup, a Citizen of New York, Kidnapped in Washington City in 1841, and Rescued in 1853, from a Cotton Plantation near the Red River in Louisiana (Auburn: Derby and Miller; Buffalo, N.Y.: Derby, Orton, and Mulligan).

Martin Robinson Delany, Origin and Objects of Ancient Free-masonry; Its Introduction into the United States, and Legitimacy among Colored Men (Pittsburgh).

James McCune Smith, "John Murray (of Glasgow)," Autographs for Freedom 1:46-50. A tribute to a Scotch abolitionist.

Frances Ellen Watkins, "Eliza Harris," Frederick Douglass' Paper, 25 December 1853. "The experience of Mrs. Stowe's Eliza Harris in crossing the Ohio on ice floes with the bloodhounds at her heels is celebrated in a ballad, called 'Eliza Harris' which suggests Whittier as well as Longfellow" (Loggins 1931, p. 246).

The History of My Life and Work: Autobiography, by Morgan London Latta, born 1853 (Raleigh, N.C.: the author, 1903). An ex-slave in North Carolina, Latta attended Shaw University and then taught school. He writes primarily of his work at Latta University in West Raleigh, North Carolina, which he founded in 1892. He was also a minister.

Lydia Maria Child, Isaac T. Hooper, A True Life (Boston: J. P. Jewell).

William Green, Narrative of Events in the Life of William Green (Formerly a Slave) (Springfield; reprinted Philadelphia: Rhistoric Publications, 1969).

Levin Tilmon, A Brief Miscellaneous Narrative of the More Early Part of the Life of L. Tilmon (Jersey City: W. W. Pratt). Tilmon was pastor of a Methodist Congregational Church in New York.

Harriet Beecher Stowe, A Key to Uncle Tom's Cabin Presenting the Original Facts and Documents upon which the Story is

Founded, Together with Corroborative Statements Verifying the Truth of the Work (London).

William Armistead, Five Hundred Thousand Strokes for Freedom, A Series of Anti-Slavery Tracts of Which Half a Million Are Now First Issued by Friends of the Negro (London: W. & F. Cash).

William Goodell, The American Slave Code in Theory and Practice. This original source collection on the slave codes was the best contemporary collection of documents, statutes, and court decisions on slavery in existence. It went through four editions in one year and became a manual for antislavery speakers (New York: American and Foreign Anti-Slavery Society).

William Hosmer, Slavery and the Church (Auburn: W. J. Moses).

Anon., The Planter: Or, Thirteen Years in the South by A Northern Man (Philadelphia: H. Hooker).

Publication in England of William Wells Brown's Clotel or the President's Daughter of Thomas Jefferson by his black house-keeper. American editions of 1864 and 1867 omitted references to Jefferson. Brown was, according to Bontemps, the first black in the United States to earn a living from his writing.

Aborted slave revolt in New Orleans.

1854

National Emigration Convention of Colored People, Pittsburgh.

Elizabeth Taylor Greenfield invited to sing before Queen Victoria.

Augustus Tolton, the first native American Catholic priest of African descent, through both parents on the continent, was born 1 April in Ralls County, Missouri of slave parentage. He was ordained to the office of priest in Rome.

The Introduction of S. W. Koelle, Polyglotta Africana (London); contained brief records of some 179 cases of enslavement; they were analyzed by P. E. Hair in "The Enslavement of Koelle's Informants" (Hair 1965, pp. 193-203).

(1854)

Harriet Beecher Stowe, <u>The Edmonston Family and the Capture of</u>
<u>the Schooner Pearl</u> (Cincinnati: American Reform Tract and
Book Society).

H. G. Adams, ed., <u>God's Image in Ebony; Being a Series of</u>
<u>Biographical Sketches, Facts, Anecdotes, etc., Demonstrative</u>
<u>of the Mental Powers and Intellectual Capacities of the Negro</u>
<u>Race</u> (London: Patridge & Oakey).

E. B. Willson [sic], <u>The Bad Friday: A Sermon Preached in</u>
<u>the First Church, West Roxbury, 4 June 1854, It Being the</u>
<u>Sunday after the Return of Anthony Burns to Slavery</u> (Boston:
J. Wilson & Son).

<u>Boston Slave Riot, and Trial of Anthony Burns</u>. Containing the
report of the Fanueil Hall meeting; the murder of Batchelder;
Theodore Parker's lesson for the day; speeches of counsel on
both sides, corrected by themselves; a verbatim report of
Judge Loving's decision, and detailed account of the embarka-
tion (Boston: Fetridge and Company). The master of Anthony
Burns refused the offer of $1,200 made by Boston citizens for
Burns's freedom.

George B. Vashon, "Vincent Ogé," a poem, <u>Autographs for Free-</u>
<u>dom</u> 2:44–60. Ogé, a Haitian educated in France, was executed
at Cap François 12 March 1791 for having initiated a rebellion
in Haiti to gain French citizenship.

The formalities of William Wells Brown's manumission were completed making it possible for him to return to the United
States where the American edition of <u>Three Years in Europe</u>
appeared as <u>Sketches of Places and People Abroad</u>. With a
memoir by the author, it was published in Boston, Cleveland,
and New York.

William Douglass, <u>Sermons Preached in the African Protestant</u>
<u>Episcopal Church of ⸳St. Thomas</u> (Philadelphia).

Frances E. W. Harper, <u>Poems on Miscellaneous Subjects</u>; with a
preface by William Lloyd Garrison. Harper was the best known
black poet of the period (Boston: J. B. Yerrington & Son,
1857, 1858, 1864, 1871).

<u>Eventide: A Series of Tales and Poems</u>, by "Effie Afton," has
been attributed to Frances Ellen Watkins Harper and probably

may be the American Negro's first attempt at the short story
form (Boston).

Frederick Douglass, "Extract from a Speech Made at New York,
May 1853," Autographs for Freedom 2:251-55.

James McCune Smith, "Freedom--Liberty," Autographs for Freedom
2:241.

William Wells Brown, "Letter from London, 29 August 1854,"
Liberator, 22 September.

Frederick Douglass, Claims of the Negro Ethnologically Considered, an address before the Literary Societies of Western
Reserve College, . . . 12 July (Rochester). Douglass's meth-
odology--reasoning from a known principle to an unknown, from
the general to the specific, or from a premise to a logical
conclusion--used in his attempt to refute racism scientifically,
was characteristic of his day. The speech indicates that
Douglass was acquainted with what scientists were saying and
writing about blacks. This commencement address was an attempt to answer these scientists in a college setting.

Hannah F. S. Lee, Memoir of Pierre Toussaint, Born a Slave in
St. Domingo (Boston).

Charles L. Reason, "Hope and Confidence," Autographs for
Freedom 2:221-29. According to Loggins, the central theme is
difficult to ascertain (Loggins 1931, p. 235).

Charles Lenox Remond, "Speech . . . Delivered May 30, 1854 . . .
before the New England Anti-Slavery Society," Liberator, 23
June.

Brantz Mayer, Captain Canot, or Twenty Years of an African
Slaver: Being an Account of His Career and Adventures on the
Coast, in the Interior, on Shipboard, and in the West Indies.
The uncut edition of the memoirs of the slave ship captain
Theodore Canot, in which he tells how Africa appeared to him,
and how he went about collecting the cream of its people for
the "civilized" New World (New York: D. Appleton and Company).

Daniel H. Peterson, The Looking-Glass: Being a True Report
and Narrative of the Rev. Daniel H. Peterson, a Colored Clergy-

(1854)

man; Embracing a Period of Time from the Year 1812 to 1854, and Including His Visit to Western Africa (New York).

Jermain W. Loguen, "Letter," Liberator, 5 May.

On Two Hemispheres: Bits from the Life Story of Lewis G. Jordan, by Lewis Garnett Jordan, born 1854.

Political Destiny of the Colored Race on the American Continent, by Martin R. Delany--copy of which was sent by Delany to each member of Congress. An attempt to encourage free blacks to emigrate to Central America. It is a study of the social condition of free blacks in the United States.

"Visit of a Fugitive Slave to the Grave of Wilberforce," by William Wells Brown, published in Autographs for Freedom 2: 70-76.

Dr. James McCune Smith received into the New York Geographical Society and Dr. John V. DeGrasse into the Massachusetts Medical Society.

Negro Emigration Convention met in Cleveland--over 100 delegates including Martin Delany; Convention adopted thirty-one point platform. They made three proposals: Martin R. Delany proposed migration to the Niger Valley of Africa; James M. Whitfield proposed to go to Central America; and Theodore Holly to Haiti. They not only made these propositions, but they actually made the necessary investigation, and at the next colonization convention in Canada in 1856, Holly made a report which resulted, eventually, in 2,000 black emigrants going to Haiti. Delany concluded eight treaties with African kings and brought evidence of land concessions and welcome. Whitfield did not actually get to Central America before the Civil War broke out.

Nehemiah Adams, A South-Side View of Slavery: Or Three Months at the South, in 1854 (Boston: T. R. Marvin; Richmond: A. Morris, 1855).

Lucien B. Chase, English, Serfdom and American Slavery; or Ourselves as Others See Us (New York: H. Long & Bro.).

Julia Criffiths, ed., Autographs for Freedom (Auburn: Alden, Beardsley & Co.; Rochester: Wanzer, Beardsley & Co.).

Black Chronology

(1854)

Jacob Dewees, The Great Future of American and Africa: An Essay Showing Our Whole Duty to the Black Man, Consistent With Our Own Safety and Glory (Philadelphia: H. Orr).

James Elmes, Thomas Clarkson: A Monograph; Being a Contribution towards the History of the Abolition of the Slave-trade and Slavery (London: Blackader).

The Journal of Charlotte L. Forten (1854-1864), by Charlotte L. Forten Grimke (New York: Dryden Press, 1953).

Journal of an expedition up the Niger and Tshadda rivers undertaken by Macgregor Laird, Esq. in connection with the British government.

Emancipation of slaves enacted in Uruguay.

Massachusetts Aid Society organized to promote emigration to Kansas of settlers opposed to slavery.

The question of slavery in Kansas and Nebraska was left to those who settled there (squatter sovereignty) thus repealing in part the Missouri Compromise. A struggle immediately ensued between the slaveholders and the abolitionists as to which party should colonize these territories first.

Portugal freed slaves on royal domains.

The Boer states and Basutoland were given up by the British.

Charles L. Reason, Hope and Confidence, a poem. Autographs for Freedom 2:221-29.

Frances Ellen Watkins, Poems on Miscellaneous Subjects (Boston). Same with additional poems (Philadelphia, 1857).

"In 1854, twenty-two years after the emancipation of slaves in the British domains, a lone black woman was active on the battlefield of the Crimea tending the sick and the wounded. Despite the obstacles which faced one with a 'duskier skin,' Mary Seacole successfully challenged Victorian prejudices against colour, class and gender. On her death in 1881, the obituary notices in The Times and The Manchester Guardian paid tribute to a woman whose personal courage and contribution to the Crimean campaign had won her wide admiration" (Alexander and Dewjee 1981, p. 45).

Black Chronology

(1854-1921)

1854-1921

> Nat Love, The Life and Adventures of Nat Love, Better Known
> in the Cattle Country as "Deadwood Dick," by Himself: A True
> History of Slavery Days, Life on the Great Cattle Ranges and
> on the Plains of the "Wild and Wooly" West, Based on Facts,
> and Personal Experiences of the Author. Relates his life as
> a railroad car worker, his slave life in Tennessee and his
> experiences as a cowboy (Los Angeles: the author, 1907).

c.1855

> Among the black Brazilian abolitionists, José de Patrocinio is
> considered beyond doubt the foremost. His activity was spread
> over a wide field embracing the press, the rostrum, and the
> political forum. He began life as a serf, an apprentice in
> the Santa Casa de Misericordia in 1868, when he was between
> thirteen and fourteen years of age. He was the spokesman of
> the abolition movement in Brazil and the principal collabor-
> ator in the manifesto of 1883 of the Confederacao Abolicion-
> ista. He died in Rio de Janeiro, 29 January 1905, indigent
> and forgotten.

1855

> Emperor Theodore III proclaimed himself King of Kings and
> Emperor of Abyssinia.

> First California Negro Convention.

> Kansas prohibited slavery.

> Boston's Jim Crow School is closed (Du Bois 1901, p. 21).
> Beginning with Massachusetts in 1855 separate schools for
> blacks and whites had been abolished in nearly all northern
> states.

> John Anderson Collins, The Slave-Mother. Written for the
> Pennsylvania antislavery fair (Philadelphia).

> William Wells Brown, St. Domingo: Its Revolutions and Its
> Patriots. A Lecture, Delivered before the Metropolitan
> Athenaeum, London, May 16, and at St. Thomas' Church, Phila-
> delphia, 20 December 1854 (Boston). Relates the rise and fall
> of Toussaint L'Ouverture.

Frederick Douglass, The Anti-Slavery Movement. A Lecture . . . before the Rochester Ladies' Anti-Slavery Society (Rochester: Lee, Mann & Co.). The speech justified Douglass's break with Garrison.

Frederick Douglass, Address . . . Delivered at the Erection of the Wing Monument, at Mexico, Oswego Co., N.Y., September 11th, 1855 (Syracuse).

James McCune Smith, "An Address to the People of the United States," in Proceedings of the Colored National Convention Held in Philadelphia, October 16, 17th and 18th, 1855 (Salem, N.J.: National Standard Office, pp. 30-33).

"The Life and Bondage of Frederick Douglass," Putnam's Monthly, a Magazine of Literature, Science and Art, 6, no. 35 (November):547. With introduction by James McCune Smith.

Samuel Ringgold Ward, Autobiography of A Fugitive Negro: His Anti-Slavery Labours in the United States, Canada, and England. The leading black abolitionist before the rise of Frederick Douglass vividly described life as a slave and his labors as an antislavery lecturer in the U.S., Canada, and England (London: J. Snow).

Frederick Douglass: My Bondage and My Freedom, with introduction by Dr. James McCune Smith (New York and Auburn: Miller, Orton & Mulligan; expanded in 1845, 1881, 1893).

Peter Randolph, Sketches of Slave Life, or, Illustrations of the Peculiar Institution, 2d ed. (Boston; reprinted Philadelphia: Historic Publications, 1969).

William C. Nell, The Colored Patriots of the American Revolution, with Sketches of Several Distinguished Colored Persons: to which is Added a Brief Survey of the Condition and Prospects of Colored Americans. With introduction by Harriet Beecher Stowe (Boston).

Life of William Grimes, the Runaway Slave, Brought Down to the Present Time, by William Grimes. Reprinted in Five Black Lives (Middletown, Conn.: Wesleyan Univ. Press, 1971, pp. 59-128).

(1855)

Slave Life in Georgia: A Narrative of the Life, Suffering,
and Escape of John Brown, a Fugitive Slave, Now in England,
by John Brown. Edited by L. A. Chamerovzow, secretary, British
and Foreign Anti-Slavery Society (London: W. M. Watts).

Samuel Blanchard How, Slaveholding Not Sinful: Slavery, the
Punishment of Man's Sin; Its Remedy, the Gospel of Christ. An
Argument before the General Synod of the Reformed Protestant
Dutch Church, October, 1855, 2d ed. (New Brunswick, N.J.:
J. Terhune, 1856).

Belle Kearney, A Slaveholder's Daughter, 7th ed. (London, New
York: The Abbey Press, c.1900).

Theodore Parker, The Trial of Theodore Parker: For the "Misdemeanor" of a Speech in Faneuil Hall against Kidnapping . . .
at Boston, April 3, 1855; with the Defence of Theodore Parker
(Boston: published for the author). The case grew out of the
Anthony Burns case; it did not come to trial, but Parker published his defense.

Passmore Williamson (Philadelphia: Pennsylvania Anti-Slavery
Society). The escape of Jane Johnson and two children, slaves
of John H. Wheeler, the trial of Williamson and others, and
refusal of state Supreme Court to issue writ of habeas corpus.

William Wells Brown, Three Years in Europe; or, The American
Fugitive in Europe. Sketches of Places and People Abroad
(London: C. Gilpin; Edinburgh: Oliver & Boyd); The Black
Man: His Antecedents, His Genius, and His Achievements (New
York and Boston, 1863); The Rising Son; or the Antecedents and
Advancements of the Colored Race (Boston, 1874); The Negro in
the American Rebellion: His Heroism and Fidelity (Boston,
1867).

William Cooper Nell, Colored Patriots of the American Revolution (Boston: R. F. Wallcut).

Robert Purvis, "Eulogy on the Life and Character of James
Forten, Delivered at Bethel Church, Philadelphia, 30 March
1842," in William C. Nell, The Colored Patriots of the American Revolution, pp. 166-81.

Josephine Brown, Biography of an American Bondman, by his
daughter (Boston: R. F. Wallcut).

1856

Buganda at height of its power under Kabaka Suna.

Colonization Convention in Canada.

Livingstone made journey from Cape Colony to Angola to the Indian Ocean, exploring Zambezi from source to mouth, and returned to England after an absence of sixteen years.

Ohio Convention of Negro Men.

Negroes endorsed the Republican candidate for President.

John Brown's raid.

Massacre of Potawatomie Creek, Kansas; slavers murdered by free-staters.

Mutesa followed Suna as Kabaka of Buganda. First contacts with British explorers. Majid succeeded Said as Ruler of Zanzibar (died 1870).

Growth of Yao power in Malawi and southern Tanzania.

Portuguese continued large scale export of captives from Angola and Mozambique to Brazil.

Charles Emery Stevens, Anthony Burns: A History. The capture and rendition of Anthony Burns in 1854 was the most famous fugitive slave case in United States history. In retelling the facts of this famous case, Charles Emery Stevens reveals why it took 22 military units to return this one fugitive from Boston to Virginia (Boston: J. J. Jewett).

Horace Greeley, A History of the Struggle for Slavery Extension or Restriction in the U.S.: From the Declaration of Independence to the Present Day. Mainly Compiled and Condensed from the Journals of Congress and Other Official Records . . . (New York: Dix, Edwards & Co.).

Thornton Stringfellow, Scriptural and Statistical Views in Favor of Slavery.

Darius Lyman, Jr., Leaven for Doughfaces: Or, Threescore and Ten Parables Touching Slavery, by a Former Resident of the South.

(1856)

William A. Smith, <u>Lectures on the Philosophy of Slavery As</u>
<u>Exhibited in the Institution of Domestic Slavery in the U.S.:</u>
<u>With the Duties of Masters to Slaves</u>, Thomas O. Summers, ed.

Despairing of resistance to the whites, a black prophet arose
among the Ama Xosa who advised the wholesale destruction of
all African property except weapons, in order that this expression of faith might bring back their dead heroes. The
result was that almost a third of the nation perished from
hunger. In British "Kaffraria" alone the Africans decreased
from 105,000 to 37,000.

Charles Sumner of the Massachusetts State Senate gave a speech,
"The Crime Against Kansas" (Washington, D.C.: Buell &
Blanchard), in the U.S. Senate condemning slavery and legislators who favored it. He was assaulted by Congressman Brooks
of South Carolina.

Elymas Rogers, a black Presbyterian minister, wrote a satiri-
cal poem, <u>The Repeal of the Missouri Compromise Considered</u>, in
which he made a reference to the Brooks-Sumner affair in the
U.S. Senate.

A demand for labor arose in Natal. The Africans refused to
leave their reserves in spite of the hut tax (tax on the homes
of Africans that had to be paid in cash). Imported labor was
demanded. England refused to send convicts or destitute
children and finally, arrangements were made for the East
Indians to provide the labor. At the same time the hut tax
was increased and forced labor on the roads required. By
1865, 6,500 Indians were at work in Natal.

<u>The Life of John Thompson, a Fugitive Slave, Containing His</u>
<u>History of 25 Years in Bondage</u>. . . , by John Thompson (Wor-
cester: J. Thompson).

Establishment of Wilberforce.

<u>Biography of an American Bondman</u>, by Josephine Brown, daughter
of William Wells Brown. Josephine, educated in France and
London, became a schoolmistress in England. Enlargement of
earlier biographies (Boston).

William Wells Brown, "Speech at the Annual Meeting of the
Massachusetts Anti-Slavery Society," <u>Liberator</u>, 8 February.

232

Benjamin Drew, The Refugee: or, The Narratives of Fugitive
Slaves in Canada; related by themselves (Boston: J. P. Jewett
& Co.; New York: Sheldon, Lamport, Blakeman).

Kate E. R. Pickard, The Kidnapped and the Ransomed, Being
Personal Recollections of Peter Still and His Wife "Vina,"
After 40 Years of Slavery (Syracuse: W. T. Hamilton).

Alexander Crummell, The Duty of a Rising Christian State to
Contribute to the World's Well-Being and Civilization, and
the Means by Which It May Perform the Same. The annual oration before the Common Council and the Citizens of Monrovia,
Liberia, 26 July, the day of national independence (London).

George W. Clark, The Harp of Freedom, a collection of abolition hymns.

The Life and Adventures of James P. Beckwourth, by James P.
Beckwourth.

James W. C. Pennington, Address Delivered at the Hartford,
August 1, 1856. Stresses the benefits of abolition to blacks
and whites as demonstrated by emancipation of blacks in British
West Indies.

1856-1915

Booker Taliaferro Washington, The Story of My Life and Work
(Naperville, Ill.: J. L. Nichols & Co., 1900). Relates his
life as a slave in Virginia, his youth in West Virginia, his
education at Hampton Institute and his career at Tuskegee
Normal and Industrial Institute as its first principal.

1857

Autobiography of a Female Slave, by Martha (Mattie) Griffiths
Browne (New York: Redfield). This may not be a genuine slave
narrative. The author became an abolitionist and freed her
slaves after she had read the speeches of Charles Sumner;
she refused to deny publicly that she was the author of this
work (Loggins 1931, p. 230ff.).

Two Speeches of Frederick Douglass. One was on the celebration of the anniversary of the emancipation of slaves in the
British West Indies and the other was about the Dred Scott

(1857)

Decision (Rochester, N.Y.: C. P. Dewey).

Twenty-Two Years a Slave, and Forty Years a Freeman, by Austin
Steward. Steward was a slave in Virginia and New York and
president of the Wilberforce Colony in Canada (Rochester,
N.Y.: W. Alling).

James Theodore Holly, A Vindication on the Capacity of the
Negro Race for Self-Government, and Civilized Progress, as
Demonstrated by Historical Events of the Haitian Revolution,
and the Subsequent Acts of That People since Their National
Independence (New Haven). Holly was born of free parents in
Washington in 1829.

William T. Catto, A Semi-Centenary Discourse Address, delivered
in the First African Presbyterian Church, Philadelphia, on
the Fourth Sabbath of May, 1857; with a history of the Church
from its first organization, including a brief notice of Rev.
John Gloucester, its first pastor (Philadelphia: J. M.
Wilson).

A Vindication was sponsored by a publishing company in Hartford organized under the auspices of a national black emigration convention for the purpose of printing "the literary
productions of colored authors, and incidentally to publish
the writings of any other class of authors when the same shall
be deemed serviceable to the great cause of humanity" (Loggins
1931, p. 199).

Solomon Northrup, Twelve Years a Slave, Narrative of Solomon
Northrup, a Citizen of New York, Kidnapped in Washington City
in 1841 and Rescued in 1853, from a Cotton Plantation near the
Red River in Louisiana, dictated to David Wilson (New York).

Frank J. Webb, The Garies and Their Friends. A Negro novel-
ist's account of pre-Civil War slaves and free Negroes in
Philadelphia; the original introduction by Harriet Beecher
Stowe arrived too late for the first edition (London and New
York: G. Routledge & Company).

Wisconsin Negroes demanded suffrage.

In the Dred Scott case the Supreme Court decided that under
the Constitution neither Negro slaves nor their descendants,
slave or free, could become citizens of the United States; it

added, as a dictum, that the Missouri Compromise was unconstitutional, and therefore a slave did not become free by
being carried to a territory where slavery had been prohibited
under the Compromise.

Frederick Douglass, Two Speeches . . . One on West India Emancipation, Delivered at Canandaigua, Aug. 4th, and the Other on
the Dred Scott Decision, Delivered in New York on the Occasion
of the Anniversary of the American Abolition Society, May,
1857 (Rochester: C. P. Dewey).

Year of the cattle killing among the Xosa. "There is nothing
in economic history that quite parallels the mass suicide of
the Ama Xosa. . . . a prophet rose in South Africa and appealed
with every cadence of tongue and billowing of emotion to the
faith and religion and hope of fighting black thousands. He
told them God would drive these white [South African] oppres-
sors into the sea and bring back the great heroes of the Kafir
nations, if only they would sacrifice to heaven the blood of
their cattle, their most dearly prized and venerated possession. The Xosa rose en masse and slaughtered their cattle by
the thousand. The cry of their hurt and the stench of their
flesh swept over the veldt; and famine fell--a hundred thousand black men starved" (Du Bois 1939, pp. 379, 380).

In Wilmington, North Carolina, a number of persons destroyed
the frame work of a new building erected by Negro carpenters
and threatened to destroy all edifices erected by Negro carpenters or mechanics. There were similar disturbances in
Virginia. In South Carolina, black mechanics were severely
condemned by the newspapers as "enemies to our peculiar institutions and formidable barriers to the success of our own
native mechanics." In Ohio, from 1820-1830 and thereafter,
the white Mechanics' Societies combined against Negroes. In
Philadelphia the series of riots against Negroes was due in
large part to the jealousy of white working men, and in Washington, D.C., New York, and other cities, riots and disorder
on the part of white mechanics, aimed against Negroes, occurred
several times (Du Bois 1902, p. 16).

Negroes in New York appealed for better schools.

French emigrant ship for Negroes, Charles-et-George, seized.

(1857)

John D. Long, Pictures of Slavery in Church and State (Philadelphia: the author).

William Anderson, Life and Narrative of William Anderson or
Dark Deeds of American Slavery (Chicago).

Ralph Roberts, "A Slave's Story," Putnam's Monthly Magazine
9 (June):614-20.

Isaac Vann Arsdale Brown, Biography of the Reverend Robert
Finley. The American Colonization Society's aim was to re-
move free blacks to Africa. This biography of the founder of
the Society provided many valuable documents on the movement's
earliest days (Philadelphia: J. W. Moore).

William Wallace Hebbard, The Night of Freedom: An Appeal in
Verse Against the Great Crime of Our Country--Human Bondage!
(Boston: S. Chism).

Hinton Rowan Helper, The Impending Crisis of the South: How
to Meet It (New York: Burdick Brothers). This book was an
indictment against slavery by a nonslaveholder of the South
and an appeal to rid the South of the leadership of slaveholders. The argument was that in a country where so few
persons actually owned slaves or had interest in slaves, if
the nonslaveholders combined against the slaveholders, slavery
would be doomed. In the South industrialism could not develop
because its unskilled slave labor had to compete with the free
labor of the North. As long as the South remained agricultural it would be dependent on others for all its supplies
except its agricultural needs. This to some extent explained
why some southerners were interested in vocational education
for blacks. The South continued to run behind the North in
commerce and industry. This book thoroughly alarmed the South.

M. Roland Markham, Alcar, The Captive Creole: A Story of the
South, in Verse (Homer, New York: J. R. Dixon).

Albert Taylor Bledsoe, An Essay on Liberty and Slavery (Philadelphia: J. B. Lippincott & Co.).

Frederick A. Ross, Slavery Ordained by God (Philadelphia:
J. B. Lippincott & Co.).

George M. Weston, The Progress of Slavery in the United States

(1858)

(Washington, D.C.: the author).

William O. Blake, <u>The History of Slavery and the Slave Trade</u>
<u>Ancient and Modern: The Forms of Slavery That Prevailed in</u>
<u>Ancient Nations, Particularly in Greece and Rome. The African</u>
<u>Slave Trade and the Political History of Slavery in the United</u>
<u>States</u> (Columbus, Ohio: O. H. Miller).

George Barrell Cheever, <u>God Against Slavery: And the Freedom</u>
<u>and Duty of the Pulpit to Rebuke It, as a Sin Against God</u>
(New York: J. H. Ladd).

1858

William C. Brownlow and Abram Pryne, <u>Ought American Slavery</u>
<u>to be Perpetuated? A Debate between Rev. W. G. Brownlow and</u>
<u>Rev. A. Pryne Held at Philadelphia, September 1858</u> (Philadel-
phia: Lippincott).

The Boers declared war on the Basutos and annexed additional
territory and livestock.

Boston blacks, in protesting the Dred Scott decision, held a
Crispus Attucks Day at Faneuil Hall.

Lincoln accepted nomination of the Republican Party.

In Angola, all Africans held in slavery would become free men
in twenty years while children born of slaves would be free.

Minnesota prohibited slavery.

<u>The Slaver Echo</u>, bound for Cuba with more than 300 Africans
on board, was captured by U.S.S. <u>Dolphin</u> and taken to Charleston, South Carolina.

Lincoln and Douglas began debates.

Arrest of Little John, a Negro, at Oberlin, Ohio under
Fugitive Slave Act; Oberlin professor arrested for rescuing
the slave.

Some 800 blacks migrated from California to the British Crown
Colony of Victoria, Vancouver Island. In 1852 the legislature
of California passed a fugitive slave act which stated that

(1858)

"in no trial or hearing under this act shall the testimony of such alleged fugitives be admitted in evidence." Therefore no freed black accused of being a slave could testify on his own behalf. A California statute required all blacks to wear collars around their necks, and this collar, fastened with a tag, had to be renewed annually (O'Brien 1942, pp. 15ff.).

James Roberts, The Narrative of James Roberts, Soldier in the Revolutionary War and at the Battle of New Orleans (Chicago: printed for the author).

Charles Lenox Remond, "Speech Delivered at the 25th Meeting of the American Anti-Slavery Society in New York City, on Wednesday, 13 May 1858," Liberator, 21 May.

E. P. Rogers, "An Extract of the Opening Sermon, Delivered . . . Before the Presbyterian and Congregational Convention, Assembled at Philadelphia (28 August 1857)," in Minutes of the Second Presbyterian and Congregational Convention (New York):pp. 15-19.

Anon., Aunt Sally; or, The Cross the Way of Freedom. A Narrative of the Slave-Life and Purchase of the Mother of Rev. Isaac Williams, of Detroit, Michigan (Cincinnati: American Reform Tract and Book Society).

"Uncle Tom Jones," Experiences of Personal Narrative of Uncle Tom Jones; Who Was for Forty Years a Slave. Also the Surprising Adventures of Wild Tom, of the Island Retreat, a Fugitive Negro From South Carolina (Boston: Farwell).

Douglass' Monthly established and continued until Douglass was able to announce in its columns Lincoln's Emancipation Proclamation.

Grand jury at Charlestown refused to indict crew of Slaver Echo.

Anthony Benezet, Views of American Slavery, Taken a Century Ago (Philadelphia: Association of Friends for the Diffusion of Religious and Useful Knowledge).

Joshua Reed Giddings, The Florida Exiles (New York: Follet, Foster & Co.; J. Bradburn, 1863). For half a century blacks and Indians in Florida united to keep United States slaveholders from crushing their peaceful society.

Memories of Childhood's Slavery Days, by Anne L. Burton, born
1858 (Boston: Ross Publishing Co., 1909). Description of
various jobs and business ventures; includes some of her
poems, favorite hymns, and an essay on race.

My Own Life Story, by Sterling Nelson Brown, 1858–1929 (Washington: Hamilton Publishing Co., 1924).

My Life and Work, by Alexander Walters, 1858–1917 (New York:
Fleming H. Revell, 1917).

Josiah Henson, Truth Stranger than Fiction: Father Henson's
Story of His Own Life (the real Uncle Tom), with an introduction by Harriet Beecher Stowe, who said "Among all the singu-
lar and interesting records to which the institution of American slavery has given rise, we know of none more striking,
more characteristic and instructive than that of Josiah Henson"
(Loggins 1931, p. 216).

The Escape: or, A Leap for Freedom, A Drama in Five Acts, by
William Wells Brown. The Escape is the first definitely known
attempt by an American black to write a play (Boston).

Mrs. Frances H. McDougall, (Whipple) Greene, ed., Shahmah in
Pursuit of Freedom: Or, The Branded Hand, translated from the
original Showiah, and edited by an American citizen (New York:
Thatcher & Hutchinson).

Thomas R. R. Cobb, An Historical Sketch of Slavery, From the
Earliest Periods, vol. 1 (Philadelphia: T. & J. W. Johnson
Company).

George S. Sawyer, Southern Institutes: Or, An Inquiry into
the Origin and Early Prevalence of Slavery and the Slave Trade.
An analysis of the laws, history, and government of the institution of the principal nations, ancient and modern, from the
earliest ages down to the present time; with notes and comments
in defense of southern institutions (Philadelphia: Lippincott).

From Farm to the Bishopric: An Autobiography, by Charles
Henry Phillips, 1858–1951 (Nashville: Parthenon Press, 1932).

(1859)

A bishop in the Colored Methodist Episcopal Church, Phillips wrote of his early life in Georgia, his education in Atlanta University, Central Tennessee College, Walden University and Meharry College, his experiences as a teacher in Tennessee, and his religious work in Memphis, Louisville, and elsewhere.

1859

Thomas Hamilton, ed., The Anglo-African 1, nos. 1-12 (January-December). The periodical lasted until March 1860. "By 1859 the free blacks were looking at themselves as a self-conscious unit in the artistic and cultural life of America" (Loggins 1931, p. 211).

Frederick Douglass, Eulogy of the Late Hon. Wm. Jay . . . Delivered on the Invitation of the Colored Citizens of New York City, in Shiloh Presbyterian Church, New York, 12 May 1859 (Rochester).

Lewis H. Putnam, A Review of the Cause and Tendency of the Issues between the Two Sections of the Country; contained a plan to consolidate the views of the people of the United States in favor of emigration of blacks to Liberia, as the initiative to the efforts to transform the present system of labor in the southern states into a free agricultural tenantry. He sought the support of the respective state legislatures, and the U.S. Congress. Putnam's solution was the emigration of blacks to Liberia (Albany, N.Y.).

Anon., Objects and Regulations of the Institute for Colored Youth, with a List of the Officers and Students, and the Annual Report of the Board of Managers, for the Year 1859 (Philadelphia).

James McCune Smith, "Civilization: Its Dependence on Physical Faith," Anglo-African 1 (January):5-17.

James W. C. Pennington, "The Great Conflict Requires Great Faith," Anglo-African 1 (October):343-45.

James W. C. Pennington, "A Review of Slavery and the Slave Trade," Anglo-African 1 (March-May):93-96, 123-26, 155-59.

James W. C. Pennington, "The Self-Redeeming Powers of the Colored Races of the World," Anglo-African 1 (October):314-20.

Besides the narratives of ex-slaves, a sizable group of free Negroes published accounts of their travels, histories of the Negro in the United States, novels, plays, magazines, and newspapers.

A resolution was introduced in Congress stating that no member of the House who endorsed the book The Impending Crisis, by H. R. Helper (about conditions in the South) was fit to be Speaker of the House and that the proposal to circulate the book as campaign material was an incipient movement of treason.

All American Missionary Association missionaries were expelled from the slave states with the arrival of John Brown into Virginia.

Roberts Vaux, Anthony Benezet: From the Original Memoir, Revised, with Additions, by William Armistead (London: A. W. Bennett; Philadelphia: Lippincott & Co.).

Free blacks of Baltimore paid $500 in school taxes but their children were not permitted to enroll in the tax supported schools.

The Life, Trial and Execution of Captain John Brown . . . With a Full Account of the Attempted Insurrection at Harper's Ferry, compiled from official and authentic sources (New York: R. W. Dewitt).

Thomas Drew, compiler, The John Brown Invasion: An Authentic History of the Harper's Ferry Tragedy; with Full Details of the Capture, Trial, and Execution of the Invaders, and of All the Incidents Connected Therewith (Boston: J. Campbell).

The Child's Anti-Slavery Book: Containing a Few Words about American Slave Children, and Stories of Slave-life (New York: Carlton & Porter, 1860).

Rev. S. H. Platt, The Martyrs and the Fugitive, or a Narrative of the Captivity, Sufferings and Death of an African Family and the Escape of their Son (New York: D. Fanshaw).

James McCune Smith, "Civilization: Its Dependence on Physical Circumstances," Anglo-African 1 (January):5-17. Discusses the effect of physical environment on a culture.

(1859)

A Narrative of the Life of Noah Davis: Written by Himself at the Age of Fifty-Four (Baltimore).

Serial publication of Martin R. Delany's novel, Blake, or, The Huts of America, was begun in the Anglo-African.

Robert Brown Elliott graduated from Eaton College.

Frances Ellen Watkins Harper, "The Two Offers," Anglo-African 1 (September and October):288-91, 311-13. A prose tale about a white woman who gives up marriage to devote her life to abolition of slavery. This may be the first attempt by a black in the U.S. at the short story form.

The Rev. J. W. Loguen, as a Slave and as a Freeman. Narrative of Real Life, by Jermain Wesley Loguen (Syracuse).

Martin R. Delany, "The Attraction of Plants," Anglo-African 1 (January):17-20.

William Wells Brown, "Letter to Mr. Garrison," Liberator, 23 September.

James Redpath, The Roving Editor: or Talks with Slaves in the Southern States (New York).

Austin Steward, Twenty-Two Years a Slave and Forty Years a Freeman, Embracing a Correspondence of Several Years While President of Wilberforce Colony, London, Canada West, 2d ed.

John Brown, with a handful of men, seized the United States arsenal at Harper's Ferry; after half his men were killed, he was captured and hanged 2 December.

Magara sailed from Charleston with Negroes from Slaver Echo, bound for Liberia.

Anglo-African published articles of blacks' struggle in California to achieve equal educational opportunities for their children.

Race riots in Panama.

New England Colored Citizens' Convention.

(1860)

Commercial Convention at Vicksburg, Mississippi recommended that all laws prohibiting the African slave trade be repealed.

Slaveholders' convention in Vicksburg, Mississippi, favored the reopening of the slave trade.

Kansas' Constitution prohibited slavery but limited suffrage to white males.

c.1860

It is estimated that blacks constituted a majority of the population, 55 to 57%, in South Carolina and Mississippi; in Louisiana, 47%; Alabama, 45%; Georgia, 44%; Virginia, 31%; Tennessee, 25%; Kentucky, 20%.

Slaveholders, by Number of Slaves, 1860

Number of Slaves Held	Number of Slaveholders
1	77,333
2-6	110,003
7-9	89,506
10-29	82,506
30-49	14,827
50-99	8,367
100-499	2,278
500 and over	14

1860

Abraham Lincoln received the electoral votes of all the free states except New Jersey but none from the slave states, and was declared President-Elect.

Rindi rules the Chaga.

President Buchanan's message declared that the threatened danger to the Union was due to continued and intemperate interference of the northern people with the questions of slavery in the southern states. Recommended a constitutional amendment which would specifically recognize slaves as property and give citizens the right to protect that property.

United States population approx. 31,450,000: 27,000,000 whites; 490,000 free Negroes; 4,000,000 slaves; 345,000 blacks in the

(1860)

North. Included among the black population were lawyers, physicians, politicians, officeholders, preachers, inventors, educators, manufacturers, and men holding responsible positions in business. Among their publications were newspapers and magazines conducted under their own editorship, letters and articles contributed to periodicals controlled by whites, speeches printed as pamphlets and reported phonographically for the antislavery and general press, sociological treatises, histories, books of travel and exploration, biographies, literary criticism, informal essays, poetry, novels, short stories and works for the stage (Loggins 1931, pp. 130-31).

William Lloyd Garrison, The New "Reign of Terror" in the Slaveholding States, For 1859-60. This book depicted the "reign of terror" antislavery spokesmen faced in the South following John Brown's raid on Harper's Ferry (New York: American Anti-Slavery Society).

The Constitution of the United States: Is It Pro-Slavery, or Anti-Slavery, by Frederick Douglass (Halifax).

"A Word for the Smith Family," Anglo-African (March). An anonymous essay on Darwin's theory of the origin of the species.

Jesse Ewing Glasgow, The Harper's Ferry Insurrection (Edinburgh).

J. W. Loguen, "Letter from his Tennessee Mistress, and Loguen's Reply," Liberator, 27 April. Loguen's mistress attempted to intimidate him into paying for his freedom.

Running a Thousand Miles for Freedom: or the Escape of William and Ellen Craft from Slavery, by William Craft (London: W. Tweedie).

What Experience Has Taught Me, by Thomas William Burton, 1860-1939 (1910).

Select Committee of the Senate, The Invasion at Harper's Ferry. This is the report made to the Senate on John Brown's invasion of Harper's Ferry, with accompanying testimony and other papers. There is both a majority and a minority report.

James Redpath, Echoes of Harper's Ferry. James Redpath, who rode with Brown's raiders in Kansas, collected this series of tributes to Brown after his execution in 1859. It includes speeches of Thoreau, Emerson, and Phillips, and Brown's own prison letters (Boston: Thayer and Eldridge).

J. Ewing Glasgow, The Harper's Ferry Insurrection: Being an Account of the late Outbreak in Virginia, and of the Trial and Execution of Capt. John Brown, Its Hero, 2d ed. (Edinburgh).

Henry Highland Garnet, "Defense of the African Civilization Society," Liberator, 27 December.

Jane Brown, Narrative of the Life of Jane Brown and Her Two Children, related to Rev. G. W. Offley (Hartford).

G. W. Offley, A Narrative of the Life and Labors of the Rev. G. W. Offley, a Colored Man and Local Preacher, Who Lived Twenty-Seven Years at the South and Twenty-Four at the North (Hartford).

Rufus W. Clark, The African Slave Trade (Boston: American Tract Society). The Dred Scott Case: Volume 1: A Legal Review of the Case of Dred Scott; Volume 2: The Dred Scott Decision: Opinion of Chief Justice Taney . . . ; Volume 3: Speech of Hon. Israel Washburn, Jun.; delivered in the House of Representatives, 19 May.

Hinton Rowan Helper, Compendium of the Impending Crisis of the South (New York: A. B. Burdick). The effects of slavery on the economic condition of the South.

Mrs. Henry R. Schoolcraft, The Black Gauntlet: A Tale of Plantation Life in South Carolina.

An appeal to Christians throughout the world by black refugees to speak out against slavery.

Appeal of blacks in New York for equal suffrage rights.

Jefferson Davis introduced in the Senate resolutions affirming state sovereignty; any attack on the domestic institution of Negro slavery was a violation of the Constitution; neither Congress nor a territorial legislature had power directly or indirectly to impair the right to hold slaves in the territories; the territories should have the right to be received into the Union with or without slavery according to their constitutions passed.

(1861)

1861

Robert Campbell, A Pilgrimage to My Motherland. An Account of a Journey among the Egbas and Yorubas of Central Africa, in 1859-60 (New York and Philadelphia). Campbell was a member of Martin R. Delany's exploration party studying the Niger Valley as a possible place of settlement for the blacks of the United States.

Alexander Crummell, The English Language in Liberia. The Annual Address before the Citizens of Maryland County, Cape Palmas, Liberia, 26 July 1860. Being the Day of National Independence (New York). Although Crummell considered English indicative of blacks' disastrous history of conquest and subjection, he suggested English as the language Liberia should adopt.

Alexander Crummell, The Relations and Duties of Free Colored Men in America to Africa. A Letter to Charles B. Dunbar, M.D., Esq., of New York City (Hartford). Crummell pointed out the advantages of life in Liberia but did not recommend it as a place for colonization. He advocated the formation of trade association for commerce with Africa.

Henry Highland Garnet, "Letter to His Wife, from Liverpool, 13 September 1861," Douglass' Monthly 4 (November):557.

James Wilkerson, Wilkerson's History of His Travels and Labors in the United States, as a Missionary . . . Since He Purchased His Freedom in New Orleans, La. (Columbus, Ohio).

Linda Brent (Harriet Brent Jacobs), Incidents in the Life of a Slave Girl, L. Maria Child, ed. (Boston: for the author).

American Anti-Slavery Society, The Anti-Slavery History of the John Brown Year. This meeting of the Anti-Slavery Society concentrated on the meaning of John Brown's famous raid on Harper's Ferry. The report of the meeting provided a primary source of information about John Brown and the views of prominent abolitionists toward his raid (New York: American Anti-Slavery Society).

Osborne P. Anderson, A Voice From Harper's Ferry: A Narrative of Events at Harper's Ferry; with Incidents Prior and Subsequent to Its Capture by Captian John Brown and His Men (Brown:

for the author). Anderson was a member of John Brown's group.

Mary Traill Spence Putnam, <u>Record of an Obscure Man</u> (Boston: Ticknor and Fields); a remarkable and little known book by the elder sister of James Russell Lowell. Written as though an actual memoir of a Southern trip in 1842, it is actually an abolitionist argument for emancipation.

Israel Campbell, <u>Bond and Free: or Yearnings for Freedom from my Green Brier House; Being the Story of My Life in Bondage and My Life in Freedom</u> (Philadelphia). Campbell was so pious he thought it was a sin for a slave to run away from slavery.

"Denmark Vesey," <u>Atlantic Monthly</u> 7 (June):728-44.

"Nat Turner's Insurrection," <u>Atlantic Monthly</u> 8 (August:173-87.

Samuel May, <u>The Fugitive Slave Law and Its Victims, Anti-Slavery Tracts</u>, no. 15 (New York: American Anti-Slavery Society).

Martin Robinson Delany, <u>Official Report of the Niger Valley Exploring Party</u>. Delany was the leader of a party of black explorers who explored the Niger Valley as a possible place of settlement for free blacks from the United States (New York).

<u>Memoirs of Samuel Spottford Clement: Relating Interesting Experiences in Days of Slavery and Freedom</u>, by Samuel Spottford Clement, born 1861 (Steubenville, Ohio: Herald Printing Company, 1908).

Negro slave escaped to Canada from Missouri in 1853; was arrested in 1860 and discharged by Canadian court.

Employment of slaves as laborers in the Union lines authorized.

Negroes in Canada approx. 13,000.

Slave revolt in Jamaica.

Annexation of St. Domingo to Spain; slavery not to be reestablished.

In Virginia, when Federal authority was established in the

(1861–1866)

southeast, the American Missionary Association asked to work among the freedmen. The first day school was established 17 September 1861 in the town of Hampton in a small house, a school formerly used by whites. The school was taught by Mrs. Mary Peake, whose father was an Englishman. She was born a free woman. Her school was the first one at Hampton and the first of its kind in the South and eventually led to the establishment of Hampton Institute (Du Bois 1935, p. 642).

1861–1866

"At the outbreak of the Civil War, President Lincoln's policy toward blacks in uniform was governed by his overriding political objective of maintaining the Union. During the beginning of the hostilities, Lincoln refrained from using black troops out of a reasonable fear that such an action would alienate border states. When the President issued his first call for 75,000 volunteers, a large number of blacks from urban centers in the North responded with enthusiasm, but Secretary of War Cameron's reply to their attempts to enlist was: "I have to say this department has no intention to call into service any colored soldiers.' However, as was the case in the American Revolution, the critical manpower shortages that developed as the war progressed caused individual field commanders to use black troops. . . . Due to the increasing need for men, a quiet change in official policy was made at the end of April 1862 when Gideon Welles, Secretary of the Navy, proclaimed to flag officers of the southern squadron that they might enlist blacks 'freely in the Navy with their consent rating them as boys at eight, nine, ten dollars a month and one ration.' In the summer of 1862 Secretary of War Stanton permitted up to 50,000 black volunteers to be assigned to labor units in the Quartermaster Corps. The Emancipation Proclamation, issued January 1, 1863, ended Union efforts to keep blacks out of uniform. Blacks joined the military readily, and Union commanders were eager by now to have the extra men. . . . Although President Jefferson Davis strongly censured Lincoln's use of black troops in combat, from 1863 onward there was considerable discussion in the South about using slaves in battle. However, the idea of putting slaves in uniform was too sharp a contradiction in the southern mind with its basic belief in black inferiority. It was not until March 15, 1865, that a desperate Confederate Congress finally passed a last-ditch law allowing black enlistments. On April 2, however, Lee surrendered, and no blacks were ever inducted into the

(1862)

Confederate States Army (C. S. A.). Nevertheless slaves provided invaluable logistical support for southern armies
throughout the entire war effort" (Smythe 1976, pp. 892, 893).

Frances Joseph Gaudet (1861-1934), He Leadeth Me (New Orleans:
the author, 1913). Narrates her childhood in Mississippi, a
lengthy account of her trip to England, France; president of
the Women's Christian Temperance Union of Louisiana and founder
of the Colored Industrial Home and School Association in New
Orleans for homeless children; pioneer for prison reform in
Louisiana.

1862

General David Hunter issued Emancipation Proclamation.

Slavery abolished in the District of Columbia.

William Douglass, Annals of the First African Church, in the
United States of America, Now Styled the African Episcopal
Church of St. Thomas, Philadelphia (Philadelphia).

George Livermore, An Historical Research Respecting the Opinions of the Founders of the Republic on Negroes as Slaves, As
Citizens, and As Soldiers. A documentary historical study of
the opinions of famous Americans on the Negro during our
nation's early years. It includes both favorable and unfavorable sentiments.

William Cooper Nell, "Speech on the Crispus Attucks Commemoration," Liberator, 28 March.

Charlotte L. Forten, "Letters, from St. Helena's Island,
Beaufort, S.C.," Liberator, 19 December.

Jeremiah Asher, An Autobiography, with Details of a Visit to
England, and Some Account of the Meeting Street Baptist Church,
Providence, R.I., and of the Shiloh Baptist Church, Philadel-
phia, Pa. (Philadelphia).

Thomas H. Jones, The Experiences of Thomas H. Jones, Who Was
a Slave for Forty-Three Years. Written by a Friend as Related
to Him by Brother Jones (Boston).

(1862)

Great Britain signed treaty with the United States for suppression of the African slave trade.

Slavery abolished in the territories of the United States.

Netherlands abolished slavery in the Dutch West Indies beginning 1 July 1863.

President Lincoln made contract with Bernard Koch to carry 5,000 Negroes to Isle of Vache, Haiti at fifty dollars each. Several schemes were devised to deport blacks, especially free blacks. With the emancipation of thousands of blacks even Abraham Lincoln thought of colonizing the freedmen outside the United States. He sent a special message to Congress explaining the necessity for Congress to appropriate the necessary money. The acceptance of black migrants was discussed with Great Britain, Denmark, France, Sweden, and all the South American countries. Only Liberia and Haiti were willing to accept them. Lincoln finally decided on the Isle of Vache, Haiti. Bernard Koch approached the government with regard to a contract for the transportation of blacks to Haiti. At the same time Koch arranged a deal with some businessmen in New York who agreed to help finance the project. When the scheme was discovered, connections were severed with Koch but the other businessmen, determined to go through with the project, hired Koch. Blacks were sent there in 1862 and for various reasons unusual suffering took place and the government sent a special investigator. The report was so unfavorable it was decided to send a boat to bring the survivors back to the United States.

Robert Purvis, "Letter to Hon. S. C. Pomeroy, Colonization Agent," Liberator, 12 September.

Act provided for education of colored children in Washington and Georgetown in the District of Columbia.

Enlistment Act provided white privates should receive $13 a month and $3.50 for clothing; blacks of the same rank, $7 and $3 respectively; blacks permitted to enlist as soldiers.

President authorized to appoint diplomatic representatives to the Republics of Haiti and Liberia.

Mutesa became King of Uganda. The Mohammedans were predominant but he was persuaded to admit Protestants and Catholics. The

Protestants, representing British imperialism, tried to convert the King; the Catholics, representing French imperialism,
tried to make him a Catholic. The King refused to accept any
of the religions.

1863

Message of President Lincoln stated there were 100,000 colored
men in service of whom 50,000 had borne arms.

Former slave William Wells Brown, abolitionist and writer,
published The Black Man, His Antecedents, His Genius, and His
Achievements, his first extensive attempt at history (New
York and Boston: the author).

President Lincoln issued a proclamation declaring that all
slaves in states or parts of states in rebellion 1 January
1863 should then be free. Hundreds of thousands of slaves
were already free by their own action and that of the invading
armies. In their cases, Lincoln's proclamation only added
possible legal sanction to an accomplished fact (Du Bois 1935,
p. 84).

Draft riots in New York City, Troy, and Boston. "In New York
City, especially the draft was felt to be unjust because the
wealthy could buy exemption for $300" (Du Bois 1902, pp. 153-
54).

In New York the three days' riot became a sort of local war of
extermination against blacks. A feeling of disloyalty to
union and bitterness toward blacks arose. A meeting was
called in Tammany Hall and Horace Greeley addressed them.
Longshoremen and employees struck at times and assaulted non-
unionists. Blacks took the place of longshoremen and were
assaulted (Du Bois 1902, pp. 153-54).

Recruitment of the 54th Massachusetts Regiment (all black) was
completed on 13 May. In July they led the successful assault
on Fort Wagner, South Carolina. This regiment served a full
year without pay rather than accept discriminatory wages.

Holland abolished the slave trade.

Frederick Douglass, Men of Color, to Arms!, broadside
(Rochester).

(1863)

Frederick Douglass, <u>Speeches of the Hon. W. D. Kelley, Miss Anna E. Dickinson, and Mr. Frederick Douglass</u>, at a mass meeting, held at National Hall, Philadelphia, 6 July, for the promotion of colored enlistments (n.d.).

Thomas Peck, "The Day of Jubilee," a poem, <u>Liberator</u>, 6 March.

Frederick Douglass, "What Shall We Do with Four Million Slaves, if They are Emancipated?," in <u>The Black Man</u>, William Wells Brown (New York and Boston), pp. 184-87.

William Cooper Nell, "Extracts from a Speech Delivered at an Emancipation Day Celebration in Boston on 1 January 1863," <u>Liberator</u>, 16 January.

On 26 January the Secretary of War authorized the Governor of Massachusetts to raise two regiments of black troops. They were the celebrated 54th and 55th black regiments--the first regularly authorized black regiments of the Civil War. Frederick Douglass and others began the work with enthusiasm and in the end, 187,000 blacks enlisted in the Northern armies of which 70,000 were killed or wounded. They fought in 213 battles.

John Hawkins Simpson, <u>Horrors of the Virginia Slave Trade and of the Slave-Rearing Plantations</u>. The true story of Dinah, an escaped Virginia slave, now in London, on whose body are eleven scars left by tortures which were inflicted by her master, her own father. Together with extracts from the laws of Virginia, showing that against these barbarities the law gives not the smallest protection to a slave, but the reverse (London: A. W. Bennett, 1863).

William and Ellen Craft, "Letters, from England," <u>Liberator</u>, 16 January.

Alexander Crummell, "The Responsibility of the First Fathers of a Country for Its Future Life and Character," delivered in Monrovia. <u>African Repository</u> 15 (September and October 1864): 257-67; 289-96.

<u>Lane Lunsford; or Another Helper from North Carolina</u>, by the Rev. William G. Hawkins (Boston). After Lunsford bought himself, he was not permitted to remain in his native city. Northern abolitionists brought him and his family to Boston

where he told his story on the abolition platform. He is
named as publisher and holder of copyright.

Harriet Beecher Stowe, "Sojourner Truth, The Libyan Sibyl,"
Atlantic Monthly 2 (April):473-81.

John Bell Robinson, Pictures of Slavery and Anti-Slavery:
Advantages of Negro Slavery and the Benefits of Negro Freedom;
Morally, Socially, and Politically Considered (Philadelphia:
for the author).

Toussaint L'Ouverture, Toussaint L'Ouverture: A Biography and
Autobiography (Boston: J. Redpath).

Mary Edmonia Lewis, black sculptor, began her portrait bust of
Colonel Robert Gould Shaw, of the 54th Massachusetts Regiment;
this established her in artistic circles. She also created
busts of John Brown and Abraham Lincoln.

After the Emancipation Proclamation schools immediately sprang
up under the army officers and chaplains. The most elaborate
system, perhaps, was that under General Banks in Louisiana; it
was established in 1863 and soon had a regular Board of Education which laid and collected taxes and eventually supported
nearly 100 schools with ten thousand pupils under 162 teachers
(Du Bois 1912, p. 17).

1864

Confederate Act provided that free Negroes and slaves could be
put into service in hospitals, on fortifications, and in production of materials of war.

The first black women to receive a medical degree were Rebecca
Lee, M.D., from New England Female College, Boston in 1864 and
Rebecca J. Cole, M.D., from Women's Medical College of Phila-
delphia, Pennsylvania, in 1867. The third black woman to re-
ceive a medical degree from an accredited medical school was
Susan Maria Smith, M.D., from New York Medical College for
Women, New York City, in 1870. Smith was valedictorian of her
class.

President authorized Union master to receive compensation not
exceeding $300 for slaves enlisting in the Union army, the
volunteer to be free.

(1864)

Letters of Phillis Wheatley, the Negro-slave poet of Boston, edited by Charles Deane and privately printed (reprinted from the Proceedings of the Massachusetts Historical Society 7:267-79).

Alexander Crummell, "The Responsibility of the First Fathers of a Country For Its Future Life and Character" and "God's Dealing with Nations and Peoples and the Lessons It Teaches," African Repository 40 (September 1864):257-67; (October 1864): 289-96; 44 (September 1867):257-63.

Alexander Crummell, Africa and America (Springfield, Mass., 1891); The Shades and the Lights of a Fifty Years' Ministry (c.1894) was an anniversary sermon preached in Washington 9 December 1894. Crummell was refused admission to the General Theological Seminary in New York because of his color. He was graduated from Queen's College, Cambridge, in 1853 and established the American Negro Academy in 1897.

Nilo Pecanha, of African ancestry, became President of the Republic of Brazil. He was born in Campos, in the state of Rio de Janeiro, 2 October, and completed his course of law in 1887.

James McKaye, The Emancipated Slave Face to Face with His Old Master, A Supplemental Report to Hon. Edwin M. Stanton, Secretary of War (New York: W. C. Bryant & Co.).

Samuel Gridley Howe, The Refugees from Slavery in Canada West, Report to the Freedmen's Inquiry Commission (Boston).

Lewis C. J. Lockwood and Charlotte Forten, Two Black Teachers During the Civil War. This book brought together the fascinating stories of two black teachers who began the tremendous task of educating ex-slaves under the Yankee missionary auspices before the end of the Civil War and before the establishment of the Freedman's Bureau.

Proceedings of the American Anti-Slavery Society at Its Third Decade, Held in the City of Philadelphia, Dec. 3rd & 4th, 1863. This report included reminiscenses of the movement by its outstanding black and white teachers. It also included an appendix, and a catalog of antislavery publications in America, 1750-1863; phonographic report by Henry M. Parkhurst (New York: American Anti-Slavery Society).

(1864)

George W. Carleton, ed., The Suppressed Book about Slavery!
An abolitionist indictment of slavery based on newspaper in-
terviews, prepared in 1857 (New York: published for Carleton).

Peter Clark, The Black Brigade of Cincinnati. After the
Emancipation Proclamation was announced, every effort was made
to keep blacks from serving in the armed forces of the Union.
The story of the black brigade of Cincinnati is the story of
one such military unit (Cincinnati).

James Willie Massie, America: The Origin of Her Present Conflict: Her Prospect for the Slave, and Her Claim for Anti-
Slavery Sympathy. Illustrated by Incidents of Travel, during
a Tour in the Summer of 1863, throughout the United States
from the Eastern Boundaries of Maine to the Mississippi (London: J. Snow).

Charles D. Drake, Union and Anti-Slavery Speeches: Delivered
During the Rebellion (Cincinnati: Applegate).

Hollis Read, The Negro Problem Solved: Or, Africa as She Was,
as She Is, and as She Shall Be; Her Curse and Her Cure (New
York: A. A. Constantine).

"The Condition and Character of Negroes in Africa," Methodist
Quarterly Review 46 (January):71-90.

Phillis Wheatley, Thoughts on His Excellency Major General Lee
Being Betray'd into the Hands of the Enemy by the Treachery of
a Pretended Friend. Proceedings of the Massachusetts Historical Society 7:166-67.

Phillis Wheatley, "Letters to Obour Tanner," Proceedings of
the Massachusetts Historical Society 7:267-79.

Frederick Douglass, "Third Decade of the American Anti-Slavery
Society," Liberator, 29 January.

Anon., Glorying in Tribulation; a Brief Memoir of Hannah
Carson, for Thirteen Years Deprived of the Use of All Her
Limbs (Philadelphia).

James Madison Bell, A Poem Entitled the Day and the War, Delivered 1 January 1864, at Platt's Hill. The poem was written
to celebrate the first anniversary of President Lincoln's

(1864)

Emancipation Proclamation (San Francisco). Bell was John Brown's chief helper in preparing for Harper's Ferry raid.

J. D. Green, Narrative of the Life of J. D. Green, a Runaway Slave, from Kentucky, Containing an Account of His Three Escapes, in 1839, 1846, and 1848 (Huddersfield).

Fugitive Slave Law of 1850 repealed.

Minnesota and Wisconsin voted against Negro suffrage.

Only six northern states allowed black men to vote: Maine, New Hampshire, Massachusetts, Vermont, Rhode Island, and New York. New York required property qualification.

Napoleon III abolished French slave traffic from Mozambique to Reunion and the Comoros.

1865

Slavery is abolished in the United States by the Thirteenth Amendment on 18 December. Slavery and involuntary servitude allowed only as punishment for crime.

The Freedmen's Bank was incorporated by Congress and had in its list of incorporators some of the greatest names in America including Peter Cooper, William Cullen Bryant, and John Jay. Yet the bank failed in 1874 owing the freedmen their first savings of over 3 million dollars.

Freedmen's Bureau established by Congress in the War Department. This Bureau of Refugees, Freedmen, and Abandoned Lands was given no money for salaries and expenses.

National Council of Congregational Churches recommended the raising of $250,000 for work among freedmen.

Prior to 1865, one seventh of blacks in the United States were free (Crisis 2, no. 1 [November 1915]:24).

Paul Jennings, A Colored Man's Reminiscences of James Madison (Brooklyn).

Frederick Douglass, "What the Black Man Wants," in The Equality of All Men before the Law, Claimed and Defended; In Speeches

(1865)

by Hon. William D. Kelley, Wendell Phillips, and Frederick
Douglass, and Letters from Elizur Wright and Wm. Heighton
(Boston):pp. 36-39.

Henry Highland Garnet, A Memorial Discourse . . . Delivered in
the Hall of the House of Representatives, Washington, D.C., on
Sabbath, 12 February 1865, with an introduction by James McCune
Smith (Philadelphia).

William Cooper Nell, "Farewell to the Liberator," Liberator,
29 December.

Frederick Douglass, "Lecture at the Dedication of the Douglass
Institute, Baltimore," Liberator, 13 October.

George Moses Horton, Naked Genius, a book of poems (Raleigh,
N.C.); "Pains of a Bachelor's Life, a poem," in Kemp P.
Battle, History of the University of North Carolina (1907),
1:604-5; "Pleasures of a Bachelor's Life, a poem," in Kemp P.
Battle, History of the University of North Carolina (1907),
1:604.

Lydia Maria Child, The Freedmen's Book. Originally used as a
textbook in schools attended by ex-slaves, this book contains
essays on slavery, black heroes, the abolition movement, and
many practical hints for everyday living (Boston: Ticknor &
Fields).

Carl Schurz, Report on the Condition of the South. Sent by
President Andrew Johnson to investigate conditions in the
South after the Civil War, Carl Schurz returned to Congress
with a report that made history as much as recorded it. It
was immediately seized by the Radicals in Congress and used
to promulgate their program of reconstruction. Washington,
Govt. Printing Office, 39th Congress, First Session, House,
Executive Document.

The United States Senate passed a motion permitting Boston
attorney John S. Rock to practice before the Supreme Court of
the United States. Rock was the first black man to be admitted
to practice before the high tribunal.

President Johnson announced his plan of reconstruction.

Confusion sown by slave trade and by increasing use of guns

(1865)

in raids and warfare continued to spread through western Tanzania and up the lower Zambezi into Central African lands.

New Ngoni states in Malawi.

Rise of European imperialist ambitions in Africa. At first hesitant and limited to a few coastal areas, the scramble for Africa developed as a rivalry between Britain and France, the two strongest European powers at that time. This rivalry drew in other European powers, including Germany, Italy, Belgium, Spain, and Portugal. Eventually they dediced to divide Africa among themselves.

Oliver O. Howard appointed Commissioner of Freedmen's Bureau.

In Lincoln's funeral procession, the Irish Immigrant Organization refused to march with blacks. New York's Council refused to permit blacks to march. It was only because of the intervention of the police commissioner that a place in the procession was assigned to blacks. Police protection was necessary to insure the safety of the black marchers.

1866

Civil Rights Bill to nullify the Black Codes passed over the veto of President Johnson; gave some civil rights to all persons born in the United States except Indians. This law eventually became the Fourteenth Amendment.

Edward G. Walker and Charles D. Mitchell, elected to the Massachusetts House of Representatives, were the first blacks to sit in an American legislative body.

Frederick Douglass, Three Addresses on Relations Subsisting between the White and Colored People of the United States (Washington).

Daniel Alexander Payne, The Semi-Centenary and the Retrospection of the African Meth. Episcopal Church in the United States of America (Baltimore).

James Madison Bell, An Anniversary Poem Entitled The Progress of Liberty . . . Delivered at the Celebration of the 3rd Anniversary of President Lincoln's Emancipation Proclamation (San Francisco).

(1866)

Jacob Rhodes, The Nation's Loss. A Poem on the Life and Death of the Hon. Abraham Lincoln (Newark).

Bill passed by Congress establishing universal male suffrage in District of Columbia, including Negroes, vetoed by President Johnson.

Race riots throughout the south; hundreds of blacks killed.

Fourteenth Amendment secured to the freedmen the right of citizenship; could not be deprived "of life, liberty, or property without due process" or denied "equal protection of the law."

Howard University organized and opened.

Act to continue the Freedmen's Bureau, which had charge of the loyal and suffering classes, black and white, in the southern states, passed over President Johnson's veto.

Blacks began to ask for suffrage. The Georgia convention in Augusta advocated a proposition to give those who could write and read well and possessed a certain property qualification the right of suffrage.

In all the trade union movements, blacks had either tacitly or in plain words been excluded from all participation but on 19 August 1866, the National Labor Union declared: "In this hour of the dark distress of labor, we call upon all laborers of what ever nationality, creed or color, skilled or unskilled, trade unionist and those now out of the union to join hands with us and each other to the end that poverty and all its attendant evils shall be abolished forever (Du Bois 1902, p. 154).

U.S. House of Representatives, Memphis Riots and Massacres. Report submitted by E. B. Washburne, Select Committee, 39th Congress, 1st Session, Report no. 101. On May 1 an outburst of violence against the black community of Memphis erupted. When the violence was brought under control two days later it was found that 48 persons had been killed (46 of them black), and 75 wounded. The Committee, after investigating the massacre, issued this report, which concluded that the Negroes played no active role after the first day, "except to be killed and abused."

(1866)

Bedford (Commander) Pim, The Negro and Jamaica, read before
the Anthropological Society of London, 1 February (London:
Trubner and Co.).

Edward Mathews, The Autobiography of the Rev. E. Mathews, The
"Father Dickson" of Mrs. Stowe's "Dred." With a preface by
Handel Cossham (London: Houlston and Wright).

William Parker, "The Freedman's Story," in two parts, Atlantic
Monthly 17, part 1 (February):152-60; Part 2 (March):276-95.

John Dungy, Narrative of the Reverend John Dungy (Rochester).

The Life of James Mars, a Slave, Born and Sold in Connecticut
(Hartford: Case, Lockwood & Co.).

1867

Thomas Wentworth Higginson, "Negro Spirituals," Atlantic
Monthly (June). Higginson recorded the words of thirty-six
hymns and two secular songs.

B. Clark, The Past, Present, and Future, in Prose and Poetry
(Toronto).

William Francis Allen, Charles Pickard Ware, and Lucy McKim
Garrison, Slave Songs of the United States, with music and
words of more than a hundred songs.

Lorenzo D. Blackson, The Rise and Progress of the Kingdoms of
Light and Darkness, or, The Reigns of King Alpha and the
Abadon (Philadelphia). King Alpha creates Adam and Eve and
puts them in charge of Earth. All goes well until King Abadon,
alias Satan is driven out of Heaven along with the wicked
angels whom he has led in a revolt against King Alpha, succeeds
in tempting Adam and Eve to disobedience (Loggins 1931, p.
306).

Z. C. Whatley, the president of the National Labor Congress,
which met in Chicago with 200 delegates present, reported "The
emancipation of the slaves has placed us in a new position,
and the question now arises, What labor position shall they
now occupy? They will begin to learn and to think for themselves, and they will soon resort to mechanical pursuits and
thus come in contact with white labor. It is necessary that

they should not undermine it, therefore the best thing that they can do is to form trades unions, and thus work in harmony with the whites" (Du Bois 1902, p. 154).

The Negro in the American Rebellion: His Heroism and His Fidelity, by William Wells Brown (Boston). Relates the role of the black soldier in the Revolutionary War and the War of 1812.

Act passed over veto of President Johnson ordering Negro suffrage in District of Columbia.

William Wells Brown, Clotelle; or the Colored Heroine, a Tale of the Southern States (Boston).

Benjamin Tucker Tanner, An Apology for African Methodism (Baltimore); In Memoriam, Dedicated to the Late Prof. O. V. Catto (n.d.).

Alexander Crummell, "God's Dealing with Nations and Peoples, and the Lessons It Teaches. A Sermon Preached in the Methodist Church, Monrovia, at the Anniversary of the Liberian Missionary Society, 21 January 1867," African Repository 44 (September):257-63.

U.S. House of Representatives, New Orleans Riots of July 30, 1866: 39th Congress, 2nd Session, Report no. 16. On 30 July 1866, a bloody riot broke out in New Orleans. This was another example of the determination of the Radical Republicans to bring about Negro suffrage, and the resistance on the part of Southerners. This Report by the Select Committee is testimony taken on this event. It makes it effectively clear that the local police were responsible for the bloodshed which resulted in some 200 casualties--almost entirely Negro and white Unionists.

Atlanta University received its charter.

Patents Issued to Black Americans:
    Dietz, W. A., Shoe, April 30, Pat. No. 64,206
    Lee, H., Animal Trap, Feb. 12, Pat. No. 61,941

1868

Lindley Spring, The Negro at Home: An Inquiry After His

(1868)

Capacity for Self-government and the Government of Whites. . . .
(New York: the author).

Lewis H. Putnam, The Review of the Revolutionary Elements of
the Rebellion, and of the Aspect of Reconstruction; with a
Plan to Restore Harmony between the Two Races in the Southern
States (Brooklyn).

Esteban Montejo, Autobiography of a Runaway Slave (New York).

Behind the Scenes: Thirty Years a Slave and Four Years in the
White House, by Elizabeth Hobbs Keckley (1824-1907) (New York,
1868).

Behind the Seams by a Nigger Woman who took in Work from Mrs.
Lincoln and Mrs. Davis (New York: The National News Company).
A satire on Elizabeth Keckley's Behind the Scenes (1868).

Black voters numbering 703,000 registered during a year as
compared with 627,000 whites.

Revolt of colored citizens of Panama.

After this date children of slave mothers in Cuba declared
free.

1868-1963

William Edward Burghardt Du Bois.

1869

Fifteenth Amendment: the right to vote shall not be denied
or abridged on account of race, color, or previous condition
of servitude.

Assembly of the insurrection in Cuba issued decree proclaiming
abolition of slavery.

Lisbon made all slaves libertos--slaves who would be paid and
treated as workers until moment of freedom.

The famous diamond, the Star of Ethiopia, was found in
Griqualand and changed hands first for 11,000 pounds sterling
and then for 25,000. The British arranged to have Griqualand

declared part of Cape Colony.

Harriet Tubman, Scenes in the Life of Harriet Tubman, as Told by Sarah Bradford (Auburn, N.Y.: W. J. Moses).

Gilbert Haven, National Sermons, Speeches, and Letters on Slavery and Its War 1850–1868 (Boston: Lee and Shepard).

Samuel J. May, Some Recollections of our Anti-Slavery Conflict. A northern minister and reformer described his abolitionist activities, including an early, bitter conflict over school integration in Connecticut (Boston: Fields, Osgood & Co.).

Frances Ellen Watkins Harper, Moses: A Story of the Nile. A narrative, in verse, of the life and adventures of Moses.

Autobiography of Rev. Francis Frederick, of Virginia, born 1809.

The Knights of Labor was founded in Philadelphia and held its first national convention in 1876. For a long time it was a secret organization, but it declared from the first that it recognized no distinctions of "race, creed or color." Nevertheless admission in all cases was subject to a vote of the local assembly where the candidate applied and at first it required only three black balls to reject an applicant (Du Bois 1902, pp. 154, 155).

Benjamin Tanner Tucker, The Negro's Origin: and Is the Negro Cursed? (Philadelphia). Attempted to show that the black man was not a mere servant and observer in ancient cultures (Loggins 1931, p. 299).

John Willis Menard, "Speech Delivered in the United States House of Representatives, 27 February 1869," Congressional Globe, Fortieth Congress, Third Session, pp. 168–85.

At the fourth annual conference of the National Labor Union in Philadelphia there were 142 representatives of whom 9 were blacks. It was decided that blacks should form their separate unions and send delegates to future conferences. The Colored National Labor Union was organized in Washington, D.C. Isaac Myers was elected president. It recommended cooperatives, loan associations, and the purchase of land.

(1869)

Race riots in Louisiana: New Orleans, Opelousas, St. Bernard Parish.

Sons of Freedom of the State of Minnesota met in convention in St. Paul. Proceedings of the convention . . . in celebration of the anniversary of emancipation, and the reception of the electoral franchise, on the first of January (St. Paul: Press Printing Company).

1869–1872

Frederick Douglass edited and conducted the weekly New National Era.

c.1870

An Address Delivered at the Laying of the Corner Stone of St. Andrew's Church, Buchanan, Bassa County, Liberia, West Africa, on the 24th February, 1870, by Alexander Crummell (Preston, England).

1870

Patents Issued to Black Americans:
    Elkins, T., Dining, Ironing Table, and Quilting Frame Combined, 22 February, Pat. No. 100,020
    West, J. W., Wagon, 18 October, Pat. No. 108,419
    Spears, H., Portable Shield for Infantry, 27 December, Pat. No. 110,599

James Madison Bell, A Poem Entitled the Triumph of Liberty; delivered 7 April 1870, on the occasion of the grand celebration of the final ratification of the Fifteenth Amendment to the Constitution of the United States (Detroit).

Hiram Rhoades Revels, "Speech Delivered in the United States Senate, March 16, 1870," Congressional Globe, Forty-first Congress, Second Session, pp. 1986–88. Revels was the first black United States Senator (Mississippi, 1870).

Blacks had at least 10 newspapers; in 1880, 31; in 1890, 154.

Lobengula succeeded Umsilikatski in Matabeleland (Rhodesia, now Zimbabwe).

Edward Bouchet received a doctorate in physics at Yale. Daedalus, Future of Negro College, p. 684.

(1871)

Act in Cuba gave freedom to slaves who had served under
Spanish flag and those who were over sixty.

United States population, approx. 38.5 million of whom 4.9
million were black.

Bill for gradual abolition of slavery in the Spanish colonies
presented to the Spanish Cortes.

American Anti-Slavery Society dissolved.

Sir Samuel Baker was commissioned to suppress the slave trade
in upper Nile region from Khartum to Gondokoro.

Hiram R. Revels, first black United States Senator from
Mississippi.

The Fifteenth Amendment granting blacks the right to vote was
ratified 30 March.

1870-1879

Joseph Hayne Rainey served in the United States Congress. He
made speeches in favor of legislation designed to enforce the
Fourteenth Amendment, the Ku Klux Act, and the Civil Rights
Bill. One of his speeches in Congress eulogized Charles
Sumner.

1871

Johns Hopkins declared in a codicil to his will dated 31 October "that the trustees of 'The Johns Hopkins Hospital' shall
apply to the legislature of Maryland for such additional
authority as they may require to enable them to educate the
orphan and destitute colored children by them received into
their charge, and shall use and employ such portion of the
nett [sic] income of the property (not exceeding one fourth
part of thereof however) (estimated at approximately eight
million dollars) devised and bequeathed to them by me, as may
be necessary to enable them to perform the duty of receiving
caring for and educating such orphan and destitute colored
children; and I do further direct that, when such authority
is obtained, the said trustees shall expend such portion of
the said one fourth part of said income as may be necessary in
the reception, care and education of said orphan and destitute

(1871)

colored children. And I also declare it to be my wish that
my said trustees shall also apply for such additional authority
as they may require, to enable them to provide proper and respective employment for such orphan and destitute colored
children so by them received and cared for, when such children
shall arrive at a suitable age. . . ."

Patents Issued to Black Americans:
    Bell, L., Locomotive smoke stack, 23 May, Pat. No. 115,153

Francis E. W. Harper, Poems (Philadelphia).

Joseph H. Rainey, "Speech on the Enforcement of the Fourteenth
Amendment, Delivered in the United States House of Representatives, 1 April 1871," Congressional Globe, Forty-Second Congress, First Session, pp. 393-95.

The law of Rio Branco (Brazil) enacted that all children of
slaves were born free, but were to serve as apprentices until
twenty-one years of age.

A teenager in Louisville, Kentucky, 12 May, staged a sit-in
on a segregated horse-drawn street car; after other blacks
joined the protest, the company agreed to integrate.

1872

Frederick Douglass nominated for Vice-Presidency of the United
States by a Socialist Party.

Act provided for discontinuance of Freedmen's Bureau.

Bill for abolition of slavery in Puerto Rico, for compensation,
brought into Cortes.

Supreme Court decision confirmed validity of slave contracts
entered into before Emancipation Proclamation.

Narrative of the Life of John Quincy Adams When in Slavery
and Now as a Freeman (Harrisburg, Penn.: Sieg, Printer &
Stationer).

Francis Ellen Watkins Harper, Sketches of Southern Life, a
series of poems (Philadelphia).

The Southern Workman founded by General Samuel C. Armstrong
and published monthly by the Hampton Normal and Agricultural
Institute, established in 1868 by the American Missionary
Society.

William Still, The Underground Rail Road. The only surviving
complete record of any station of the Underground Railroad.
Compiled by the Negro secretary of the Philadelphia "station,"
it details the hardships and dangers with which escaping
slaves were faced and it gives a moving portrait of the determination of individuals to gain their freedom. The list of
Underground Railroad operators given by Siebert contained 128
names of blacks. In Canada and in the northern United States
there was a secret society known as the League of Freedom
which especially worked to help slaves run away. Harriet
Tubman was one of the most energetic of these slave conductors
and brought away several thousand slaves. William Lambert, a
black man, was reputed between 1827 and 1862 to have aided in
the escape of 30,000 (Philadelphia).

Frederick Douglass, U.S. Grant and the Colored People (Washington).

Alexander Crummell, "Obligations of the American Black Man for
the Redemption of Africa . . . To Colored Students, Undergrad-
uates, at Xenia, Lincoln, Howard and Other Colleges in the
United States of America, on Matters Pertaining to the Conversion of Africa," African Repository 48 (February):55-61;
(June):162-68; (August):234-38.

Joseph H. Rainey, "Speech on Education, Delivered in the
United States House of Representatives, February 3, 1872,"
Appendix to the Congressional Globe, Forty-Second Congress,
Second Session, pp. 15-17.

Patents Issued to Black Americans:
    Elkins, T., Chamber commode, 9 January, Pat. No. 122,518
    Byrd, T. J., Improvement in holders for reins for horses,
    6 February, Pat. No. 123,328
    Byrd, T. J., Apparatus for detaching (horses) from
    carriages, 19 March, Pat. No. 124,790
    Byrd, T. J., Improvement in neck yokes for wagons, 30
    April, Pat. No. 126,181
    Marshall, T. J., Fire extinguisher, 26 May, Pat. No.
    125,063

(1872–1876)

McCoy, E., Lubricator for steam engines, 2 July, Pat. No. 129,843 and 6 August, Pat. No. 130,305
Bell, L., Dough kneader, 10 December, Pat. No. 133,823

1872–1876

Blacks were kept from voting by force and intimidation; whites were motivated to vote as employers wished by engendering race hate and fear. Stringent laws on vagrancy, guardianship, labor contracts were enacted. As a result of discretion given judges and juries in cases of petty crime, blacks were arrested on the slightest pretext and the labor of convicts leased to private parties.

1873

Richard T. Greener, black graduate of Harvard College, employed as professor of metaphysics at the University of South Carolina.

Howard University Library received the antislavery collection of Lewis Tappan, comprising about 2,000 printed items on the American Colonization Society and its activities, the African slave trade and its suppression, and on the abolition of slavery. Included also were writings of black men of the eighteenth and nineteenth centuries.

Slavery is abolished in Puerto Rico.

Patents Issued to Black Americans:
McCoy, E., Lubricator, 27 May, Pat. No. 139,407

Frederick Douglass, Address Delivered . . . at the Third Annual Fair of the Tennessee Colored Agricultural and Mechanical Association on Thursday, 18 September 1873, at Nashville, Tennessee (Washington).

Gold mask captured by British from Kofi Kakari, King of Ashanti.

The Sultan of Zanzibar signed a treaty with Great Britain for the abolition of the slave trade.

James Williams, The Life and Adventures of James Williams, a Fugitive Slave: with a Full Description of the Underground

Railroad. James Williams describes his slave life in Maryland, his escape to Pennsylvania in 1838, his work for the
Underground Railroad, his experiences as a California gold
miner, a businessman in California and Nevada, and a worker
for the African Methodist Episcopal Church in Sacramento (San
Francisco: Women's Union Print).

Islay Walden, Walden's Miscellaneous Poems, Which the Author
Wishes to Dedicate to the Cause of Education, and Humanity,
2d ed. (Washington). Walden, born a slave in North Carolina,
we are told, derived his knowledge from hearing hymns sung in
church. After the Civil War, Walden wandered through Pennsylvania and New Jersey. A church in New Brunswick, New
Jersey, raised funds to send him to Howard University where
he may have been a student when he published his first volume
of poetry (Loggins 1931, p. 333).

The History of William Webb, by William Webb, born 1836
(Detroit: Edbert, Hocktra).

Ellwood Griest, John and Mary: Or, The Fugitive Slaves; a
Tale of South-Eastern Pennsylvania (Lancaster: Inquirer
Printing & Publishing Co.).

Harry (Henry) Bleby, Josiah: The Maimed Fugitive: A True
Tale.

Joel Tyler Headley, The Great Riots of New York, 1712-1873;
Including a Full and Complete Account of the Four Days' Riot
of 1863.

1874

William C. Nell, Negro antislavery worker and author, died.

Charlotte L. Forten, "The Angel's Visit," in William Wells
Brown, The Rising Son (Boston):p. 475.

Richard T. Greener, Charles Sumner, Benjamin Williams Arnett,
ed. (Charleston, S.C.).

Proceedings of the Semi-Centenary Celebration of the African
Methodist Episcopal Church of Cincinnati, held in Allen
Temple, 8, 9, and 10 February (n.d.).

(1874)

David Augustus Straker, Citizenship, Its Right and Duties-- Woman Suffrage; a Lecture Delivered . . . at Hillsdale, Washington, D.C. 13, 14 April 1874 (Washington).

Whites rioted against blacks in Vicksburg, Mississippi, killing thirty-five.

Richard H. Cain. "Speech on Civil Rights, Delivered before the United States House of Representatives, 10 January 1874," Congressional Record 2:565-67.

James T. Rapier, "Speech on Civil Rights, Delivered in the United States House of Representatives, June 9, 1874," Congressional Record 2:4782-86.

William Wells Brown, The Rising Son, or The Antecedents and advancement of the Colored Race (Boston). Reprints much of the material in The Black Man and the Negro in the American Rebellion.

Archibald H. Grimke received a law degree from Harvard in 1874.

Lewis Hayden, A Letter from Lewis Hayden, of Boston, Massachusetts, to Hon. Judge Simms, of Savannah, Georgia (Boston).

Robert Brown Elliott, Congressman from South Carolina, defense of the Civil Rights Bill, Congressional Record 2 (6 January):407-10.

Robert Brown Elliott, Sumner Memorial Meeting, Oration Delivered in Faneuil Hall, April 14, 1874, under the Auspices of the Colored Citizens of Boston, with the Address of Edward G. Walker, President of the Meeting, and a Sketch of the Proceedings, 1874 (Boston).

Charles H. Jones, Africa: The History of Exploration and Adventure, As Given in the Leading Authorities from Herodotus to Livingstone (New York: Hurst & Co., 1881; first published in 1875).

1875

Patents Issued to Black Americans:
Ashbourne, A. P., Process for preparing coconut for domestic use, 1 June, Pat. No. 163,962

Ashbourne, A. P., Biscuit cutter, 30 November, Pat. No. 170,460
Nash, H. H., Life preserving stool, 5 October, Pat. No. 168,510
Fisher, D. A., Joiners' clamp, 20 April, Pat. No. 162,281

Civil Rights Act (Sumner's Bill) decreed privilege of equal rights and enjoyment in inns, public conveyances, theatres, and other public places of amusement without distinction of color. It forbade exclusion of Negroes from jury duty.

Alexander Crummell, The Social Principle among a People, and Its Bearing on Their Progress and Development. A Discourse Delivered on Thanksgiving Day, 25 Nov. 1875, in Saint Mary's Chapel, Washington, D.C. (n.d.).

Olive Gilbert, Narrative of Sojourner Truth, a Bondswoman of Olden Time, Emancipated by the New York State Legislature in the Early Part of the Present Century; with a History of Her Labors and Correspondence Drawn from Her "Book of Life" (Boston: author).

Patrick Healy resigned after nine years as the President of Georgetown University in Washington, D.C.

Between 1875 and the turn of the century, Michael Healy was an important representative of the United States government between San Francisco and the Alaska Territory. He was born in Georgia in 1840, the acknowledged son of Michael Morris Healy, an Irish immigrant planter, and Eliza Clark Healy, his slave and wife. Michael followed in the footsteps of his brothers James Hugh, Patrick, and Sherwood in attending the College of the Holy Cross in Worcester, Massachusetts.

Blanche K. Bruce of Mississippi served in the United States Senate from 1875 to 1881, the only black during Reconstruction to serve a regular term in the Senate. Seven blacks were elected to the 44th Congress as Representatives: John R. Lynch, Mississippi; J. T. Walls, Florida; Jeremiah Haralson, Alabama; John A. Hyman, North Carolina; Charles E. Nash, Louisiana; J. M. Rainey and Robert Smalls, South Carolina.

1876

Mirambo of Unyamwezi in western Tanzania was at height of his power.

(1876)

It was clear that the American South was determined to maintain
white supremacy at all cost. They were effectively assisted
in this endeavor by the outcome of the disputed presidential
election in 1876, in which Rutherford B. Hayes was the Republican candidate and Samuel Tilden was the Democratic candidate.
This disputed election was settled in Congress by the Compromise of 1877, in which Hayes was finally declared the win-
ner. In effect, the Compromise of 1877 saw the Republican
Party (the so-called Party of Emancipation) abandon the Negroes
to former slaveholders. It was felt by the party leaders to
be necessary to avert another civil war. Nevertheless, for
all practical purposes this compromise signaled a return toward
slavery which was to characterize the relations between blacks
and whites for decades to follow. The remaining troops were
withdrawn from the South, and the South was accorded complete
home rule and other political favors. The most important
favor to the Southerners was the promise that the compromise
brought in the area of race: "It did assure the dominant
whites political autonomy and nonintervention in matters of
race policy . . ." (Woodward 1951, p. 246).

Henry George Tuke, compiler, The Fugitive Slave Circulars. A
short account of the case of Sommersett [sic] the Negro, and
of Lord Mansfield's celebrated judgment, under which slavery
in England received its death blow. Also of Forbes v. Cochrane,
extending the doctrine of Sommersett v. Steuart to slaves on
board British public ships, with a note of other cases on the
subject. Full reprints of Sommersett v. Steuart, and Forbes
v. Cochrane. Copies of the original and amended Fugitive
slave circulars, with a reference to the slave trade note of
1873, and a note as to the right of searching slave vessels
(London: Stanford).

Patents Issued to Black Americans:
    Fisher, D. A., Furniture castor, 14 March, Pat. No.
    174,794
    McCoy, E., Steam cylinder lubricator, 1 February, Pat. No.
    173,032
    McCoy, E., Steam cylinder lubricator, 4 July, Pat. No.
    179,585
    Carrington, T. A., Range, 25 July, Pat. No. 180,323

Levi Coffin, Reminiscences of Levi Coffin, the reputed president of the Underground Railroad; a brief history of the
labors of a lifetime in behalf of the slave, with the stories

of numerous fugitives who gained their freedom through his instrumentality, and many other incidents (Cincinnati: Western Trade Society).

Blanche Kelso Bruce, "An Address, Delivered in the United States Senate, 3 March 1876," Congressional Record 4:2101-4. A plea for civil rights.

Uncle Tom's Story of His Life: An Autobiography of the Rev. Josiah Henson (Mrs. Harriet Beecher Stowe's "Uncle Tom") from 1789-1883 (London); an enlarged version of Truth, Stranger than Fiction (1858).

George Washington Williams, The African Negro, from 1776 to 1876, Delivered 4 July 1876, at Avondale, Ohio (Cincinnati).

Frederick Douglass, "Oration of Frederick Douglass," in Inaugural Ceremonies of the Freedmen's Memorial Monument to Abraham Lincoln, Washington City, 14 April 1876 (St. Louis): pp. 16-26.

1877

The case of Hall v. de Ceur stated that a state could not prohibit segregation on a common carrier; in the case of Louisville, New Orleans, and Texas Railroad v. Mississippi (1880), the Court ruled that a state could constitutionally require segregation on carriers. These rulings of the Supreme Court foreshadowed the Plessy v. Ferguson case in 1896 when the Court ruled that separate facilities for Negroes and whites were not a violation of the constitutional guarantees of the Thirteenth and Fourteenth Amendments. "If one race be inferior to the other socially, the Constitution of the United States cannot put them upon the same plane." This ruling set the pattern for attitudes toward treatment of Negroes in the United States that still persist. It became known as the "separate but equal" ruling of the Supreme Court, and the nation became more concerned with the separation of Negroes than with equality.

Islay Walden, Walden's Sacred Poems; hymns in perfectly executed meter with a sketch of his life (Loggins 1931, p. 333).

Albery A. Whitman, Not a Man and Yet a Man. More than 250 closely printed pages. Opens by introducing Rodney, a slave.

(1877)

Rodney rescues Dora, who is taken captive by the Indians, and she falls in love with him. Rodney is turned over to a slave trader to be sold to a slave owner in Florida where he falls in love with another slave. They finally get to Canada and freedom (Loggins 1931, pp. 388ff.).

Early Recollections and Life of Dr. James Still, by James Still, born 1812 (Philadelphia).

1878

Patents Issued to Black Americans:
   Taylor, B. H., Rotary engine, 23 April, Pat. No. 202,888
   Dorsey, O., Door-holding device, 10 December, Pat. No. 210,764
   Lavalette, W. A., Printing press, 17 September, Pat. No. 208,208
   Winters, J. R., Fire escape ladder, 7 May, Pat. No. 203,517
   Davis, W. R., Jr., Library table, 24 September, Pat. No. 208,378

The Colored Cadet at West Point: Autobiography of Lieut. Henry Ossian Flipper, U.S.A., First Graduate of Color from the United States Military Academy, by Henry Ossian Flipper, 1856-1940 (New York: Homer Lee & Co.).

James Trotter, Music and Some Highly Musical People (Boston).

1879

Patents Issued to Black Americans:
   Winters, J. R., Fire escape ladder, 8 April, Pat. No. 214,224
   Binga, M. W., Street sprinkling apparatus, 22 July, Pat. No. 217,843
   Balles, Wm., Ladder scaffold support, 5 August, Pat. No. 218,154
   Elkins, T., Refrigerating apparatus, 4 November, Pat. No. 221,222

The Zulu were finally defeated at Ulundi.

William Lloyd Garrison died.

Frederick Douglass, Speech on the Death of William Lloyd

Garrison, at the Garrison Memorial Meeting in the 15th Street Presbyterian Church, Monday 2 June 1879 (Washington: n.d.).

William H. Curd, An Apology for the American People; a Reason and an Apology for American Slavery; a Duty (Chicago: B. Hand & Co.).

Martin R. Delany, Principia of Ethnology: The Origin of Races and Color, With an Archaeological Compendium of Ethiopian and Egyptian Civilization, from Years of Comparative Examination and Enquiry (Philadelphia, 2d ed., 1880). Book attempted to show that the essential properties of color are the same for the color of the whitest and the blackest.

J. Willis Menard, the first black elected to Congress, published Lays in Summer Lands, a collection of forty-six poems (Washington, D.C.).

William Lloyd Garrison, "A Eulogy by Wendell Phillips at Garrison's Funeral," Old South Leaflets no. 79, 28 May 1879.

"Angelina Grimke Weld," Unitarian Review 12 (December):671ff.

Jacob Stroyer, Sketches of My Life in the South (Salem, Mass.: Salem Press). Stroyer lived from 1846-1908.

Autobiography of John Malvin, 1795-1880. A narrative containing an authentic account of his fifty years' struggle in the state of Ohio in behalf of the American slave and the equal rights of all men before the law without reference to race or color (Cleveland: Leader Printing Company).

1880

Patents Issued to Black Americans:
   Waller, J. N., Shoemaker's cabinet or bench, 3 February, Pat. No. 244,253
   Scrottron, S. R., Adjustable window cornice, 17 February, Pat. No. 224,732
   Ashbourne, A. P., Refining coconut oil, 27 July, Pat. No. 230,518
   Pinn, T. B., File holder, 17 August, Pat. No. 231,355
   Johnson, P., Eye protector, 2 November, Pat. No. 234,039

Spain abolished slavery; became effective in 1886.

(1880)

Life of Norvel Blair, a Negro Citizen of Morris, Grundy County, Illinois (Joliet, Ill.: Joliet Daily Record Steam Press).

The Life, Experience, and Gospel Labors of the Rt. Rev. Richard Allen (n.p., n.d.).

My Southern Home: or, The South and Its People, by William Wells Brown (Boston). Series of made-up memoirs of his childhood and impressions of his travels in the South after the Civil War.

Richard T. Greener, "The Emigration of Colored Citizens from the Southern States," Journal of Social Science 11 (May):22-35. Greener was the first black graduate of Harvard College, a lawyer, and United States Consul in Vladivostok.

Frederick Douglass, "The Negro Exodus from the Gulf States," Journal of Social Science, 11 (May):1-21.

Alexander W. Wayman, My Recollections of African M.E. Ministers, or, Forty Years' Experience in the African Methodist Episcopal Church (Philadelphia).

1881

Life and Times of Frederick Douglass. Douglass relates his early life as a slave, his escape, his life up to 1881. Introduction by George L. Ruffin (Hartford, Conn.: Park Publishing Co.).

Patents Issued to Black Americans:
    Wormley, James, Life saving apparatus, 24 May, Pat. No. 242,091
    Campbell, W. S., Self-setting animal trap, 30 August, Pat. No. 240,309
    Johnson, P., Swinging chairs, 15 November, Pat. No. 249,530
    Nichols and Latimer, Electric lamp, 13 September, Pat. No. 247,007

William Saunders Scarborough, first recognized black classical scholar, author of First Lessons in Greek; Adapted to the Greek Grammars of Goodwin and Hadley, and Designed as an Introduction to Xenophon's Anabasis and Similar Greek (New York and Chicago).

(1882)

Frederick Douglass, <u>John Brown. An Address . . . at the Four-</u>
<u>teenth Anniversary of Storer College, Harper's Ferry, West</u>
<u>Virginia, 30 May 1881</u> (Dover, N.H.). Proceeds to the founding
of a John Brown Professorship in Storer College.

Frederick Douglass, "The Color Line," <u>North American Review</u>
132 (June):567-77.

Mohammed Ahmad, a black Kushite born in Dongola Province,
announced publicly that he was the Mahdi. He led the Sudan in
revolt, determined to resist a hated religion and Egyptian
oppression.

David Smith, <u>Biography of Rev. David Smith, of the A.M.E.</u>
<u>Church: Being a complete History Embracing Over Sixty Years'</u>
<u>Labor in the Advancement of the Redeemer's Kingdom on Earth,</u>
<u>including "The History of the Origin and Development of Wil-</u>
<u>berforce University."</u> Xenia, Ohio: Xenia <u>Gazette</u>. Smith was
a former slave in Maryland. The history of Wilberforce is
written by Daniel Payne.

c.1882

George Washington Williams published his <u>History of the Negro</u>
<u>Race in America, 1619-1880</u> (New York & London: G. P. Putnam's
Sons).

1882

Alexander W. Wayman, <u>Cyclopaedia of African Methodism</u> (Baltimore).

John Jasper, <u>The Sun Do Move!</u> The Celebrated Theory of The
Sun's Rotation around the Earth, as Preached by Rev. John
Jasper, of Richmond, Va., With a Memoir of His Life (New
York).

Theophilus Gould Steward, <u>Genesis Re-read; or, The Latest Con-</u>
<u>clusions of Physical Science, Viewed in Their Relation to the</u>
<u>Mosaic Record</u>, to which is annexed an important chapter on the
direct evidences of Christianity, by Bishop J. P. Campbell,
D.D., LI.D. (Philadelphia). An attempt to reconcile the
Biblical story of creation and the theory of evolution.

Alexander Crummell, <u>The Eulogy on Henry Highland Garnet,</u>

(1882)

D.D. . . . Delivered . . . 4 May 1882 (Washington).

Joseph T. Wilson, Emancipation: Its Course and Progress from 1481 B.C. to A.D. 1875; voice of a New Race. An attempt to give a general survey of the history of blacks from 1481 B.C. to 1875 A.D. It is an enlargement of a pamphlet with the same name published in 1881 (Loggins 1931, pp. 272, 400).

Alexander Crummell, The Greatness of Christ (New York). A volume of twenty sermons.

John F. Slater gave to a board of trustees, $1 million for "the uplifting of the lately emancipated population of the Southern States and their posterity, by conferring upon them the blessings of Christian education" (Du Bois 1902, p. 39).

Patents Issued to Black Americans:
    Little, E., Bridie-bit, 7 March, Pat. No. 254,000
    Richardson, A. C., Hame fastener, 14 March, Pat. No. 255,022
    Tregoning and Latimer, Globe supporter for electric lamps, 21 March, Pat. No. 255,212
    Purvis, W. B., Bag fastener, 25 April, Pat. No. 250,850
    Latimer, L. H., Manufacturing carbons, 17 June, Pat. No. 252,386
    McCoy, E., Lubricator, 28 March, Pat. No. 255,443
    McCoy, E., Lubricator, 18 July, Pat. No. 261,166

1883

Patents Issued to Black Americans:
    McCoy, E., Lubricator, 9 January, Pat. No. 270,238
    Scottron, S. R., Cornice, 16 January, Pat. No. 270,851
    Purvis, W. B., Hand stamp, 27 February, Pat. No. 273,149
    Reynolds, H. H., Window ventilator for railroad cars, 3 April, Pat. No. 275,271
    Cooper, J., Shutter and fastening, 1 May, Pat. No. 276,562
    Washington, Wade, Corn husking machine, 14 August, Pat. No. 283,173
    Bailey, L. C., Combined truss and bandage, 25 September, Pat. No. 285,545
    Thomas, S. E., Waste trap, 16 October, Pat. No. 286,746

George Washington Williams wrote a letter to the New York Globe, published in its issue 16 June, proposing that an

(1883)

American Negro History Society be organized. Societies with a combination literary-historical outlook had existed among blacks since 1840 but they were local rather than regional or national.

Mohammed Ahmad massacred the army of the Englishman Hicks Pasha, 10,000 strong at Chekan. He defeated the governor of Fashoda in the mountains of southern Kordofan and then seized Kordofan.

John Mercer Langston, Freedom and Citizenship, a volume of selected speeches and addresses from 1858-1880 (Washington, D.C.).

Life and Public Service of Martin R. Delany, by Frances E. Rollin Whipper (who wrote under the name Frank A. Rollin) included, "International Policy towards the African Race" (pp. 313-27); "A Speech Delivered in Cleveland in 1854" (pp.· 327-67); "Reflections on the War" (pp. 309-13) (Boston).

Frederick Douglass, "The Condition of the Freedman," Harper's Weekly 27 (8 December):/82-83.

Frederick Douglass, Address . . . Delivered . . . 16 April 1883. On the Twenty-First Anniversary of Emancipation in the District of Columbia (Washington).

The Life of William J. Brown (1814-1885), of Providence, Rhode Island: with Personal Recollections of Incidents in Rhode Island. He was a shoemaker and Baptist minister (Providence: Angell & Co.).

Supreme Court decision declared the Supplementary Civil Rights Act of 1875, giving colored persons equal privileges in hotels, inns, theatres, and public conveyances, unconstitutional except in the District of Columbia and the territories.

C. W. Larison, Silvia Du Bois, a biography of a slave who whipt her mistress and gained her freedom (Ringos, N.J.: C. W. Larison.

William Still, Underground Rail Records, Revised Edition, with a Life of the Author, Narrating the Hardships, Hairbreadth Escapes and Death Struggles of the Slaves in their Efforts for Freedom (Philadelphia).

(1883)

R. C. Smedley, History of the Underground Railroad in Chester and the Neighboring Counties of Pennsylvania. The first effort by a nonparticipant to evaluate the working of the famous railroad to freedom. It included many source documents vital to an understanding of the times (Lancaster, Penn.: Office of the Journal).

Lydia Maria Child, Letters of Lydia Maria Child, a leading children's writer of her day and a staunch antislavery disciple. This book reveals many hidden aspects of the crusade to which she dedicated her life (Boston & New York: Houghton, Mifflin & Co.).

Alexander Crummell, A Defense of the Negro Race in America, from the Assaults and Charges of Rev. J. L. Tucker, D.D., of Jackson, Miss., in His Paper before the "Church Congress" of 1882, on "The Relations of the Church to the Colored Race." Prepared and published at the request of the colored clergy of the Protestant Episcopal Church (Washington).

1884

Edwin Archer Randolph, The Life of John Jasper, Pastor of the Sixth Mt. Zion Baptist Church, Richmond, Va., from His Birth to the Present Time; with His Theory on the Rotation of the Sun (Richmond).

Benjamin Tucker Tanner, An Outline of Our History and Our Government for African Methodist Churchmen Ministerial and Lay (Philadelphia).

George Washington Williams, The Negro as a Political Problem (Boston: Oration).

James Walker Hood, The Negro in the Christian Pulpit; or, The Two Characters and Two Destinies, as Delivered in Twenty-One Practical Sermons (Raleigh).

John Jamison Moore, compiler, History of the A.M.E. Zion Church, in America. Founded in 1796, in the City of New York (York, Penn.).

Howard University Dental School established.

The Founding of the Congo Free State was zealously fostered by Leopold of Belgium and in 1908, it was annexed to Belgium.

Black Chronology

The "scramble" for African colonies was on and within a quarter of a century Africa was virtually in the hands of Europe. In this division the British Empire gained a network of possessions extending from the Anglo-Egyptian Sudan down to South Africa, with valuable holdings on the East Coast and in Somaliland. France was next with a larger area, but a smaller population. Her spoils reached from Morocco and Algeria, including the Algerian Sahara, to the French Congo, and on the Eastern Coast comprised Madagascar and French Somaliland. Germany, late in entering the game of colonization, contrived none the less to become mistress of four very valuable colonies: Togoland, Kamerun, South-West Africa, and East Africa. Italy's and Spain's possessions were much smaller, embracing, for the former, Eritrea and Italian Somaliland, and for the latter, Rio de Oro and the Muni River Settlements.

Patents Issued to Black Americans:
  Mitchell, C. L., Phoneterisin, 1 January, Pat. No. 291,071
  Johnson, W., Egg beater, 5 February, Pat. No. 292,821
  Purvis, W. B., Paper bag machine, 12 February, Pat. No. 293,353
  Blue. L., Hand corn shelling machine, 20 May, Pat. No. 298,937
  Woods, G. T., Steam boiler furnace, 3 June, Pat. No. 299,804
  Church, T. S., Carpet beating machine, 29 July, Pat. No. 302,237
  Reed, J. W., Dough kneader and roller, 23 September, Pat. No. 305,474
  Woods, G. T., Telephone transmitter, 2 December, Pat. No. 308,817

Oldest American Negro medical association, the Medico-Chirugical Society, organized in Washington, D.C.

Albery A. Whitman, The Rape of Florida, reprinted in 1885 as Twasinta's Seminoles; or, The Rape of Florida (St. Louis: Nixon-Jones Printing Co.).

T. Thomas Fortune, Black and White: Land, Labor, and Politics in the South (New York). Fortune's book is an economic study of the southern black twenty years after emancipation, in which he defends organized labor. Blacks are encouraged to join with other members of the working classes by seeking training in industry (Loggins 1931, p. 285).

(1884)

The <u>A. M. E. Church Review</u> established.

1884-1885

"Except for the years between 1914 and 1918, they [the powers
of western Europe] were . . . able to control their rivalries
in Africa within a general agreement among themselves. No
matter how much they might quarrel elsewhere, they were usually
careful not to quarrel in Africa. The broad limits of expansion for each of the interest powers--for Britain, France,
Germany, Belgium (though as yet only through its king), Italy,
Portugal and Spain--were defined with little trouble at the
Berlin colonial conference of 1884-5. An effective agreement
on partition had in fact long preceded this conference. In
North Africa the French had established their 'priority of
interest' as early as 1830 with a sudden invasion of Algeria.
This was continued at the eastern end of the Mediterranean by
Britain, for whom Lower Egypt and the Red Sea had become of
major importance as a channel of communication with the British
empire in India. Here the British, following on the revolt of
Arabi Pasha, finally asserted their primacy over the French by
an invasion of 1882. This was ostensibly aimed at restoring
the earlier Anglo-French financial control of Egypt. But
having got into Egypt, the British stayed, declaring a protec-
torate in 1914 and finally evacuating the country only in the
wake of the Second World War and the rise of a new Egyptian
nationalism. Meanwhile, the French had established a pro-
tectorate over Tunisia in 1883. Twenty years later, partly as
the outcome of a deal with Britain which confirmed the latter's
free hand in Egypt, France turned her attention to Morocco.
In 1904 this ancient country was divided into 'zones of influence' by France and Spain, and colonial subjection soon
followed. The same process was repeated elsewhere, and often
against the same tough resistance" (Davidson 1968, pp. 242,
243).

1885

<u>Sunshine and Shadow of Slave Life: Reminiscences as Told by
Isaac D. Williams to "Tege"</u> [pseud.] (East Saginaw, Mich.:
Evening News Printing and Binding House).

T. Thomas Fortune, <u>The Negro in Politics</u>, is "a spirited
attack on Frederick Douglass's tenet that for the colored
American 'the Republican party is a ship, all else is the
ocean'" (Loggins 1931, p. 286).

(1885-1890)

Just before the original dental school for blacks at Howard University graduated its first class, of the 15,000 dentists in the United States not more than twenty-five were black. Less than half of this number were graduates of dental schools. Some of these practitioners became members of the original faculties of Howard University and Meharry Medical College.

Patents Issued to Black Americans:
    Sampson, G. T., Sled propeller, 17 February, Pat. No. 312,388
    Cosgrove, W. F., Automatic stop plug for gas oil pipes, 17 March, Pat. No. 313,993
    Creamer, H., Steam feed water trap, 17 March, Pat. No. 313,854
    Woods, G. T., Apparatus for transmission of messages by electricity, 7 April, Pat. No. 315,308
    McCoy, E., Steam dome, 16 June, Pat. No. 320,354
    McCoy, E., Lubricator, 16 June, Pat. No. 320,379
    Goode, Sarah E., Folding cabinet bed, 14 July, Pat. No. 322,177
    Carter, W. C., Umbrella stand, 4 August, Pat. No. 323,397

The Mahdi seized Omdurman, a suburb of Khartoum, and later entered Khartoum over the mud of the dammed river and killed Chinese Gordon.

Mohammed Ahmad, master of four-fifths of the Egyptian Sudan, died of typhoid fever.

Anglo-German agreement signed in London defined British and German spheres of influence in East Africa.

Bishop Turner and Congressman Morgan of Alabama tried to re- vive migration to Africa; one ship load of 200 sailed in 1885.

1885-1890

Before 1895 black physicians, in imitation of the prevailing attitude of physicians toward dentists generally, disregarded black dentists as factors in health service and as a rule ex- cluded them from professional association. In 1895 black physicians, dentists, and pharmacists, organized the National Medical Association.

(1886)

1886

Slavery abolished in Spanish dominions.

Brazil provided for gradual emancipation of slaves according to law of 1885.

Meharry Medical College established in Nashville, Tennessee; one of the first medical schools for blacks.

Harriet, the Moses of Her People, by Sarah Bradford (New York); about Harriet Tubman.

Patents Issued to Black Americans:
    Flemming, R. F., Jr., Guitar, 3 March, Pat. No. 338,727
    Marshall, W., Grain binder, 11 May, Pat. No. 341,589
    Richardson, W. H., Cotton chopper, 1 June, Pat. No. 343,140
    Latimer, L. H., Apparatus for cooling and disinfecting, 12 January, Pat. No. 334,078
    Scottron, S. R., Pole tip, 21 September, Pat. No. 349,525
    Headen, M., Foot power hammer, 5 October, Pat. No. 350,363
    Davis, I. D., Tonic, 2 November, Pat. No. 351,829
    Brown, Henry, Receptacle for storing and preserving papers, 2 November, Pat. No. 352,036

Rufus Lewis Perry, 1835–1895, The Cushites; or The Children of Ham as seen by the ancient historians and poets. A paper read by Rev. Rufus L. Perry . . . before the Brooklyn Literary Union with an introduction by T. McCants Stewart, Brooklyn Literary Union c.1886 (Brooklyn, N.Y.: Literary Union). Perry also wrote "L'homme d'apres la science et le Talmud," in Articles and Addresses by Negroes.

Frederick Douglass, "The Future of the Colored Race," North American Review 142 (May):437–40.

Julia A. J. Foote, A Brand Plucked from the Fire; an Autobiographical Sketch (Cleveland: published by the author). An African Methodist Episcopal evangelist preacher who grew up in Schenectady and Albany, New York, Foote focused on her religious life and travels in the northeast and Canada. She began preaching after a mystical experience in Boston.

David Augustus Straker, Reflections on the Life and Times of Toussaint L'Ouverture, the Negro Haytien (Columbia, S.C.).

T. McCants Steward, Liberia, the Americo-African Republic;
Being Some Impressions of the Climate, Resources, and People,
Resulting from Personal Observations and Experiences in West
Africa (New York).

J. W. Stevenson, How to Get and Keep Churches Out of Debt, and
Also a Lecture on the Secret of Success in the Art of Making
Money (Albany).

Benjamin William Arnett, The Black Laws· speech of B. W. Arnett
in the Ohio House of Representatives, 10 March.

Samuel W. Clark, The Negro Mason in Equity: a Public Address,
Authorized by the M. W. Grand Lodge of Free and Accepted Masons
for the State of Ohio and Its Jurisdiction, for the Purpose of
Placing before the World the Historical Facts Upon Which the
Negro Mason in America Bases His Claim to Legitimacy and Con-
sequent Rights.

Life of Reverend Thomas James by Himself (Rochester, N.Y.:
Post Express Printing Co.). James lived from 1804-1891.

1887

Charles W. Chestnutt, "The Goophered Grapevine," Atlantic
Monthly 60 (August):254-60; "Po' Sandy," Atlantic Monthly 61
(May 1888):605-11; "The Conjurer's Revenge," Overland Monthly
13 (June 1889):623-29; "Hot-Foot Hannibal," Atlantic Monthly
83 (January 1889):43-56; "Dave's Neckliss," Atlantic Monthly
64 (October 1889):500-8.

William J. Simmons, Men of Mark, Eminent, Progressive and
Rising. Biographical dictionary of blacks in the United
States.

T. Thomas Fortune issued an appeal for a Negro National Organization, which he repeated in 1889. Afro-American League--
changed to Afro-American Council--met in Chicago in 1890.

Joseph H. Morgan, History of the New Jersey Conference of the
A.M.E. Church, from 1872-1887, and of the Several Churches as
Far as Possible, from Date of Organization; with Biographical
Sketches of Members of the Conference (Camden).

Patents Issued to Black Americans:
    Robinson, J., Dinner pail, 1 February, Pat. No. 350,852
    McCoy, E., Lubricator, 8 February, Pat. No. 357,491

(1888)

Creamer, H., Steam traps, 8 March, Pat. No. 358,964

Stewart, E. W., Machine for forming vehicle seat bars, 22 March, Pat. No. 373,698

McCoy, E., Lubricator attachment, 19 April, Pat. No. 361,435

Gregory, J., Motor, 26 April, Pat. No. 361,937

Stewart, E. W., Punching machine, 3 May, Pat. No. 362,190

Lewis, E. R., Spring gun, 3 May, Pat. No. 362,096

Shorter, D. W., Feed rack, 17 May, Pat. No. 363,089

McCoy, E., Lubricator for safety valves, 24 May, Pat. No. 363,529

Woods, G. T., Relay instrument, 7 June, Pat. No. 364,619

Woods, G. T., Polarized relay, 5 July, Pat. No. 366,192

Woods, G. T., Electro-mechanical brake, 16 August, Pat. No. 368,265

Hawkins, R., Harness attachment, 4 October, Pat. No. 370,943

Thomas, S. E., Waste trap for basins and closets, 4 October, Pat. No. 371,107

Miles, A., Elevator, 11 October, Pat. No. 371,207

Woods, G. T., Telephone system and apparatus, 11 October, Pat. No. 371,241

Woods, G. T., Electro-magnetic brake apparatus, 18 October, Pat. No. 371,655

Woods, G. T., Railway telegraphy, 15 November, Pat. No. 373,383

Woods, G. T., Induction telegraph system, 29 November, Pat. No. 373,915

Stewart and Johnson, Metal bending machine, 27 December, Pat. No. 375,512

1888

James M. Simms, The First Colored Baptist Church in North America. Constituted at Savannah, Georgia, January 20, A.D. 1788. With Biographical Sketches of the Pastors (Philadelphia).

E. K. Love, History of the First African Baptist Church, from Its Organization, January 20th, 1788, to July 1st, 1888 . . . (Savannah).

Theophilus Gould Steward, The End of the World; or, Clearing the Way for the Fullness of the Gentiles . . . With an Exposition of Psalm 68; 31 (Philadelphia). "An extravagant prophecy" presented "in pompous language" (Loggins 1931, pp. 300-1).

(1888)

David Augustus Straker, <u>The New South Investigated</u> (Detroit: Ferguson Printing Company).

Robert B. Forten, "Rome," in Daniel Alexander Payne, <u>Recollections of Seventy Years, 1811-1893</u> (Nashville, Tenn.), p. 52. Payne knew intimately most of the black leaders of his day. He was associated with most of the religious, educational, and social movements of his period. <u>Recollections of Seventy Years</u> therefore includes much of the history of blacks during the nineteenth century (Loggins 1931, p. 264).

Patents Issued to Black Americans:
    Blackburn, A. B., Railway signal, 10 January, Pat. No. 376,362
    Creamer, H., Steam traps, 17 January, Pat. No. 376,686
    Blackburn, A. B., Spring seat for chairs, 3 April, Pat. No. 380,420
    Cherry, M. A., Velocipede, 8 May, Pat. No. 382,351
    McCoy, E., Lubricator, 29 May, Pat. No. 383,746
    McCoy, E., Lubricator, 29 May, Pat. No. 383,745
    Woods, G. T., Overhead conducting system for electric railway, 29 May, Pat. No. 383,844
    Woods, G. T., Electro-motive railway system, 26 June, Pat. No. 385,034
    Woods, G. T., Tunnel Construction for electric railway, 17 July, Pat. No. 386,282
    Benjamin, Miss M. E., Gong and signal chairs for hotels, 17 July, Pat. No. 386,286
    Thomas, S. E., Casting, 31 July, Pat. No. 386,941
    Woods, G. T., Galvanic battery, 14 August, Pat. No. 387,839
    Woods, G. T., Railway telegraph, 28 August, Pat. No. 388,803
    Cornwell, P. W., Draft regulator, 2 October, Pat. No. 390,284
    Thomas, S. E., Pipe connection, 9 October, Pat. No. 390,821
    Clare, O. B., Trestle, 9 October, Pat. No. 390,753
    Blackburn, A. B., Cash carrier, 23 October, Pat. No. 319,577
    Hyde, R. N., Composition for cleaning and preserving carpets, 6 November, Pat. No. 392,205
    Coolidge, J. S., Harness attachments, 13 November, Pat. No. 392,908
    Johnson, W. A., Paint vehicle, 4 December, Pat. No. 393,763
    Winn, Frank, Direct acting steam engine, 4 December, Pat. No. 394,047

(1888)

Creamer, H., Steam trap feeder, 11 December, Pat. No. 394,463

George Washington Williams, <u>A History of the Negro Troops in the War of the Rebellion</u> (New York: Harper & Bros.). Begins with a survey of the black's role in the ancient and modern European wars and then gives in detail, with documented facts, the role of the various black organizations which rendered actual service in the Civil War (Loggins 1931, p. 279).

Joseph T. Wilson, <u>The Black Phalanx</u> (Hartford). In 1882 Wilson was chosen by the post of the Grand Army of the Republic to write a history of the role his regiment had played in the Civil War. The book however gives resumes of the role of black soldiers in the Revolutionary War, the War of 1812 as well as in the Civil War.

John Wallace, <u>Carpetbag Rule in Florida</u> (Jacksonville, Fla.).

Daniel Alexander Payne, "The Mournful Lute, or, the Preceptor's Farewell," in Daniel Alexander Payne, <u>Recollections of Seventy Years</u>, pp. 29-34.

Father Augustine Tolton, born in Illinois of slave parents, was the first black priest appointed in the United States. He was ordained at the Propaganda in Rome, in 1888. He was pastor of St. Monica's Church in Chicago.

Elisha Winfield, <u>Life of the Rev. Elisha W. Green</u>. Elisha Green was a former slave who became one of the founders of the Kentucky Normal and Theological Institute, now the State University of Louisville; eleven years moderator of the Mt. Zion Baptist Association; five years moderator of the Consolidated Baptist Educational Association and over thirty years pastor of the Colored Baptist Churches of Maysville and Paris (Maysville, Ky.: Republican Printing Office).

Slavery is abolished in Brazil. There were approximately 725,000 slaves in Brazil at this time.

The total number of slaves imported is not known. It is estimated that nearly 900,000 came to America in the sixteenth century, 2.75 million in the seventeenth century, 7 million in the eighteenth, and over 4 million in the nineteenth--perhaps 15 million in total. Probably every slave imported represented,

(1888)

on the average, five corpses in Africa or on the high seas.
The American slave trade, therefore, meant the elimination of
at least 60 million Africans from their fatherland. The
Mohammedan slave trade meant the expatriation or forcible
migration in Africa of nearly as many more. It would be conservative, then, to say that the slave trade cost Africa 100
million people.

References Cited

Ahuma, S. R. B. A. Memoirs of West African Celebrities . . . 1700-1850. Liverpool: D. Marples, 1905.

Alexander, Ziggi, and Dewjee, Audrey. "Blacks in Britain: Mary Seacole" History Today 31 (September 1981):45.

Berrudez-Plata, Cristobal, et al., eds. Catalogo de Pasajeros a Indias durante los siglos xvi, xvii y xviii redactado pai el personal facultivo del Archivo General de Indias. Seville and Madrid: Imprenta Espasa-Calpe, S.A., 1930-.

Blake, William O. The History of Slavery and the Slave Trade, Ancient and Modern. Columbus, Ohio: H. Miller, 1859.

Breasted, J. H. Ancient Records of Egypt. New York: Russell & Russell, 1962.

Brignano, Russell C. Black Americans in Autobiography. Durham, N.C.: Duke University Press, 1974.

Catterall, Helen T. Judicial Cases Concerning American Slavery and the Negro. 5 vols. New York: Octagon Books, 1968.

Chamberlain, A. F. "The Contribution of the Negro to Human Civilization." Journal of Race Development 1 (April 1901):483-84.

Conway, M. D. "Benjamin Banneker." Atlantic Monthly 11 (January 1863):79-84.

Corwin, Arthur F. Spain and the Abolition of Slavery in Cuba, 1817-1886. Austin and London: University of Texas Press, 1967.

Coupland, Reginald. East Africa and Its Invaders. Oxford: Clarendon Press, 1938.

David, A. Rosalie. The Egyptian Kingdoms. New York: E. P. Dutton, 1975.

Davidson, Basil. Africa in History: Themes and Outlines. New York: Macmillan, 1968.

Davidson, Basil. African Kingdoms. New York: Time-Life Books, 1966.

Davidson, Basil. A History of East and Central Africa. Garden City, N.Y.: Doubleday Anchor, 1969.

Dictionary Catalog of the Schomburg Collection of Negro Literature and History. Boston: G. K. Hall, 1962.

Diffie, Bailey W. Prelude to Empire: Portugal Overseas before Henry the Navigator. Lincoln: University of Nebraska Press, Bison Books, 1960.

Diggs, Irene. "The Negro in Viceroyalty of Rio de la Plata." Journal of Negro History 36, no. 3 (1951):286, 287.

Diggs, Irene. "Zambi and the Republic of Os Palmares." Phylon 14, no. 1 (1953):63.

Donnan, Elizabeth. Documents Illustrative of the History of the Slave Trade to America. Vol. 1. New York: Octagon Books, 1969.

Drake, Thomas E. Quakers and Slavery in America. Magnolia, Mass.: Peter Smith.

Du Bois, W. E. B. Black Folk: Then and Now. New York: Henry Holt & Co., 1939.

Du Bois, W. E. B. Black Reconstruction in America, 1860-1880. New York: Harcourt, Brace & Co., 1935.

Du Bois, W. E. B., ed. The Common School and the Negro American. Atlanta University Publications, no. 16. Atlanta: Atlanta University Press, 1912.

Du Bois, W. E. B. The Negro. New York: Henry Holt & Co., 1915.

Du Bois, W. E. B., ed. The Negro Artisan. Atlanta University Publications, no. 7. Atlanta: Atlanta University Press, 1902.

Du Bois, W. E. B., ed. The Negro Church. Atlanta University Publications, no. 8. Atlanta: Atlanta University Press, 1903.

Du Bois, W. E. B., ed. The Negro Common School. Atlanta University Publications, no. 6. Atlanta: Atlanta University Press, 1901.

Du Bois, W. E. B. The Philadelphia Negro. Boston: Ginn & Co., 1899.

Du Bois, W. E. B. <u>Suppression of the Slave-Trade</u>. Vol. 1. Cambridge, Mass.: Harvard University Press, 1896.

Du Bois, W. E. B. <u>World and Africa: Inquiry into the Part Which Africa Has Played in World History</u>. New York: Viking Press, 1947.

Edwards, Paul. "Black Personalities in Georgian Britain." <u>History Today</u> 31 (September 1981):41-42.

Edwards, Paul. "The History of Blacks in Britain." <u>History Today</u> 31 (September 1981):33.

Foley, Albert S. <u>God's Man of Color</u>. New York: Farrar, Straus & Co., 1955.

Gould, Joseph F. "In Moslem Spain." <u>Crisis</u> 7, no. 6 (April 1914): 298.

Gray, Richard. "The Vatican and the Atlantic Slave Trade." <u>History Today</u> 31 (September 1981):37.

Grove, George. <u>Dictionary of Music and Musicians</u>. Edited by J. A. Fuller-Maitland. London: St. Martins Press, 1900.

Hair, P. E. "The Enslavement of Koelle's Informants." <u>Journal of African History</u> 6 (1965):193-203.

Handlin, Oscar. <u>Race and Nationality in American Life</u>. Garden City, N.Y.: Doubleday & Co., 1957.

Hansberry, William L. "Sources for the Study of Ethiopian History." Washington, D.C.: Howard University Studies in History, 1930.

Harris, Shelton H. <u>Paul Cuffe</u>. New York: Simon & Schuster, 1972.

Huggins, Willis N., and Jackson, John G. <u>An Introduction to African Civilizations</u>. New York: Negro Universities Press, 1969.

Hull, Richard W. <u>Munyakore: African Civilization before the Batuure</u>. New York: John Wiley & Sons, 1972.

Imbert, H. <u>Les Negritos de la Chine</u>. Hanoi-Haiphong: Impr. d'Extreme-Orient, 1923.

Jocelyn, Susan E. W. "The Story of the Amistad." <u>Crisis</u> 9, no. 3 (January 1915):138ff.

July, Robert W. <u>History of the African People</u>. New York: Scribner's Sons, 1970.

References Cited

Lane-Poole, E. Stanley. History of Egypt in Medieval Ages. London: Methuen & Co., 1901.

Lanuza, José Luis. Morenada. Buenos Aires: Emecé Editores, S.A., 1946.

Loggins, Vernon. The Negro Author. New York: Columbia University Press, 1931.

Long, Edward. History of Jamaica. Vol. 2. London: T. Lowndes, 1774, pp. 475-80.

MacDermott, T. H. "From a Jamaican Portfolio--Francis Williams." Journal of Negro History 2 (April 1917):147-60.

Maroon, Fred J., and Newby, P. H. The Egypt Story. New York: American Heritage Publishing Co., n.d.

Nuermberger, Ruth Ann Ketring. The Free Produce Movement: A Quaker Protest Against Slavery. Durham, N.C.: Duke University Press, 1942.

O'Brien, Robert W. "Victoria's Negro Colonists--1856-1866." Phylon 3, no. 1 (1942):15ff.

Parks, Henry Bamford. A History of Mexico. Boston: Houghton Mifflin Co., 1938.

Pereda Valdes, Ildefonso. Negros esclavos y negros libres. Montevideo, 1941.

Petrie, William Mathew Flinders. A History of Egypt from the Earliest Times to the XVIth Dynasty. 6 vols. London: Methuen & Co., 1894; New York: Scribner's Sons, 1895-1901.

Porter, Dorothy. Early Negro Writing, 1760-1837. Boston: Beacon Press, 1971.

Randall-McIver, David, and Thompson, Arthur. Ancient Races of the Thbaid. London, 1905.

Rogers, Joel Augustus. Sex and Race. Vol. 1: The Old World. New York: J. A. Rogers, 1942.

Rogers, Joel Augustus. World's Great Men of Color. New York: Macmillan & Co., 1947.

Saco, José Antonio. Historia de la Esclavitud de la Raza Africana en el Nuevo Mundo. 4 vols. Havana: Cultural, S.A., c.1938.

Savage, W. Sherman. "The Influence of John Chavis and Lunsford Lane on the History of North Carolina." Journal of Negro History 25, no. 1 (January 1940):14.

Schurz, William Lytle. The Civilization of Latin America. New York: E. P. Dutton & Co., 1954a.

Schurz, William Lytle. This New World. New York: E. P. Dutton & Co., 1954b.

Singer, Ronald. "The Sickle Cell Trait in Africa." American Anthropologist 55 (1953):637,638.

Slave Trade. Vols. 1-94. British Parliamentary Papers 61. Shannon: Irish University Press, 1969.

Smythe, Mabel M., ed. The Black American Reference Book. Englewood Cliffs, N.J.: Prentice-Hall, 1976.

Spratlin, V. B. Juan Latino, Slave and Humanist. New York: Spinner Press, 1938.

Steward, Theophilus Gould. Haitian Revolution, 1791-1804. New York: Thomas Y. Crowell Co., 1914.

Tax, Sol, ed. Horizons of Anthropology. Chicago: Aldine, 1964.

Thiers, Adolphe. French Revolution. Vol. 2. Translated by D. Forbes Campbell and H. W. Herbert. Philadelphia: J. B. Lippincott & Co., 1861-1868.

Thomas, John L., ed. Slavery Attacked. Englewood Cliffs, N.J.: Prentice-Hall, 1965.

Usherwood, Stephen. "The Abolitionists' Debt to Lord Mansfield." History Today 31 (March 1981):40.

Wallace, David Duncan. The History of South Carolina. 4 vols. New York: American Historical Society, 1934.

Wallace, David Duncan. South Carolina: A Short History, 1520-1948. Chapel Hill: University of North Carolina Press, 1951; Columbia: University of South Carolina Press, 1961.

Weigall, Arthur E. P. B. A Guide to the Antiquities of Upper Egypt from Abydos to the Sudan Frontier. London: Methuen & Co., 1910.

References Cited

Woodson, Carter G. The Negro in Our History. 6th ed. Washington, D.C.: Associated Publishers, 1939.

Woodward, C. Vann. Reunion and Reaction. Boston: Little, Brown & Co., 1951.

Index

Indonesians, 12
Innes, William, 173
Innocent VIII, 40
Innocent XI, 81
Iron Age, 8, 10, 11, 14, 15, 20, 25, 33

Jackson, Andrew, 89, 204
Jacques I, 141
James I, 67
James, John, 178
Jamison, M. F., 208
Janjira, 10
Janssonius, Joannes, 69
Jasper, John, 147, 277
Jay, John, 256
Jefferson, Thomas, 118, 129, 131, 140, 190, 205, 207, 210, 223
Jekyll, Joseph, 98
Jenkins, Levi, 207-8
Jennings, Paul, 256
Joao de Barros, 37
John II, 37, 39
John Saffin's Tryall, 90
Johnson, Andrew, 257, 258, 259, 261
Johnson, John F., 197
Johnson, William, 217
Johnstone, Abraham, 135
Jones, Absalom, 124, 137, 144, 148
Jones, Charles C., 194
Jones, Edward, 160
Jones, Thomas H., 214, 249
Joseph II, 96

Kashta the Kushite, 6
Kasim Ibn Hammud, 21
Kasr-al-Kabir (Alcazar), Battle of, 62
Kearney, Belle, 230
Keckley, Elizabeth, 262
Kettridge, Frank E., 201
Kilwa, 18, 26, 43, 44, 50, 116
Kimball, J. Horace, 184
Knight, Joseph, 118
Knights of Tabor, 201
Koch, Bernard, 250
Koelle, S. W., 119, 223
Kossuth, Louis, 219
Ku Klux Act, 265

Kuk Lux, 200
Kush, X-Group culture in, 12
Kushites, 8, 9, 10

Lacaussade, Auguste, 152
Laing, Samuel, 199
Laird, Macgregor, 227
Lambert, William, 109, 267
Lander brothers, 165
Lane, Isaac, 175
Lane, Lunsford, 194
Langston, John M., 163
Latino, Juan, 48, 61
Latta, Morgan L., 222
Lawrence, George, 148
Lay, Benjamin, 84, 100
Lecture on the Haytien Revolutions (Smith), 192
Lectures on American Slavery (Douglass), 215
Ledesma, Manuel A., 169
Lee, Hannah F. S., 225
Lee, Jarena, 210
Lee, Rebeca, 253
Lee Boo, Prince, 154
Legare, Hugh, 197
Legion of Liberty and Force of Truth, 198
Leopold of Belgium, 280
Leo the African, 45, 69
Leo X, 57
Leo XI, 41
Letters from a Man of Color (Forten), 148
Letters on American Slavery (Rankin), 173
Letters (Sancho), 98
Letters to Catherine E. Beecher (Grimke), 184
Lewis, John W., 218
Lewis, Mary E., 253
Lewis, R. B., 198
Liberator, 166, 171, 189, 191, 192, 194, 196, 200, 202-3, 209, 214, 218, 225, 226, 232, 250
Liberia Herald, 168
Liberia (Innes), 173
Liberty Almanac, 198
Liberty Cap, The (Follen), 203
Liberty Minstrel, The (Clark), 197